The New Museum

Selected Writings
by John Cotton Dana

Edited by William A. Peniston
Preface by Mary Sue Sweeney Price
Introduction by Stephen E. Weil

The New Museum: Selected Writings by John Cotton Dana

The Newark Museum Association
49 Washington St.
P.O. Box 540
Newark, NJ 07101-0540

The American Association of Museums
1575 Eye St. N.W., Suite 400
Washington, DC 20005-1105

Library of Congress Cataloging-in-Publication Data

Dana, John Cotton, 1856-1929.
The new museum : selected writings / by John Cotton Dana ; edited by William A. Peniston ; preface by Mary Sue Sweeney Price ; introduction by Stephen E. Weil.
p. cm.
Includes bibliographical references and index.
ISBN 0-9321201-64-0
1. Museums. I. Peniston, William A., 1959- II. Title.

AM5.D354 1999
069–dc21

99-044326

The New Museum

Selected Writings
by John Cotton Dana

Edited by William A. Peniston
Preface by Mary Sue Sweeney Price
Introduction by Stephen E. Weil

Washington, D.C.

Table of Contents

I. Preface

By Mary Sue Sweeney Price

A good museum attracts, entertains, arouses curiosity, leads to questionings—and thus promotes learning.” In this succinct statement, John Cotton Dana, founder and first director of The Newark Museum, summarized his entire philosophy on the purpose of his “new museum,” what he hoped would be the philosophy of all museums. It was the culmination of several decades of thought by a man who spent most of his professional career as a library and museum director.

Born in Woodstock, Vt., into an old New England family, Dana graduated from Dartmouth College in 1878 and then headed west to Colorado, where he eventually became the director of the Denver Public Library. An innovative librarian at a time when public libraries were just beginning to develop in this country, Dana advocated open stacks, service to children, foreign language materials for immigrants, and business information for professionals. As director of the Newark Public Library from 1902 to 1929, he applied these same principles of progressive education to the museum field, galvanizing a willing coterie of collectors, businessmen, and civic leaders to found The Newark Museum Association in 1909.

As we celebrate the 90th anniversary of The Newark Museum, its current Trustees and staff are pleased that the American Association of Museums proposed this publication of Dana’s pithy, challenging, and farsighted writings on museums

---

Mary Sue Sweeney Price is director, The Newark Museum, Newark, N.J.

and their central role in American society. Although editor William A. Peniston, the museum's librarian, has concentrated on Dana's statements regarding the museum field in general, the book also includes his writings on the relationship between museums and art patronage. Dana was a prolific writer, frequently publishing short statements in popular journals, but *The New Museum* includes only his more substantial contributions. He also frequently restated his most strongly held convictions; thus it has been impossible to avoid some repetition. We did exclude the more dated materials, especially Dana's reviews of contemporary literature on museums.

The first part of *The New Museum* reprints Dana's major contribution to the museum field, which he made in a series of short pamphlets published between 1917 and 1920. This includes his conceptualization of the "new museum," which he discussed in a critique of the existing state of museums in the first quarter of the 20th century, appropriately entitled "The Gloom of the Museum." The second part of the book presents in chronological order Dana's other writings on museums in general, so that the reader may more fully understand the development of his thought.

The third part, "The Experiment of The Newark Museum," highlights the extraordinary achievements that Dana accomplished as the director of this institution from 1909 to 1929. It demonstrates that Dana's theories were solidly grounded upon his experiences in building outstanding collections, mounting innovative exhibitions, and serving his community. The fact that Dana realized that these activities were not antithetical, but instead mutually sustaining, was another indication of his genius.

The last two sections of this volume are devoted to Dana's thoughts on museum education and the arts, respectively. Museum education was one of Dana's chief concerns, and his theories on the topic are probably one of his most lasting contributions to the modern development of American museums. He instituted many innovative programs for children and adults alike, and his ideas included the establishment of branch museums, a lending collection of objects for schools, and an activities club for young adults. These ideas are still very much part of The Newark Museum's mission as we continue to support the Educational Loan Collection and the Junior Museum.

"Museums and Art" reveals Dana's unique understanding of the museum's role as a patron of contemporary art, especially the applied arts, for which he developed a sustained interest and a personal passion. In addition, his belief that "Art has always flourished only where it is asked to flourish and if we wish for a renaissance of art in America, we must be its students and patrons" led to the establishment of a pioneering American art collection in Newark that today is considered among the finest in the country.

Stephen E. Weil's introduction is a thoughtful reflection on Dana's influence on the American museum profession by one of today's leading theorists on museums, and we are tremendously appreciative of his commentary and his time and effort on this project. We also wish to thank Hugh H. Genoways and Mary Anne Andrei for their annotated bibliography, which includes descriptions of many of the essays we were unable to include in this collection. Their fine summaries will be of interest to all readers of *The New Museum*, and their thorough research into Dana's writings will help serious scholars locate some of the more obscure citations.

We also acknowledge the support of the staff at the American Association of Museums: John Strand and Jane Lusaka, who oversaw the production of this publication, and Melissa Miller, who designed it. In addition, Charles Cummings at the Newark Public Library helped us locate some of these essays, and we are grateful to him and his staff. Finally, William Peniston's willingness to assume the major responsibility of selecting and arranging these materials is deeply appreciated. On behalf of all those who will benefit from this volume, I thank him for his thoughtful and dedicated editorial work.

II. Introduction

By Stephen E. Weil

For museum workers of my generation, John Cotton Dana (1856-1929) was largely a legend. His last full-length biography was published in 1940. The little that most of us knew about his career came primarily from the chapter devoted to him in Edward P. Alexander's 1983 *Museum Masters: Their Museums and Their Influence.* The larger part of his writings—originally published in the most fugitive of forms—had disappeared from view. The only thing readily extant was the edited reprint of *The New Museum* included in the special Dana issue of *The Museologist* that Barbara H. Butler edited for the Mid-Atlantic Association of Museums in 1988. Even the last few living links to Dana had dissolved. Gone from the scene were such senior colleagues as Dorothy Dudley and Dorothy Miller, both at the Museum of Modern Art, who had apprenticed under Dana in the groundbreaking museum studies program he initiated at The Newark Museum in 1925. Now, with the publication of this anthology, both Dana and his work are restored to us. The occasion is joyous, and the discourse of our field will forever be the richer.

As perhaps befitted his New England Puritan ancestry and early legal training, Dana was hardheaded and eminently practical, little given to sentimentality and prepared to unleash his curmudgeonly and coruscating wit at any sign of pretense. His own turn-of-the-century description of himself was as "an agnostic . . . an egotist, a

---

Stephen E. Weil is emeritus senior scholar, Center for Museum Studies, Smithsonian Institution, Washington, D.C.

pessimist and an anarchist." That description notwithstanding, readers of this volume will find a certain sweet and distinct idealism repeatedly shining through his otherwise acerbic prose. There were two things in which Dana appeared to have a particular faith. One was in the capacity of museums in the United States to better themselves, to dispel the gloom into which he believed they had sunk through their slavish imitation of inappropriate European models. The other was in the power of beautifully wrought objects—as grand as works of art or as humble as pots and pans—to enrich the lives of individuals at every level of society.

With respect to the "betterment" of museums, Dana found a hopeful analogy in the institution to which he had devoted his earlier career: the public library. Writing in 1921, he recalled that 40 years earlier the management of libraries had been based on the proposition that "a library should first of all strive for size, completeness, and for the reverence of the unlettered and the respect of the learned." During the intervening decades, he had watched the library—indeed, he himself had played a pivotal role in its transformation—evolve from "a closed temple of 'wisdom undisturbed' to an open workshop of delight and learning." The proper measure of this newly evolved library was not what it owned but what it did, not the size or completeness of its collection but its capacity "to be of immediate practical aid to all of the community that supports it." Dana thought that museums should strive to emulate this model, "to be of direct and useful service to those who found and maintain them—the general public." For Dana, it was only a matter of time before the management of every museum would come to its common sense and realize that its most promising future lay not in mindlessly amassing ever more objects but in providing a "full and rich utility" to its community.

Dana's belief in the positive role that beautiful objects might play in everyday life was in dramatic contrast to the enormous scorn he repeatedly directed toward the then-burgeoning and older-style art museums of New York, Philadelphia, and other metropolitan centers. Typical is his description of how the European-style art museum had been misguidedly replicated in the United States in the form of a public institution:

> [When the] common people found that they had, through taxes, money held in common and at their own disposal through their elected servants, they decided to use some of it to buy museums for themselves. Unfortunately, no one was at hand to tell them that they would get no pleasure or profit out of the kinds of museums which kings, princes, and other masters of people and wealth had constructed; and so, being ruled by precedent or fashion, as were also their rich donors, their important citizen-trustees, and their architects, they voted for, or silently approved, spending public money

for the old kinds of museums. They cared more to be in the fashion than they did to get something useful and enjoyable.

In condemning those museums—together with the older European works of art that they principally displayed—Dana offered several arguments. First, he said, it was pointless to devote a museum entirely to the display of objects that had no connection to the lives of most of its potential visitors. Second, the belief that these works of art might nevertheless exert some beneficial influence—to think that "museum pieces need only to be seen to produce in those who see them a certain elevation of soul, a definite impulse to better living, and a beautiful and helpful broadening of the mind"—was a delusion. Finally, more than simply pointless, to display only such works to the exclusion of everything else was actually pernicious. It must inevitably suggest to the public that only things that were old, rare, costly, and mostly of foreign origin were capable of providing visual delight. And that, in turn, could only undermine the public's potential understanding of how much satisfying design and beauty might be inherent in the everyday object produced in their own time and country and frequently available at modest prices.

In Dana's view, the true work of the museum as a service institution was in enriching the quality of its visitors' lives, not in accumulating masterpieces for its own greater glory. One way in which it could do that was by helping its visitors to cultivate their own individual sensibilities in such a way that beautiful objects could provide them with pleasure and serve as the source of a satisfying lifelong interest. The old art museum, with its emphasis on certifiably important objects that virtually none of its visitors could ever hope to connect with, did not offer such cultivation. The new museum that Dana envisioned would do precisely that. "In art matters," he wrote, "it is more important to be sensitive than to be knowing; it is better worthwhile to feel that a thing is right for you and to get pleasure with the feeling than it is to know who made it and when, where it was made and under what conditions, who has owned it, who now owns it, what he paid for it, and what great critics have said of it."

This missionary sense—that the museum has both the capacity and the obligation to be a life-enhancing institution—is the hallmark of all Dana's writings. Sometimes, as in *The New Museum,* he described the museum's role in positive terms. Its "one and obvious task," he wrote, is "adding to the happiness, wisdom and comfort of members of the community." At other times he defined it through negation, specifying what—in his view—the museum was not and ought not be. He rejected as baseless conventions an entire host of then-current notions about museums: what he called the "old doctrine that a museum, like beauty, is its own excuse for being"; that the museum ought to serve principally as a storehouse to safeguard humankind's common heritage; that the museum ought to serve primarily as a place in which curators can educate and even (his word) "entertain" themselves. Above all, he rejected the idea that simply to collect objects was to create a museum. Objects were easy to get, but objects alone were not a museum. They "merely form a 'collection.'" The worth of a museum, he repeatedly said, was in its use.

Dana's prescience was awesome. He articulated as nobody previously had done the informal nature of learning in museums. He foresaw the need of museums, schools, and libraries to collaborate. He emphasized—long before marketing concepts had become current—the importance of connecting program decisions to the needs and interests of the museum's community. "Learn what aid the community needs," he said, and "fit the museum to those needs." He speculated on the extent to which a museum might be an enterprise that could be better managed as a business. He explored the possibility of branch museums and other forms of outreach. He understood how advertising and public relations might be used to further institutional goals.

In some instances, Dana's ideas only came to fruition years later and in the hands of others. At the Museum of Modern Art (which opened just four months after his death in 1929), Dana's notion of showing well-designed and readily available objects of everyday utility achieved its fullest realization in the series of "Good Design" exhibitions that Edgar Kaufmann, Jr., mounted in the early 1950s in cooperation with Chicago's Merchandise Mart. Dana's belief that a museum should be community-based rather than discipline-based was ultimately to find its most complete expression in the Anacostia Neighborhood Museum that the Smithsonian Institution opened in 1967. When that museum's founding director John R. Kinard described it as encompassing "the life of the people of the neighborhood—people who are vitally concerned about who they are, where they came from, what they have accomplished, their values and their most pressing needs," one could almost hear Dana speaking through him.

Other ideas of Dana's are only now starting to be realized. Of those, perhaps the most startling was his anticipation of a basic truth that the museum community has only just begun to grasp some seven decades after his death: that there must be some demonstrable relationship between the support that a museum receives from its community and the value that the museum is able to return to the community in exchange. In 1920 Dana wrote:

> All public institutions (and museums are not exceptions to this rule) should give returns for their cost; and those returns should be in good degree positive, definite, visible, measurable. The goodness of a museum is not in direct ratio to the cost of its building and the upkeep thereof, or to the rarity, auction value, or money cost of its collections. A museum is good only

> insofar as it is of use. . . . Common sense demands that a publicly supported institution do something for its supporters and that some part at least of what it does be capable of clear description and downright valuation.

Although Dana was rarely explicit about the kinds of values he envisioned the museum returning to the community—if pressed, he might have responded that those values were, in every case, something to be negotiated between a specific museum and its particular community—they would probably have all fallen within the boundaries cited earlier from *The New Museum*—that they must somehow add to the community's happiness, wisdom, and comfort. However, as to what the final configuration of such a museum might be, Dana was specific. No such final configuration was possible: "A finished museum is a corpse, and so is a finished collection. In common with all other institutions, a museum to be of any value must grow; and it must do more than that—it must change its objects, their manner of presentment, and its method of management that it may meet the ever changing needs of a changing order of society."

If Dana's writings had been more widely available in the years after his death, might the history of this country's museums somehow have been different? Conceivably, they might still have come out where they are today—with their focus shifting in large measure from collections care to visitor services—but perhaps they could have done so sooner and with less anguish. Only now, with Dana's writings in hand, can we realize how much we missed him, how badly we needed to hear his views. John Cotton Dana, welcome back. From this point on, no serious conversation about museums may ever again be possible without your participation.

III. The New Museum

The New Museum

Note of Introduction

My interest in museums has been quite different and intense for nearly 20 years. As I studied them, their work, and the buildings which housed them, and read what has been written concerning them, I concluded that, like the libraries of 40 years ago, they were far less used than they should be; that they did not make much impression on the taste, manners, or activities of those who visited them, and that they soon would be either entirely neglected or very greatly changed in content, intent, and activities. The latter seemed to be quite the inevitable course; and still further study showed that certain changes, all making for greater usefulness, were well under way throughout the whole museum world.

As librarian of the Newark, N.J., Free Public Library, I found I was able to assist in establishing about eight years ago what might be called a museum of museum experiments.

In 1914, five years after the founding of this Newark museum, I set down briefly and printed—first in letters to *The New York Times* and later in the *Newarker*, the house organ of the Public Library—certain ideas upon museum construction, collections, and management. These ideas then roughly formulated have, in the last three years, taken more definite form. Finally, I decided to publish the results of my study, observation, and experiments in a series of small volumes and to give them the general title of *The New Museum*. It seemed to us that the story of our experiments with the Newark Museum—a museum which we wished to make useful to the city as a quite definite educational enterprise—might be helpful to others, and that to set forth that story would be a useful experience for ourselves.

Here is No. 1 of *The New Museum* series.

J. C. Dana
Newark, N.J.
April 1917

The New Museum Series, no. 1. Woodstock, Vt.: The Elm Tree Press, 1917.

PART I: WHY THIS SERIES IS BEGUN: THE OLD MUSEUM AND THE NEW

There are about 80 live museums in the United States. Of these, indeed, it is doubtful if the term "live" can be properly applied to more than 50. Of the total of 600 institutions in the country which assume the name museum, only the number above noted combine the essentials of museum existence—a home, collections properly so called, an income, and, most important of all these essentials, such activities as may fairly be supposed to produce beneficial effects in their respective communities.

The above data are gathered from the three reports on museums which Mr. Paul M. Rea, director of the Museum of Charleston, S.C., has published in recent years through the U.S. Bureau of Education.

Mr. Rea says quite plainly that these few live museums are doing all the work in the museum field which is worthy of serious consideration. If, then, we assume that a good museum is a proper and helpful institution to any community which may establish and maintain the same; and if we note that there are in this country several thousand towns and cities without museums, good or poor, alive or dead; and if we note that other figures in Mr. Rea's reports show that the number of active museums is increasing quite rapidly, we arrive inevitably at these conclusions: (1) that the museum idea is abroad; (2) that in many communities the wish to establish a museum of some kind is in the minds of at least a few of the more public-spirited citizens; and that, consequently, (3) there is now a wide-spread, if not an intense and popular, demand for suggestions on museum founding and on the elements of museum management.

The literature of this subject is quite meager. Of all that has been written on it, by far the greater part consists of histories of museums, of descriptions of their contents or perfunctory museum reports, of elaborate and technical discussions of individual objects, and of methods of installing costly special objects or special groups. Notable exceptions to this statement are G. Brown Goode's Report on the U.S. National Museum for 1892-3 and other writings by him, and the 10 annual volumes of the *Proceedings of the American Association of Museums.*

Our Search for Information

From the very beginnings eight years ago of our still modest enterprise, we have felt the need of sources of information on such topics as these:

- How to organize a museum association.
- How to stimulate interest in a local museum.
- How to construct a museum which shall interest and help its community.
- How to record acquisitions.

- ✦ How to install the simpler and commoner classes of museum objects.
- ✦ How to store safely and compactly objects which are not in use.
- ✦ How to prepare and display modest temporary exhibits.
- ✦ How to secure such printing of labels, lists, etc., as befits a museum.
- ✦ How to get expert museum advice and competent museum workers.
- ✦ How to discover the latest and best things that have been published on museum work of each and every kind.

These and many other queries we have met and answered as best we could. Our problems have not been large ones in the sense that they involved large expenditures; they have been large in the sense that they were broad and fundamental, that is, of the kind that every museum must meet in beginning its career.

We have felt so keenly the lack of printed information which gave clear, precise, and definite answers to our many queries that we decided several years ago that, if fortune favored us by keeping our museum alive and growing, we would in due course set down in print our own experiences, the results of our inquiries, studies, observations, and experiments. And it is precisely because we are young, inquisitive, and, we hope, unprejudiced, and have felt so keenly our own ignorance and our own shortcomings, that we are willing to run the risks that go with the offering of advice and suggestion, especially by the young and inexperienced. Often it is those who are just beginning to learn who can give most help to others who are but one step behind them in the learning process.

Our Opposition to Museum Conventions

Another aspect of our museum attitude has helped so to embolden us as to make us willing to put down for others that which we are in the very process of learning for ourselves, and that is our frankly confessed opposition to most of the accepted museum conventions. This opposition is addressed not so much to conventions of management as to conventions of purpose.

We decided, quite early in our history, that the art gallery type of museum would be, for our city, not at all worth the money it would cost to establish and maintain. Special local conditions were in part responsible for this conclusion. Newark is only nine miles from New York, and any Newarker who wishes can, at the cost of 50 cents and three hours time, make a long visit either to the world's best museum of science or to its best museum of art. This cost in money and time will be, in a few years, even less than it is today. To set up in Newark a poor imitation of either of these great institutions—poor at least in its contents and in its home a mere ostentatious product of a foolish desire to add the façade of a marble palace to the city's insignia of culture—to do these things seemed to us foolish and wasteful and unproductive of good results.

The Kind of Museum Newark Seems to Need

Obviously the thing needed by Newark in the museum field was something which should supplement locally the great storehouses of wonderful, beautiful, and educational objects in the collections of the city next door, the richest city in the world, and a city of which Newark each year becomes more essentially a component part. This supplement, so we felt and still feel, should be adapted with special care to the needs of the people of Newark; through careful study it should be made something the people of Newark would use and, using, would find pleasure and profit therein. It should not be constructed in its home, or in its collections, or in its activities after any preconceived pattern. What Newark men and women and children would welcome and would use to add to the interests of their lives and to the improvement and general efficiency of their business and work-a-day lives—this we thought should be slowly and carefully discovered by study, observation, and trial—and so the museum would grow. To build first an expensive home, a palace, a temple or any grandiose and permanent structure on the conventional lines of so-called museum architecture was, so we seemed clearly to see, to do a foolish, wasteful, antiquated thing—a thing possible only to those who knew little of modern community life, still less of American educational practice, and least of all of modern museum ideas. Vast sums, it is true, are invested in some of our large cities (and relative large sums in some of our smaller cities) on buildings and collections of museums of the conventional art gallery type, and sums also very large are spent on the maintenance of the same. But a very brief study of these museums and of the use made of them in adding to the pleasure, to the broadening and enlightening, and to the definite education of their respective communities, convinced us that they are among the least effective products of community enterprise that American development has brought forth. We came to a like conclusion concerning conventional scientific and historical and industrial collections, and little more: gratifying to a few, awesome to a few, tiresome to many, and helpful to almost none.

The Coming of the New Museum Idea

The same open-minded study (did we not believe it was open-minded we would never presume to offer to our colleagues any suggestions whatever) which seemed to us to demonstrate the general futility of conventional museums of whatever character, brought to our attention a movement within the museum field which precisely fell in with the notions we had already acquired concerning museum work.

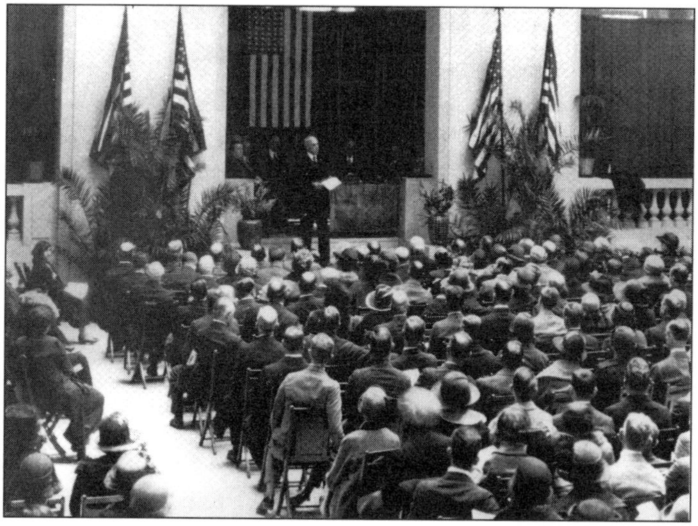

John Cotton Dana speaks at the cornerstone ceremonies for The Newark Museum, 1925.

This movement or activity within certain museums, suggested long ago by Mr. Goode and hinted at broadly by a few students long before his day, has scarcely yet embodied itself in a museum. It is too new, on the one hand, and the old "art gallery" and "collections" ideas of museums are still too powerful, on the other hand, to permit it to express itself fully in an active, complete, and well-rounded institution. There are seeming exceptions to this statement here and there, which will be alluded to later.

This new movement with which we have tried to identify ourselves and in which we have tried to do our part is difficult of description. It is not directed to the erection of Greek or Renaissance façades in parks or corners remote from a city's center. It is not concerned with the construction, behind those façades, of a few grand courts and galleries. Its galleries or work and study rooms are not to be invested with that ancient and ghastly fetish, a top light—something which one may properly hope to escape when he enters a modern building. It is not friendly to that "museum" atmosphere which is depressing and numbing to the sensitive visitor in direct ratio to the self-conscious grandeur and refinement of its architectural container. Nor does this new museum method aim at the acquisition of rare and priceless objects with which to fill rows of cold and costly cases, all peculiarly well fitted, if they do nothing else, to aggravate the foolish pride of the thoughtless citizen; nor at the acquisition of so many objects within any one field as to make a museum distinctly a museum of a certain kind.

The Value of Mere Collections

Parenthetically it should be said—lest some misunderstand our attitude toward the preservation of rare and beautiful objects, toward the creation of art galleries, toward the making of science collections and collections in any field whatever—that all these things are manifestly useful and have their proper place. We merely hold to the theory that in most cases their immediate utility is vastly over-rated; that their cost is out of proportion to their value; that their managers usually too greatly exalt their acquisitions and forget the entertainment and instructions of those for whom they were professedly acquired; and that their presence, and the dominance of the conventions which go with them, make very difficult the introduction of homelier, more attractive, and more useful objects and methods into the museum world.

Most of us prefer to copy. It is one of the limitations of wealth that it cannot be original in its exercise of one of its prime functions, the practice of conspicuous wastefulness. The rich like to collect what other rich have collected. They add the lust of possession to the practice of patronage of art or science. They think of "grand" public homes of the public's treasures only in terms convention has fixed. Hence remote palaces full of things whose accepted merits in beauty, rarity, age, and cost are excelled only by the paucity of their visitors.

But, as it is well for the public to become possessors of the rich and rare, and as the rich will supply them only under certain architectural and administrative conditions, it is obvious that it would be quite as foolish as it would be unwise to oppose the growth of the conventional museum.

Our attitude of criticism which is, we fully realize, quite negligible as such, is born merely of the belief that a better type of museum, a museum properly so-called, indeed, is possible, is in fact inevitable, and that some of the energy and money which now goes to the old kind of museum store-house may well be diverted to the new kind of museum work-shop. And that belief is expressed in this pamphlet as a partial explanation of the character of the constructive suggestions we make later.

The General Theory of the New Movement

The general theory of the new movement we are trying to describe seems to be this:

Each community can use to good advantage a certain quantity of material in formal and informal training through the eye. This training, this visual instruction, every member of every community is gaining in some measure every working moment of his life. In each community there is a tendency toward rather special and somewhat limited interests in the visual field, by reason of the special industrial, commercial, and educational activities of that community. We believe that it will pay any community to add to its educational apparatus a group of persons which shall form the staff of a local institution of visual instruction and to put in the hands of these persons modest sums with which they shall acquire, label, describe, arrange for show, and prepare for lending such objects as careful study and experiment shall suggest in the expectation that staff and objects combined will do for the community these things at least, and, one may hope, in time many others:

1. Entertain—and be ready to try to interest and instruct—such as may have the wish and the time to visit casually the institution's headquarters.
2. Entertain and more definitely and generally instruct—in classes and conducted groups, by labels, leaflets, handbooks, talks, and illustrated lectures—such adults as may be induced to come to see special exhibits, also at the institute headquarters.
3. Entertain, interest, and still more definitely instruct children who may be sent to the institute's headquarters from schools on stated occasions and for certain specific observations the objects observed and the talks and the reading expounding the objects being closely related to school work and to the age and stage of mental development of each group that comes.
4. Prepare for schools single objects and groups of objects with such labels, leaflets, lantern slides, and instructors as the proper use of each may demand, and lend these to schools as the school authorities may designate, all being fitted, of course, to make easier the work of teaching and to make broader and more effective the work of the pupils.
5. Place in schools—as opportunity and fit occasions and the felt need of teachers, supervisors, and the management may indicate—single objects and large and small collections of objects, fully labeled and accompanied by pictures, leaflets, and pamphlets; all being such as may entertain and instruct both teachers and pupils, and particularly such as may be found to give constant and almost daily assistance in adding interest and value to studies and in broadening the experiences of pupils and in awakening new interests in them. These to be changed as use and circumstance suggest.
6. Place in convenient and easily accessible rooms (like store rooms on business streets and in special rooms with separate entrances in school buildings) single objects and small, well-rounded collections in art, science, industry, ethnology, and other fields, such as experience shows will attract a large number of visitors. Manage these branch institutes when possible as veritable independent teaching centers, with leaflets and cards descriptive of the museum's work and

its acquisitions for distribution, and with skilled attendants who can describe and instruct as opportunity offers.

7. Discover collectors and specialists and experts in the community and secure their cooperation in adding to the museum's collections; in helping identify, describe, and prepare labels and leaflets; in arousing the interest of young people in the museum's work and in finding such boys and girls as may wish to make collections of objects of any kind for themselves or for the museum.

   This development of the collecting habit among the young, with its accompanying education of powers of observation, its training in handwork, its tendency to arouse interests theretofore unsuspected even by those who possess them, its continuous suggestions toward good taste and refinement which lie in the process of installing even the most modest of collections, and its leadings toward sound civic interest through doing for one's community a helpful thing—this work of securing the cooperation of boys and girls, making them useful while they are gaining their own pleasure and carrying on their own education, is one of the coming museum's most promising fields.

8. Lend to individuals, groups, and societies, for any proper use and for any reasonable length of time, any of the museum's objects, whenever it is clear that things thus lent will be of more service to the community than when they are resting, relatively unseen and unused, in the museum's headquarters.

9. Prepare and display, at the headquarters, at branches, and in schools, carefully selected objects which are products of the community's activities in field, factory, and workshop. These will be local industry exhibits. They may be so small as to show in a very easily transported case a few of the major steps in the manufacture of a simple object. They may include merely a group of completed objects, interesting for their beauty or complexity, or for the high technical skill of the craftsman who made them. Or they may be so extensive as to fill every available inch of space the museum controls and to illustrate many aspects of one field of industry, and so general as to give a bird's-eye view of all the industries of the whole community. These may be planned to attract and interest the business man, or to draw to them the women, or to arouse in young people a healthful curiosity in the activities of their community and the results of the daily labor of men and women—their fathers, mothers, brothers, and sisters, in the field, the store, and the factory.

10. Keep the museum and its activities continually before the community in the daily press, and publish and distribute as many leaflets, posters, broadsides, and cards descriptive of the museum's acquisitions as conditions seem to warrant. At the

proper time publish leaflets and booklets, based on the museum's material, proper to be used as reading lessons in the schools.

11. Connect the work the museum may do, its objects, and all the activities of its staff, with all the resources of the public library. In doing this, many books and journals will be displayed near objects on view, references to books and journals will be made on labels and in leaflets of all kinds, and the library will be asked to show placards and notes and to distribute things the museum may publish descriptive of its purposes and activities.

✦

The activities thus very briefly described form a small part only of the work that, as we conceive it, the coming museum will do. Though they are suggestions only, they seem to demonstrate their reasonableness merely by the statement of them. They are ample, in our opinion, to show to the open-minded that the new museums are to be museums properly so-called—homes and workshops of the Muses. They are not to be storage warehouses, or community attics, or temples of dead gods, or copies of palaces of extinct nobility, or costly reproductions of ancient temples, or grand and elaborate structures which are of service only as evidences of conspicuous waste by the rich and as ocular demonstrations of the unwise expenditure of public funds.

The New Museum an Institute of Visual Instruction

The coming museum, being entitled to the ancient name by virtue of its activities, will ultimately be called The Museum, though it will be for a time quite properly conceived of by many as an Institute of Visual Instruction. Museums of the old kind, we contend, are truly not museums at all. They are "collections" of variable extent and cost, and of slight definite utility. They will become each year a little less considered, less esteemed, and less used; or they will, as is the case with some of them already, transform themselves slowly into living organisms, with an abundance of teachers, with ample workshops, classrooms, and spaces for handling the outgoing and incoming of objects which they lend. In the new museums, as in the old ones which are informed with the new spirit, the experts will use their expertness partly on objects, as now; but they will sweeten much of it generously with the simple syrup of sympathy and use it for the pleasure and profit of the common man.

We have purposely presented emphatically the difference between the museum of today and the museum we are trying to develop, and shall try in this series to foreshadow, in the hope that, in so far as our emphasis is disturbing, in so far will the differences we mention be more clearly seen.

Many Old Museums Are New in Part

These differences, it should again be said, are not of our creation. We found the new movement active in many institutions old and young. Indeed, there are few museums today—few at least of the very small number which Mr. Rea tells us are alive—in which the management does not claim that it is doing the new work and developing into the new kind.

That is, to say over once more what we have already said, of the activities above prophesied for the new museum, there are few, if any, which are not being somewhere carried on or being promised for the future.

We have simply conceived of a museum as a living thing, definitely living as is the school; and upon this conception we have grafted such activities of present day museums as one may properly call alive, and have added such others as the thought of a museum as an active "institute of visual instruction" inevitably brings to mind.

Of the things named above, or suggested elsewhere in this volume, we are doing very, very few. Our limitations, psychological and social, are many; our financial limitations are very definite and narrow. We have placed here, in this the first number of our Museum Series, this statement of what we believe a museum should try to be, only because we felt that unless we made our position in this fundamental quite clear, the experiences we shall set forth and the suggestions we shall make would not be accepted as we intend them, and the spirit in which we present them would not clearly be understood.

This Is Not a Museum Manual

Once more: What we are putting down for publication is by no means entirely the product of either our own experience or our own invention. We have studied museum literature; we have visited museums; we have gathered where we could, and we shall try to give due credit always.

✦

Again it should be said that we plan to put into these publications such of a learner's acquisitions as we hope may be useful to other learners. We are not compiling complete museum manuals. We had hoped that workers in old, rich, and experienced museums, far better equipped for the purpose than we are, would undertake what we are doing, but they do not. We dare hope that, by setting forth plainly the lessons we have learned and the principles we have been forced to accept, we can help the beginner. We can hope to do little more.

Our Experience in Museum Work

As to some of the elements of museum management in general and of our fitness to speak of them, perhaps this should be said: For 15 years, seven of them before our museum was organized, we did in the library many of the things that are done in modern museums. We had several unused rooms. In these, in 10 years, there were held about 5,382 meetings, large and small, of 662 different civic and educational organizations, with a total attendance of 167,335. Perhaps no library in the world, and certainly no museum, ever enjoyed so ample an experience as was ours in the management of a center for the voluntary expression by the community of its civic and self-educational impulses. We cared for all these meetings. We helped to make the library a welcome place for them. And from them we learned much in the line of public service.

In the same years we prepared or supervised and directed the installation and the public visitation of 74 exhibitions. These ranged from paintings of the best type to book-plates, guns, and school handiwork. They were visited by 300,000 persons. The installation of every one of them was carefully studied and as carefully carried out as funds permitted; and on the printing of posters, announcements, and catalogs, no time was spared to make it as good as our judgment could dictate and as our local printer could produce.

The management of these many meetings and exhibitions was in the hands of the library staff—not the same throughout in personnel, but the same in intent and skill—that has managed all the museum's affairs since its foundation. Our experience, then, and our learnings in those elements of museum work which we plan to include in this series have not come solely from the management for a few years of a very small museum.

Hence, in part, the boldness which permits us to put into print some of the things we have found helpful.

PART II: BEGINNING A MUSEUM

The introduction to this pamphlet makes it plain that we think the kind of museum best worth having in your community is the kind that is alive and active, is doing some rather definite work in the field of entertainment and of enlightenment and education. But it is demonstrated by that marvelous volume of museum biographies, *The Dictionary of American Museums* (published in 1920 by the Buffalo Museum of Natural Sciences for the American Association of Museums), that museums are not born of definite educational or recreational intent as often as they are of the moods of hobby-riding collectors, of self-centered enthusiasts, and of the memorial-seeking rich. Perhaps this is well. The world needs variety more than it needs standards. There can be no standards in museums. Museums must be born of enthusiasm and grow through unselfish devotion; and enthusiasm and unselfish devotion must be permitted to choose their own objectives and their own methods.

If, then, you find in your community a few who are like-minded with yourself in believing that your fellow citizens would be amused and instructed if they had one of those vague entities, a museum, added to their other public institutions, you will be wise to proceed somewhat as follows:

From print, conversation, and correspondence, discover how museums have found their beginnings in towns like yours. Nothing will here be better worth your investigation than the volume of museum biographies above referred to.

Next, write to museums nearby and ask if they have any suggestions to make. Not infrequently it happens that enthusiastic collectors are giving aid, sympathy, and collections to a museum in another town than their own, all unknown to their fellow citizens.

Before writing to museums, consult the list of them herein and see if any on the list seem, by proximity or character, to be especially well fitted to assist you. Your state museum may be quite ready to give you aid as well as advice.

Having gained a few data on methods of museum-founding, make careful inquiry in your own community to discover collectors, hobby-riders, scientists, teachers seeking such help as a museum can give, and public-spirited men and women of means who have museum leanings or are open to all suggestions for general advancement.

Then get the ear of the newspapers and ask them to print a few notes on the advantages of museums, laying particular stress on the good points of the kind of museum that you think would most interest the museum-minded persons you have discovered.

If the indications are favorable, call a general meeting of all who would care to hear a discussion of the subject of a local museum.

This first discussion is of great importance; rather, it is of great importance that it fit the situation precisely. If you import a speaker for the occasion, let him not be an expert in any part of the field your coming museum may promise to cover. Such a speaker will be naturally inclined to dwell on his own specialty, and thus to fit the inclinations of only a few of your audience. The best way is to have all the speaking done by your own acquaintances in the community itself. Select for the purpose men and women, old and young, who already have an interest in the subject, and let each tell briefly why he or she looks with favor on the museum idea, and what seem to be the indications that others will oppose it. If an outsider is called in to start the movement, he should be thoroughly familiar with local conditions and possibilities and should talk chiefly on a museum's general influence, on the specific steps that should be taken in organizing it, and, perhaps, on the absolutely indispensable items of expense that must be met in its earlier years.

If the attendance and the interest in the discussion seem to warrant it, the organization of an association to promote a local museum can be effected at once. You can frankly confess that you hoped for good results from the meeting and had come prepared therefor.

The proceedings could then take the following course:

You suggest that a chairman be appointed and you name a proper person for the position. Then ask if your nomination is seconded and, if it is, put his election to vote.

He takes the chair and you suggest that a person you name act as secretary, and he is elected also.

Not infrequently, on occasions like the one we are considering, the person most interested, or most given to management, simply says that if there is no objection he will ask Mr. Blank to act as chairman and Mr. So-and-so as secretary. This saves time and is usually quite satisfactory.

You now say that you purpose to offer to those present two motions and to put in nomination five persons as officials; but that before you do this you wish to call to the attention of all the fact that, while your proceedings may seem highhanded, or cut-and-dried, or both, it should be noted that, though your proposals may result in the creation, within five minutes, of a complete organization, that organization will be tentative only, and may be modified or set aside entirely if, after a short trial, it is not found to be satisfactory.

You then move that it is the sense of the meeting that it should proceed with the formation of an organization for the founding and maintenance of a museum in the community.

This is carried.

You then say that in conference with some of those present and with others not present, and after a study of like institutions in other places, you have prepared a form of organization which the secretary will read.

He reads as follows:

The Anyplace Museum League

1) The name of this organization is the Anyplace Museum League.
2) Its purpose is to establish and maintain at Anyplace a museum for the reception and exhibition of articles of art, science, history, ethnology, industry, and tech-

nology, and for the promotion of education by the use of such articles in any proper place, and for the encouragement and management of the study of the arts, industries, and sciences, and to those ends it shall acquire, as occasion permits, such real estate and personal property as may be convenient and necessary for the purpose.

3) The officers shall be president, vice president, secretary, treasurer, and director.
4) These officers shall form the executive committee, which shall have full charge of all affairs of the league when the league itself is not in session.
5) The duties of the several officers shall be those usually assigned thereto in organizations of the character of this one.
6) Anyone may become a member on payment of the annual dues of one dollar, but shall cease to be a member one year and one month after the date of receipt of said dues by the treasurer.
7) The annual meeting for the election of officers shall be held on --- ---.
8) Regular meetings shall be held on the --- of each month except in July, August, and September.
9) The president can call a special meeting at any time and must call one on the written request of three members.
10) This constitution can be amended at any regular or annual meeting by a majority vote if notice of proposed changes has been given at the next preceding meeting.

You can call attention to the brevity and simplicity of the proposed form of organization, and to the fact that it can be easily changed, or even voted out of existence. You can very wisely add that, in discussing the subject with friends of the movement, it seemed better to organize at once, no matter how simply, and to let better plans and methods come by trial and experience, than to attempt to arrive at the last word of wisdom by the machinery of committees and prolonged discussions. Also you can very properly say that if and when the property and activities of the league become important, more elaborate regulations, and probably a charter, will be needed and will undoubtedly be forthcoming.

You can then move that this constitution be adopted.

We assume that it is adopted.

You then say that you will, as you have promised, suggest the names of the officers. You say, of course, that you do this with some reluctance and only after discussing the matter with those you will name and with several others who had expressed themselves as interested in the organization, and that, of course, your presentation of the names is a nomination only, and that other nominations will be welcome and quite as proper to be made as your own.

Your nominees will be, we assume, elected.

Advice on their selection may seem superfluous, but it is not generally understood that activity and ready attention to public, as well as private, business, are more important in the persons who are to launch and manage a new public enterprise, than are age, wealth, or literary or scientific leanings. Much is to be done in the beginning, even of a small and humble organization in a small community. The president should be aggressive. He need not be a leading citizen. As time goes on and work develops, all your leading citizens will be given opportunities to play parts in the enterprise far better worth the taking, in view of their own powers and circumstances, than is the presidency of an infant experiment.

The director is, or should be, the moving spirit behind the institution. He should be given such powers as are held by the general manager of every successful business enterprise. Collectors and experts and ultra-enthusiastic hobby-riders do not make good managers. They find irksome the attention to details which the proper conduct of such an office imposes. Moreover, they are already prepared, in most cases, to give the best of their abilities and their special activities to the promotion of those features of the museum's growth which particularly interest them.

The director should have common sense, enthusiasm for education in all its forms, and an eagerness to learn of the good work a museum can do for a community, and a desire to see that good work done by the museum in his charge. In almost every community, large or small, today, it will be easier to find a woman than a man who is fitted to the director's task and is willing to take it.

It is not probable that the beginnings of a museum organization will ever be found as simple as indicated above. Human currents and counter-currents are too strong—especially, perhaps, in small places. In large towns, there are almost always in existence organizations like academies, scientific societies, literary clubs, and public welfare groups which have either already begun to make collections or are eager to do so. Sometimes, one of these may wisely be asked to take over the first of the town's museum's activities. Sometimes, several of them, at a joint meeting, can form a stronger museum promotion body than can any general gathering.

There are so many variations in the conditioning circumstances that no general rules of procedure can be laid down.

A study of the social, civic, and educational activities of any community will usually disclose, and quite clearly, the best method for initiating the museum movement therein.

If a museum of the old type has already been established, and if, as is quite apt to be the case, it has hardened into a cake of ancient and outgrown customs, it may be advisable to start on a rival institution; though usually it is better to build anew on the old than to attempt to overthrow the old or to outbuild it.

In many school buildings will be found the rudiments of collections, usually in the field that was once vaguely designated as natural history; and often a series of remains left by enthusiastic teachers who, when they taught a few years ago in the building, gathered such material as they could that promised to help make studies more alive and attractive to their pupils. These traces of museum effort in schools are usually worth taking into the new movement, and with them would often go the interest and cooperation of such teachers as have come to realize the great helpfulness of visual aids to instruction in almost any subject.

These school collections also point to the fact that the new organization may safely count in its work on the sympathy and cooperation of nearly every teacher in the community. Indeed, it often happens that a broad-minded teacher, man or woman, is easily the best person to be found to act as director in the museum's early years.

The rapid increase of public library buildings in recent decades has given a great impetus and a still greater opportunity to the new museum movement. A library lends books with pictures in them. It can equally well lend pictures which are not in books.

Pictures form one of the most effective parts of the equipment of a new museum. A library which lends them is already a lending museum in fact, even though not in name.

The Newark Library had a collection of 400,000 pictures covering thousands of subjects, and lent them by thousands before it developed within itself a museum proper. In nature study it is not admitted by many that 25 colored pictures of the same bird, costing not to exceed 25 cents for the lot, are superior as visual aids in teaching—especially if to the 25 pictures one mounted specimen of the same bird can be added to a whole group of mounted specimens of the same kind. Indeed, it is doubtful if a new museum in a small community can do any better work with its first funds than to supply its local library with inexpensive sets of pictures, mount and label them, systematize their arrangement, and cover the cost to the library of storing and lending them.

Even the small library building can find room for the collections and the activities of a new museum in its earlier stages.

The word museum will long continue to arouse in the minds of most the thought of ancient, rare, curious, and beautiful things. Full advantage should, of course, be taken of this universal mental habit. A young organization in a small town can very wisely direct some of its energy in its early days to securing the loan or gift of these ancient, rare, curious, and beautiful objects, and can often advantageously house them in public buildings. In the little town of Pomfret, Vt., with only 600 inhabitants scattered over 36 square miles of hills and valleys, the librarian of the public library—though well advanced in years and though her library was housed in the tiniest of buildings—easily brought together a most interesting historical collection of papers, manuscripts, books, pictures, paintings, portraits, and old household utensils. Inevitably, this work of gathering will go on, and in due course this little community will have its museum of history, biography, pioneer life, and natural sciences, even though no museum organization ever appears on the scene.

In many another town, like work can and should be done. The library, often a fire-proof building, can store all that may come to it and, with a little assistance from a cooperating museum body, can display always a part of its treasures at least, and this can continuously encourage the growth of the little stream of contributions. To these "old attic" features of the museum's work, it can, at very little cost, add some of the minor activities hinted at in the introduction to this pamphlet.

From the agricultural and other departments of the state; from the state university and from private colleges; from the state's museum; from semi-public and public-service corporations; from mines, mills, and factories; from private collections; from scientific enthusiasts and from collecting enthusiasts among boys and girls, the museum can gather at very slight expense more material than it can, at first, advantageously use, unless it finds it possible to raise a sufficient annual income to pay a director and one or two assistants. To give a specific suggestion of what may be done in this line, we note that in one of the pamphlets issued on the work of the Newark Library, "High School Aids in Visual Instruction," is a long list of firms and organizations which furnish, free to all who ask with a definite purpose, interesting collections of material, chiefly in the field of manufacturing, mounted and labeled for display.

As already indicated, in speaking of the use of pictures, the new museum will no sooner have gathered a few objects of interest than it will begin to make use of them. The rarities, the curios, the old portraits—most of the contributions in fact that come in as the result of the prevalence of the idea that a museum is the "Community's Old Attic"—these can all be stored, kept with great care, and displayed as often as possible.

But the live part of the museum's acquisitions—the material which is for use and not simply for gazing—this will soon demand for its storage, arrangement, labeling, and preparation for study and lending more space than a library in most towns and villages can spare for the purpose.

Perhaps the objects acquired after the old museum method can remain in the library and there receive their proper modicum of admiration and wonder and impart their full share of museum fatigue. Museum work proper can meanwhile be transferred to a spare corner in a school house or to a convenient room near the town or village center. Here the director and her aids—all, perhaps, beginning as volunteer workers—will meet to plan for acquisitions.

Parenthetically it should be noted that if we seem here to be dealing at too great detail with very small matters in a very small community, we can properly make reply that in view of the new museum's needs, the procedure for even the largest community should be somewhat in the manner we are going to outline. The whole purpose of the work is new for a museum, at least, and its elements are much the same whether funds available and population to be served be large or small.

The moment, then, that a museum of the modern type has a staff—even if it consists of one person only—and working space and a modicum of funds for the purchases and current expenditures, the staff, with the approval of the proper officials, should proceed to discover the museum's possible field of usefulness. Here is not a question of acquiring rarities, or curios, or high-priced objects of any kind and placing them where those who are interested may come and see them. Here, on the contrary, is the task—one may properly say the duty—of learning what kinds of objects presented in what kinds of ways and accompanied by what kinds of printed or oral expositions will fill a definite need and serve a definite purpose in the community. The old-style museums are founded on the assumption—itself a mere product of obedience to precedent—that the presence in a community of rare and expensive objects in fields either of art or science gives that community not only a certain prestige in the world but also a certain mental éclat, a certain aspiration, a certain integument of culture, a certain open sesame to the realm of refinement.

This assumption is vigorously championed everywhere. Acting under it, communities are still taxing themselves to get, and are asking private benefactors to get for them, marble palaces filled with those so-called emblems of culture—rare and costly and wonder-working objects. The natural history of this mother of the old-style museums, this sublime faith in the civic value of curios to the general public, is interesting and instructive. Here is no place to set it forth. We can only say that, frankly, we cannot discover advantages to any community from the presence in it of one of these culture-fetishes at all commensurate with its cost. It serves no definite and expressed needs. It is alien to its community in every respect of that community's life, save in that of its unfounded traditions. That it is, in our opinion, well that these things come into the public's possession, we have already clearly stated.

The new museum, on the other hand, does not build on an educational superstition. It examines its community's life first and then straightway bends its energies to supplying some of the material which that community needs, and to making that material's presence widely known, and to presenting it in such a way as to secure for it the maximum of use and the maximum of efficiency in that use.

The more modest the new museum is in its staff and resources, the wiser it is to begin its inquiries in the field of formal education. Aids in teaching, over and above the text book, are always too few. The studies even of the primary classes can all be made more interesting and more easily and thoroughly mastered with the help of things. The teachers, the supervisors, and the superintendent can tell what are the objects; of the many different kinds which they would gladly add if they could to their teaching tools; which best combine the advantages of being useful, low in cost, easily transported, and not easily damaged by use.

If the community is a large one, it may be wiser to begin by supplying a few things to the high schools. Here the pupils who will use what the museum can lend are few and a few copies of the same things will supply the demand.

In this educational work, wherever it may begin in the city's educational system, the fundamental principle of the new type of museum—which is the fitting of acquisitions and activities to actual demands—should, of course, be closely followed. Many objects will come in as gifts and loans which will have no relation to this educational work, though it is astonishing how much of what the old type of museum—seeking only the unique, old, and costly—would consider quite useless and even unworthy of acquisition, has an admirable utility in the vast field that opens to the museum of the new type.

The early exhibits of a new museum need not conform at all to the conventions. One could be made of the handwork of pupils in the schools; another of the needlework, from plain sewing to the finest embroidery, of the women of the town; another of cherished heirlooms from homes of the older families; and still another of the "collections"—from birds' eggs and stamps, to kites and models of flying machines—of boys and girls.

A preeminently good field from which to draw resources for a first exhibit is the community itself—its history and present condition. A "community exhibit," being in effect a modest community survey thereof, would include maps old and new; old records; diagrams of growth; statistics of nativity, occupations, etc.; town reports from the earliest date; pictures of the town of all periods; charts and diagrams on the town's income and expenditures, on the public institutions, its roads, water supply, etc.—incipient budgets, in effect; pictures or objects illustrative of its flora, fauna, etc.; in fact anything which would help to give any resident a clearer view of the history, the advantages, and the needs of his community—with, of course, suggestions to old and young as to specific things they can do to make the town a better place in which to live and do business.

Loan exhibits are easily secured. They are often particularly useful in a museum's early days, before it has acquired many interesting objects of its own and before it has a staff which can give time to the preparation of exhibits of local materials even of the simplest kind.

Your state museum may be glad to lend a complete exhibit of some kind, adapted in size and character to your needs and equipment.

The Federation of the Arts of Washington, D.C., lends many exhibits, some of them small and easily shown, others more elaborate.

In Massachusetts, for many years, a Library Art Club has distributed each year among the libraries which form its membership many interesting exhibits for temporary display.

Many individual artists and firms making or handling interesting products are ready to prepare collections—from oil paintings to campaign badges and buttons—and to lend them to any responsible organization. Many libraries and a few museums are glad to be of help in the same way.

The Newark Library prepared an exhibit illustrating the craft and art of bookbinding and lent it to be shown in more than 40 institutions. It has lent many other small collections. The Newark Museum recently prepared an exhibit on the art of making posters and another on the printing of Mr. Bruce Rogers, and both of them are now on their travels.

Cases will be needed in which to show objects which are rare or valuable or are easily injured by dust or handing. But so many exhibits can be shown without cases that the lack of them need not check the museum's early activities.

When cases become absolutely necessary they can sometimes be borrowed, and it is always possible to buy them second-hand. The best kinds are always very expensive, whether new or second-hand.

What Shall the New Museum Collect?

First of all, ideas.

We have already mentioned, incidentally, many of the classes of objects which a museum may wisely gather. Notably, it should collect pictures, and a pamphlet in the Newark "Library Economy Series" on the picture collection in that library describes very fully and in very specific detail methods of collecting, arranging, and managing pictures of almost every kind, and tells how to make them available for almost any purpose.

It should look for collections of hobby-riding specialists and enthusiastic gatherers, especially those which have been carefully identified and labeled.

It should collect things to illustrate the community's history, like household utensils, wills, deeds, letters, early pamphlets, and portraits of the first settlers.

It should try to find collections already made which illustrate the flora, fauna, geology, and mineralogy of the region and the origin and development of its industries and of its social, civic, and religious societies.

If such material as we have already mentioned has not already been collected, the museum should try to find those who will take up one and another division of the field in which it lies and encourage them to work therein.

It should gather material illustrative of the community's manufacturing enterprises and at the same time try to get objects from other places, other countries, and earlier times of like nature to that which it gathers at home. Here it will enter the field of applied art, and this will cultivate persistently whenever opportunities are given.

Painting and sculpture it should not neglect, of course; though the importance to the community, and so to the effectiveness in these fields, has not been shown to be as great as enthusiastic admirers of them have assumed them to be.

But, above all other things, the new museum should begin by collecting ideas.

No one man knows how a museum should be managed that it may, with the funds available, reach the maximum of efficiency in its one and obvious task of adding to the happiness, wisdom, and comfort of the members of its community. We say no one man has this knowledge; indeed, with perfect assurance we can say that this particular parcel of knowledge has not yet been wrought out of experience. It does not exist.

But concerning it there are many ideas—we are, in fact, humbly trying to set down some of them in the series of which this book is the first—and it is these ideas on museums and their management which we are sure those who are beginning to erect a museum of a new type should try to collect before they collect anything else whatsoever.

We have ventured to repeat ourselves more than once in preparing this outline of hints on museum beginnings. Our own experience has led us to do this. We needed to be told; but we had to learn by experience. Because we had to go through that experience once, we hope it may help others to escape a like experience if we indulge somewhat in repetition.

Advice That Would Have Helped Us

It is better to spend money in making good use of one thing than in acquiring another thing. The worth of a museum object is in its use. One common insect, for example, properly displayed with appropriate accompaniments showing its growth, its habits, its harmfulness or helpfulness, with readable and easily understood labels, is far more attractive and useful than is a case of 40 insects, each scientifically named only and set in wearisome rows. One good painting, well lighted, with seats convenient for those who wish to inspect it, with an accompanying pamphlet of simple, straightforward description and comment, can do more for education in the understanding and appreciation of the method and purpose of the world's great painters than is done (save for a very few students) by rows of paintings in huge galleries.

A scrap of printed cotton accompanied by proper text, pictures, charts, and suitably related objects, can throw more light on the subject of textiles for 99 out of 100 visitors than can long rows of examples of the finest "museum specimens" of old and rare fabrics.

Properly to display an object—so to present it, that is—as to make it tell an interesting and instructive story calls for the use of time and brains. You can, therefore, well be sparing in the use of money for purchasing objects; whereas, if you do not spend money freely in the purchase of museum brains, you can make no progress toward the construction of a new museum.

The elements of the arts of listing, classifying, storing, displaying, and labeling objects in museums will be set forth in future pamphlets in this series as clearly and definitely as our study, our experience, and our powers of observation, invention, and statement permit. We venture to add here a few suggestions that seem to us fundamental and that may be found helpful, even in the early days of the most modest institutions.

A Few Fundamental Notes

1) Centralize authority. A museum cannot be well managed by a board of directors. No business can.
2) Museum purposes and methods change daily, as do all other community enterprises in these days. Therefore, do not try to develop a museum after a plan. Learn what aid the community needs; fit the museum to those needs.
3) Beware of "experts" in the museum field.
4) The present dominance of oil paintings in the museum world is responsible for much of the present-day inutility of museums. Sacrifice little of the museum's means or exhibit space to paintings.
5) Accept with thanks everything offered without conditions; accept nothing with conditions.
6) The community maintains schools for education. Attach the museum to the schools; do not let it try to compete with the schools.
7) Welcome enthusiastic collectors as collaborators in the museum. They gather and

store and are laughed at for their pains—and are not disturbed thereby. Time will almost always prove them benefactors.

8) The worth of a museum is in its use.
9) To do something with loving care is better for a man, and far better for a child, than to gaze in wonder at what another has done.
10) Encourage the young to help make their museum.
11) Art is a result, not a cause.
12) Art has no laws; the works of art we most admire are unique and beyond all laws.
13) If there were laws of art production and if we discovered and followed them, we would build art-producing mechanisms. We cannot.
14) The schools have definite aims and pursue them, and all the people in their youth are compelled to feel their influence. The museum can reach only those whom it can attract. This fact alone is enough to compel it to be convenient to all, wide in its scope, varied in its activities, hospitable in its manner, and eager to follow any lead the humblest inquirer may give.
15) Get good museum workers; let one of them at least be experienced in teaching; find a space for display; get an insect, a bird, an animal, a plant, a lithograph, a plaster cast, a spinning wheel, a tea cup, a bit of rock, a mineral, a dozen of the things made commercially in your community, a typewriter, an appropriation for printing, a friend in the local newspaper, set your museum brains at work upon these objects, and in a few weeks you can open a museum which every intelligent person will rejoice to see.
16) Remember, always, that the very essence of the public service of a public institution is the public's knowledge of the service that institution can give; therefore advertise, advertise, and then advertise again. Advertising is the very life-blood of all the education a museum can give.

The Gloom of the Museum

Prologue

Today, museums of art are built to keep objects of art, and objects of art are bought to be kept in museums. As the objects seem to do their work if they are safely kept, and as museums seem to serve their purpose if they safely keep the objects, the whole thing is as useful in the splendid isolation of a distant park as in the center of the life of the community which possesses it.

Tomorrow, objects of art will be bought to give pleasure, to make manners seem more important, to promote skill, to exalt handwork, and to increase the zest of life by adding to it new interests; and these objects being bought for use will be put where the most people can most handily use them: in a museum planned for making the best use of all it contains, and placed where a majority of its community can quickly and easily visit it.

PART I: HOW THE ARTS HAVE BEEN INDUCED TO FLOURISH

The story of an art epoch in the life history of a people seems to resolve itself into something like this:

Character and circumstances lead the people into conquest. It may sound better, though it means the same, to say that character and circumstances bring out a few men of genius who lead and rule the people and take them on to conquest. The conquest means wealth, and this is true whether the conquest be of other peoples by leadership and force of arms, or of the land's natural resources and of methods of producing and using power.

Always a few gain most of the wealth and hold most of the power. The conquest being somewhat well assured, these few have leisure. They search for occupations and

---

The New Museum Series, no. 2. Woodstock, Vt.: The Elm Tree Press, first printing, 1917, second printing, 1927.

things and indulgences which may give them pleasure. Whatever else these occupations, objects, and indulgences may be, they must be such as the common people cannot have; for the rich and ruling class must always keep itself distinct from the lower classes in its pleasures and pastimes, just as it always did in its leadership in war and government. These distinctive recreations and diversions and admired objects of the powerful and rich have always been of about the same character. War is first choice; if not war of the higher kind in which is involved the existence of the tribe, family, city, dukedom, principality, kingdom, or nation over which the rich and powerful in question rule, then a war of petty conquest, mean in itself, but permitting some braggadocio, keeping up the clan spirit and exalting the ruling class. Lacking a vigorous and dangerous war on battlefields to engage all their activities, the rulers have often turned to hunting—to hunting in a form which nature, or special laws, or the rules of the game make somewhat dangerous; for if it does not at least seem dangerous, those who engage in it will not appear brave to the lower classes. The form of hunting chosen is usually one which is quite inaccessible to the poor and weak. Big game near home, and better still at a good distance; falconry, the right to use falcons being easily restricted to the few; fox hunting on horseback; dangerous athletic sports; and latterly automobiling, ballooning, and flying—these have all had or shall have their vogue.

Another obvious method of distinguishing their life from that of the common people has been the possession of distinctive residences beyond all need in size, number, cost, and adornment. It is through these residences that the rich and powerful have chiefly been led to become patrons of the arts. The wish to make full use of the religious habits of the ruled has often led the rich to build and adorn churches; and always, of course, the need of expensive and peculiar dress has been an occasion for calling in the aid of artisans of certain kinds. The study of literature, language, history, and the fine arts has also often been a recreating of the rich, though usually these studies have been pursued by proxy. As unusual native ability has almost always been one of the essentials to success in acquiring wealth and power, it is not strange that an occasional member of the class of the ruling rich has shown marked ability in letters and the arts, or at least in appreciation of them. But pursuit of art and letters has usually ended with little more than such a patronage of them as would bring in return ample adulation, a reputation for learning, and glorification in history.

Comparative security, then, after a series of profitable wars, finds the rich and powerful compelled to engage in expensive sports, to build large and expensive residences, and to decorate them and to adorn elaborately their own persons that there may be no lack of distinctions between themselves and the common people. The demand for architects, painters, sculptors, gold and silversmiths, ironworkers, and artisans of all kinds thus at once arises; and a demand also for teachers, poets, orators, and historians to make a pretense of love of learning.

It is worth noting here that in former days these workers produced without the intervention of machinery; that the rich have usually been ready to adopt the older methods in art productions if for any reason they were inaccessible to the poor; and that today admiration for the handmade is largely born of a desire to have something which, being unique in its kind, will impart a little of the old leisure-class exclusiveness to its owner.

The patronage of the arts, with the consequent development thereof, has varied in extent in the rise to wealth and leisure of the leaders among different peoples, as circumstances dictated, but its origin seems always to have been about the same. Whenever this patronage has appeared—whenever, that is, the demand for objects of art has arisen—the supply has been forthcoming.

Fashion among the rich has sometimes prevented the results of this patronage of art from showing themselves very plainly in the country of the rich. In our day, for example, the fashion is to import from abroad and to say that good artwork cannot be produced at home; so we have a Barbizon painting factory in Paris, makers of antiques in Italy, and a digging up of gone-by utensils and furniture in all European and Asiatic countries. These old things cost more in the first place, the tariff makes them more expensive still, and their ownership gives considerable of the ruling-class distinction. Were it to become the fashion to patronize American designers and craftsmen in all lines and to give artists and architects a free hand instead of insisting on conformity to the ancient ways as interpreted by the ignorant rich, we would have a larger art demand in America; the supply would raise prices and wages; art study would be encouraged; more men of genius, skill, and training would come here from abroad; and we would begin our own renaissance.

Those who know Mr. Veblen's delightful book on "The Theory of the Leisure Class" will see that I have borrowed from him in my statement about the character of the diversions and the conspicuous waste of the rich.

But our renaissance does not come. We have an aristocracy based on wealth, with accompanying power. This aristocracy feels the same need that aristocracies have always felt of acquiring ancient, rare, and costly objects that the possession of them may mark them as superior to the poor and weak. They find that the easiest way to acquire such objects is not to cause them to be produced by artists and artisans of their own country—America—but, as already noted, to purchase them in older countries. What had already given distinction to their owners in France, Italy, England, and Germany is seen at once to be peculiarly well fitted to give a like distinction here.

Hence the products of our own people are definitely held in no esteem as honorific possessions. Art in America does not flourish.

I have used the foregoing remarks, taken from a paper published in the *Independent* seven years ago, as a preface to the essay which follows on the gloom of the museum in the hope that they will make still more self-evident the statements in the latter concerning the origin of American museums of art. The kinds of objects—ancient, costly, and imported—that the rich feel they must buy to give themselves a desired distinction are inevitably the kinds that they, as patrons and directors of museums, cause those museums to acquire. Veritably, most of our great museums look with open scorn on the products of American artists and artisans.

The peculiar sanctity of oil paint on canvas has been graciously extended in some small degree to New World products, and our great museums occasionally buy, more often receive as gifts, and still more often receive as loans for exhibition the works of American painters. But most of our richer museums of art, that in Chicago being a notable exception, follow the dictates of the rich. They very evidently do not think it is the proper function of a museum of art to promote, foster, or patronize American talent.

The new museum, for the development of which this series is designed, will hold that its first duty is to discover talent and encourage its development here at home.

The rich and powerful collect foreign things and insist that foreign things only shall be enshrined in the museum they patronize. The poor follow the rich in this thinking. The attempt to modify this state of affairs is not one that is full of hope. But the growing habit of cities to maintain their own museums will surely tend to democratize them; and if, in the beginnings of the museums that are now coming into existence, the suggestions for making them immediately and definitely useful to their founders and patrons—the public—which we find today so widely approved among museum workers are quite generally adopted, the day will soon come when many public museums will look upon the promotion of American art as one of their most important functions.

PART II: THE GLOOM OF THE MUSEUM, WITH SUGGESTIONS FOR REMOVING IT

Prefatory Note

The art of museum construction, acquisition, and management is in its infancy. No one can say with authority how that art will be developed in the next few years. But on this much at least the public may congratulate itself: that museum authorities now feel that their respective establishments should be, above all things, attractive in a sane and homely way to the public which owns them.

Art museums of necessity have the faults of their ancestry, and these faults are so obvious that even a layman like myself may see them, and the plain statement of such of them as a layman dares to say he sees may help to move the intelligent part of the public to set to work to correct them.

Throughout this discussion I have art museums almost solely in mind.

How Museums Came to Be So Gloomily Beautiful

One need visit only a few of the older museums of art and archaeology in Europe to understand why most American museums of the same subjects are so ineffective.

In Europe, these older museums have objects of great importance to students of art, of history in general, of the history of art, of social development, and of the history of invention and discovery. Large groups of these objects were first collected many years ago by wealthy and powerful individuals: princes, kings, emperors, and members of the nobility. These collectors were usually entirely selfish in their acquisition, rarely looking beyond their own personal pleasure or the aggrandizement of their immediate families. They collected that they might possess, not that they might use, or that others might use, the things collected for the pleasure and advancement of the world at large.

As the idea of general welfare crept into and modified the government of any given country, the ruling powers of that country in many cases confiscated or purchased these collected treasures, added other purchases and gifts to them, made them so-called public collections, and deposited them for safekeeping in national and municipal buildings. These buildings were for the most part erected for other purposes than the reception and proper display of works of art and archaeology. This fact usually made it possible to install collections in them only under such conditions of space and light as prevented either logical or artistic arrangement and made both casual observation and careful study of most of the objects a burden instead of pleasure.

As the collections were of very great value—consisting usually of originals which no money could replace, which should therefore be guarded with the utmost care—the first thought in regard to them was their preservation; their utilization being a secondary and rather remote affair.

Why Museum Buildings Are Temples and Palaces

The character of the buildings which, as time went on, were here and there erected to house these collections of priceless originals, was determined by several factors. As most of the collections had found their first homes in the palaces of rulers or members of the nobility, it was quite naturally concluded that their new homes should also be in the style of the local palace or royal residences. As the things collected were objects of art, it seemed obvious that they should be housed in artistic buildings, and as for several centuries it has been difficult for architects or those having power over art collections to conceive of an artistic building save in terms of Greek or Renaissance architecture, nearly all special museum buildings imitated either the Greek temple or the Italian palace.

In Europe, therefore, we find museums to be either old buildings of the royal palace type or later constructions copying the palace or the Greek temple; containing priceless originals in all lines of art, craftsmanship, and archaeology; arranged as the characters of the several buildings compel; guarded with extreme care; dutifully visited by serious-minded tourists; and used sparingly by a small number of special students.

New America Copies the Old Europe, Of Course

This, roughly speaking, was the museum idea as it embodied itself in Europe when the subject of museums began a few decades ago to be taken up seriously in America. It was inevitable that the first wish of all our museum enthusiasts should be to produce imitations of the European institutions. Those institutions were, in most cases, long established and greatly admired, and they furnished the only illustrations of the museum idea.

Moreover, collections more or less well suited to form the beginnings of art museums had been made here, after the European manner, by a few of the rich; some of these had fallen by gift or will to public use, accompanied not infrequently by the requirement that they be permanently housed in art buildings which were inevitably fashioned after the European type.

The promoters of art museums in America had no choice in the matter. The approved examples of Europe, the precedents already established in America in accordance with those examples, the unanimous votes of architects and trustees on what it is that makes a building a fit home for works of art, and the voice of so much of the general public as had ever seen or heard of European museums—all these factors united to complete the erection here of the kind of museum building which now oppresses us.

Why Museums Are Way Off in the Woods

The prevalence of the European idea of a museum determined not only the character of our museum buildings but also their location. As they must be works of art, and as temples and palaces need open space about them to display their excellences, and as space in the centers of towns is quite expensive, donors, architects, trustees, and city fathers all agreed that the art museum building should be set apart from the city proper, preferably in a park with open space about it. Distance from the center of population and the difficulty most citizens would encounter did they attempt to see the museum's contents were given no weight in comparison with the obvious advantages of display of the building's outer charms.

The Museum of Religious Gloom

A city may with perfect propriety set itself to the task of making a collection of rare and ancient original products of man's craftsmanship, spending, for example, $10,000 for a piece of tapestry, $100,000 for a painting, $30,000 for a marble statue, $20,000 for a piece of porcelain, and so on; it may add to these by gift and may place them all in a one-story, poorly lighted, marble, fireproof building set in a park remote from the city's center. But it ought to do this with a full comprehension of the fact that, while it is in so doing establishing a "Museum of Art" in the sense in which that phrase is most often used today, it is not forming an institution which will either entertain or instruct the community to an extent at all commensurate with its cost. In such an establishment the city will have an "art museum" of the kind which the citizen points out with pride to visiting friends; which appears in the advertising pamphlets of the local boards of trade; which is the recipient of an occasional painting or other work of art from a local art patron; which some strangers and a few resident women and children occasionally use to produce in themselves the maximum of fatigue with the minimum of pleasure; which will offer through the opening of loan collections a few opportunities each winter for society to display itself and demonstrate its keen aesthetic interests.

Rarity and High Price Make Things More Beautiful

The European examples which were so disastrous in their effect on the character and location of our museum buildings had an unfortunate influence also on the character and arrangement of their contents.

In the order of events in Europe, as already noted, one country after another and one city after another came into the possession of treasures of art and archaeology—priceless originals—which it was the duty of the authorities to preserve with the utmost care. Our own art museum enthusiasts, imitating their predecessors, sought also to form collections of unique and costly objects. A delusion like that which everywhere possesses the art novice as to the relative value of real oil paintings, however atrocious, and colored lithographic reproductions of paintings, however excellent, possessed those who made private art collections and those who selected and purchased objects for our museums. Art museum objects were not chosen for their beauty or for the help they might give in developing good taste in the community, but for their rarity, their likeness to objects found in European museums, and for their cost.

The older collections on the continent are naturally largely historical and archaeological. This seemed sufficient reason for making our collections of the same kind.

The wish to form collections which should illustrate the development of this or that special form of art also influenced greatly the character of our early museums.

But the wish to make them, like their European models, include a large number of things peculiar, unique, not copies, not obtainable by others, and costly, was probably the chief factor in making our museums mausoleums of curios.

The objects acquired being rare and costly, it was inevitable that they should be very carefully safeguarded, placed where they could be seen only (and that not very adequately), and never handled and examined closely.

American Museums Today

That this rough outline of recent museum history in America is fairly correct is amply demonstrated by present-day American museums themselves. They are usually housed in buildings fashioned to look like Greek temples or Renaissance palaces, which are very poorly adapted to the proper installation of collections and very rarely well planned for growth. These buildings are set apart from the city whose citizens they are built to serve, often in remote parks. The objects in them are very largely second-rate original artworks, usually with large additions of things historical or archaeological of little art value. Many of the buildings are so expensive to administer and to light and to heat that the managers can keep them open to the public only a small part of the hours when the public can best visit them. They are visited by few, that few being made up largely of strangers passing through the city; and the objects displayed are used for practical, everyday purposes and are looked to for suggestions applying to daily life by a very small number of persons, and by them very rarely.

Museum Failures Are Not Chargeable to Specific Persons

It may be said that if this development of American art museums into remote palaces and temples—filled with objects not closely associated with the life of the people who are asked to get pleasure and profit from them, and so arranged and administered as to make them seem still more remote—it may be said that if this development has been as natural and inevitable as has been suggested, then no one can be charged with responsibility for the fact, and not much can be done to correct the error.

It would indeed be difficult to lay the burden of this unfortunate line of development on the shoulders of any persons who may be specifically named. It would be difficult also to correct the mistake already made. No one, for example, would quite dare to suggest (taking up the point only of location) to the citizens of Boston, New York, Buffalo, and Cincinnati that they can much better afford, in the long run, to move their museums into the centers of daily movement of population and thereby secure a tenfold enlargement of their use and influence, than they can to go on paying large sums for their maintenance in relative idleness where they are now.

And it would be idle to attempt to persuade architects and trustees and a public, bound to accept the architectural conventions of their time, that when they use the outward presentations of one-story buildings designed for housing gods in a perpetual twilight as the peripheries of well-lighted and convenient and easily warmed and controlled spaces for the display of precious objects to thousands of visitors, they show a certain magnificent courage, but not good architectural traits, not originality, and not common sense.

But, in spite of the depressing influence of fashion and of the architectural paralysis induced by the classic burden in these matters, one may hope that all museums hereafter built need not conform to the old ideas, and that some of the museums already in existence can be so modified as to be far more useful and influential than they are today.

The Art of Museum Making in Its Infancy

The art of making museums which will be largely used by those who pay for them and will please and profit all who visit them is in its infancy. No one ventures to describe definitely the ideal American art museum. A few suggestions may at least provoke helpful discussion.

Museums Should Be Central

An art museum should be so located that it may be reached by a maximum number of persons with a minimum expenditure of time and money. It should be near the center of the city which maintains it—not its population center but its rapid transit center—and as near as possible also to its more important railway stations that strangers may visit it quickly and cheaply.

It may be said that a collection of art objects properly housed in a beautiful building gains somewhat in dignity and importance and in its power to influence beneficially those who visit it if it is set apart a little from the city's center of strenuous commercial and material life; holds itself somewhat aloof, as it were; detaches itself from the crowd; and seems to care to speak only to those whose desire for its teachings is strong enough to lead them to make some sacrifice of time and money to enjoy them.

The suggestion is a specious one. This theory of the fitness of remoteness is born of pride and satisfaction in the location and character of museums as they are. The buildings are remote and are religious or autocratic or aristocratic in style; their administrators, perhaps in part because of this very aloofness and sacrosanct environment, are inclined to look upon themselves as high priests of a peculiar cult, who may treat the casual visitor with tolerance only when he comes to worship rather than to look with open eyes and to criticize freely; and the trustees are prone to think more of their view of the proper museum atmosphere than of museum patronage, more of preservation than of utilization.

This same theory as to the preciosity which remoteness may confer, applied to art in general and carried to its logical conclusions, would forbid the expenditure of public funds or private gifts on the beautifying of streets or bridges or public buildings. Under its application, one might say that a commercial city should be built in the coldest, baldest possible style, and that beautiful façades of homes, office buildings, and factories should be erected as façades only in remote parks and boulevards, there to be solemnly visited and viewed by those who truly care to exalt their souls and purify their intellects.

The Museum Building: Some of Its Obvious Qualities

The museum building located in the city's center should satisfy the fundamental conditions of all good architecture: It should be large enough for its purpose; it should be constructed of the materials, proper in its day, which are best adapted to its form and size; it should be in harmony with its surroundings; and it should be as beautiful as the highest technique and the best taste of the time can make it.

A building of steel and concrete in a modern American city is not made an appropriate home of the fine arts by placing on its front the façade of one or the façades of half a dozen Greek temples or of 15th-century Italian palaces. It is impossible to believe that the best Greek architects, if they were the masters in good taste we suppose them to have been, would have continued to make their buildings look as though they were built of columns of stone, with huge girders and cross-beams of the same material, long after they had learned to use steel and concrete in construction.

In time we shall learn to insist that great public buildings like libraries and museums be erected as such and not as imitations of structures developed for quite other purposes, in other cities, in other times, and under limitations as to material and method by which we are no longer bound.

A modern museum building for an American city is a distinct problem in arrangement and a difficult one not to be solved by the adoption for its exterior of a type, however beautiful, which in origin and development never bore the slightest relation to the subject of museums.

It may be said that the contents of art museums are in part priceless, cannot be replaced, must be so housed as to make their destruction by fire impossible, and that, therefore, the only safe location for a museum is in a park, far from all other buildings. In reply it may be said that the high value put on many of the objects in art museums is largely fictitious, born of the rivalry of rich collectors and even of rich museums in their search for objects of honorable uniqueness; that a few students could truly feel their loss; but that as instruments of human enlightenment and happiness they are by no means priceless. Next, it may be noted that it is doubtful if any art museum authorities have yet erected a remote building on the contents of which they can get fire insurance rates as low as they could get them on the same contents housed in a fireproof building in the center of their city. There are risks in remoteness as well as safeguards. It should also be said that if a city wants a warehouse for the storage of art treasures, build it by all means; but do not encumber it with the fine, open spaces of a public park. But if it wants an institution of the newer museum type, something from which can be derived pleasure, surely, and profit if the gods permit, then let that be built where it can be easily made use of, in the city's center.

In a great city the museum building could properly be several, perhaps many, stories high, and if open space about it were quite impossible for financial reasons, light could be had from courts. Nearly all rooms would then be lighted from one side, as nearly all exhibition, study, and lecture rooms should be.

The Vast Extent of Museum Collections Leads to Obscurity

The objects gathered in art museums will continue to include the works of men's hands in all materials, for all purposes, of all countries, and for all time. Students of every form of art will continue to ask that museums include not only the products of that art when it was at the highest point of its development, but also its products in every stage of its growth and of its decline. Museums—that is, some of the large museums at least—must continue to be not only museums of many arts, but also of the histories of those arts, and therefore of archaeology and of ethnology.

But as time goes on, many collections, thus expanding naturally into other fields than that of art, will become unwieldy, overloaded with objects of interest only to the very special student, mere confusing masses of seemingly unrelated objects to the ordinary visitor. They will lose all effectiveness in what should be their special field—that of suggesting to the observer that a certain refinement of daily life is worth all it costs—and, to the would-be promoter of this refinement, that certain special methods in this, that, and the other field have been successful once and may be successful again. That is to say, art museum collections continually tend to lose the power of doing that which they were designed to do, which is to say to us that manners and feelings are important parts of life. For the objects which have to do with age-long gropings after good things will always tend to become so numerous as to hide the good things themselves.

The Undue Reverence for Oil Paint

The extreme veneration now paid by museum authorities to great paintings will surely become weaker as the possibilities of a museum's influence become better understood. Painting in oil upon canvas is not a craft that makes a strong appeal to the average man, save through the stories it tells. Its value, after all, is almost entirely pictorial. As mere pictures—which is all that they are to the average observer of ordinary intelligence, plus the interest born of their age, their history, and their cost—they each year suffer more and more from the competition of other pictures not done in oil on canvas, found in posters, in journals and newspapers, and in the cinema. In due course the oil painting will take its place in museums with other products of men's hands simply as one of the many things of high beauty and great suggestiveness produced in perfection only by men of special talent who have been able to master a difficult technique.

This fact will in time be recognized and acted upon: that the oil painting has no such close relation to the development of good taste and refinement as have countless objects of daily use. The genius and skill which have gone into the adornment and perfecting of familiar household objects will then receive the same recognition as do now the genius and skill of the painter in oils. Paintings will no longer be given an undue share of space, and on them will be expended no undue share of the museum's annual income. It is doubtful if any single change in the general principles of art museum management will do as much to enhance museum influence as will this placing of the oil painting in its proper relation with other objects.

The Subordination of Painting and the Promotion of Applied Art

If oil paintings are put in the subordinate place in which they belong, the average art museum will have much more room for the display of objects which have quite a direct bearing on the daily life of those who support it, visit either the main buildings or its branches, and make use of its collections. One need not be specific; the museum will show by originals or replicas what has been done by other people to make more convenient and attractive all the things that we use and wear and see day by day, from shoes to signposts and from table knives to hat pins. As the museum gives more space and more attention to these things, it will quite inevitably also display the objects in which its own city is particularly interested. It will have no absurd fear that it will be commercialized and debased if it shows what is being done today in the field of applied art in its own city and in other parts of the world. It will take no shame from the fact that it is handling and installing and displaying articles made by machinery for actual daily use by mere living people. One of the grotesqueries of expertness in museum work today is the reverential attention paid to products of craftsmanship which are (1) old, (2) rare, (3) high in price, (4) a little different from all others, and (5) illustrate a change in method of work or in the fashion of their time. Still more depressing is this reverence when it is accompanied, as it often is, with indifference, or scorn, or fear of commercial taint, toward products of craftsmanship which are (1) modern, (2) common, (3) not high in price, (4) a copy of the old, rare, and priceless.

What could be more ludicrous than the sight of those who, openly devoted to the worship of beauty, treat with scorn modern reproductions of old things which they have pronounced beautiful, even if they copy the old so well that only labels and microscopes can distinguish one from the other, or even if, not professing to be exact reproductions, they show originality and high skill in design, are technically quite perfect, and either disclose the taste of the time or are factors in the betterment of that taste.

Surely a function of a public art museum is the making of life more interesting, joyful, and wholesome; and surely a museum cannot very well exercise that function unless it relates itself quite closely to the life it should be influencing; and surely it cannot thus relate itself unless it comes in close contact with the material adornment of that life—its applied arts.

The necklace found on an Egyptian mummy is unique, old, and costly. But even if presented to a museum by someone of wealth and influence, it still may be hideous and it may have no suggestion whatever for the modern designer. If it has certain suggestive value in this line, it thereby becomes just as well worthy of its place in the museum as is a necklace made yesterday in a neighboring city. Being unique, it should be kept. Its origin gives it an archaeological value. But if it is admitted to a museum of art, it need not stand in the way of the display in the same museum of modern necklaces which may interest many and may give suggestion and stimulus to modern designers.

Of course, it is not the Egyptian mummy's necklace which stands in the way of the display of modern necklaces, but the spirit of curators, experts, directors, and trustees. They become enamored of rarity, of history, and, in this specific instance, of necklaces as indicative of steps in civilization. They become lost in their specialties and forget their museum. They become lost in their idea of a museum and forget its purpose. They become lost in working out their idea of a museum and forget their public. And soon, not being brought constantly in touch with the life of their community through handling and displaying that community's output in one or scores of lines, they become entirely separated from it and go on making beautifully complete and very expensive collections, but never construct a living, active, and effective institution.

Is the Department Store a Museum?

A great city department store of the first class is perhaps more like a good museum of art than are any of the museums we have yet established. It is centrally located; it is easily reached; it is open to all at all the hours when patrons wish to visit it; it receives all courteously and gives information freely; it displays its most attractive and interesting objects and shows countless others on request; its collections are classified according to the knowledge and needs of its patrons; it is well lighted; it has convenient and inexpensive rest rooms; it supplies guides free of charge; it advertises itself widely and continuously; and it changes its exhibits to meet daily changes in subjects of interest, changes of taste in art, and the progress of invention and discovery.

A department store is not a good museum, but so far are museums from being the active and influential agencies they might be that they may be compared with department stores and not altogether to their advantage.

The Museum as the Teacher and Advertiser

To make itself alive, a museum must do two things: It must teach and it must advertise. As soon as it begins to teach, it will of necessity begin to form an alliance with present teaching agencies, the public schools, the colleges and universities, and the art institutions of all kinds. It is only by bearing in mind the history of its development and the part that imitation has played in that development that one can understand how American communities have been able to establish, build up, and maintain great collections of works of art, beautifully and expensively housed and administered, which yet have almost no cooperative relations with all the other educational and social-betterment institutions of the same communities. Teaching tends to become dogmatic. Dogmatism in art is injurious, but museum teaching need not be dogmatic. Indeed, museums might well be less dogmatic than they now are. They buy high-priced paintings and spend vast sums for rare brocades, pottery, ancient wood carvings, and whatnot, and then set these (with an ample air of assurance of wisdom which may very well be called dogmatic) before their constituents, saying, "Look, trust the expert, and admire." Far less dogmatic would it be to set side by side in a case ancient and rare modern and commercial pottery, and say, "Here are what some call the fine products of the potter's art when it was at its best in Italy long ago, and here are products of the potters of America today. You will find a comparative study of the two very interesting."

Would there be anything debasing in such an apposition? Would it be less dogmatic than is nearly all museum presentation of itself today?

By no right in reason whatever is a museum a mere collection of things, save by right of precedent. Yet precedent has so ruled in this field that our carefully organized museums have little more power to influence their communities than has a painting which hangs on the wall of some sanctuary, a sanctuary which few visit and they only to wonder as they gaze and to depart with the proud consciousness that they have seen. Some of the best of our museums, spending many thousands per year on administration and many other thousands on acquisitions, are now pluming themselves on the fact that they employ one—only one—person to make their collections more interesting to the thousands who visit them; that they have a hall in which during a winter a few lectures are given; and that they publish a bulletin recording their progress in piling up treasures, and catalogues which are as devoid of human interest as a perfect catalogue can be.

Museums of the future will not only teach at home, they will travel abroad through their photographs, their textbooks, and their periodicals. Books, leaflets, and journals—which will assist and supplement the work of teachers and will accompany, explain, and amplify the exhibits which art museums will send out—will all help to make museum expenditures seem worthwhile.

Why Not Branch Museums?

Museums will soon make themselves more effective through loan exhibits and through branches.

The museum is in most cases so remote from the city's center that even if it were to rival in attractiveness the theater, the cinema, and the department store, the time and money it takes to reach it would bar most from ever paying it a visit. It should establish branches, large and small, as many as funds permit, in which could be seen a few of the best things in one and another field that genius and skill have produced; in which could be seen the products of some of the city's industries, placed beside those of other cities, of other countries, and of other times; in which thousands of the citizens could each day see—at the cost of a few minutes only of their time—a few at least of the precious objects which their money has been used to collect.

Even though the main museum building is centrally situated, the need of branches—in a large city, at least—is quite obvious. The small branch would be more effective in the appeal it could make to many visitors than the main building could ever be. A half hour in the presence of one fine painting, a dozen Greek vases (with perhaps a few of other times and countries for comparison), one great piece of sculpture—each of these with ample descriptive notes and leaflets—would arouse more genuine feeling and a deeper interest than an aimless stroll through rooms full of the world's best art products.

These branches need not be in special buildings. Often, a single room conveniently located would serve as well as, or even better than, an elaborate and forbidding structure. How the idea would be worked out in detail no one can say. Apparently it has never been tried. But there seems to be no reason other than that found in precedent why the art treasures of a city—its own property, bought by itself to illuminate and broaden and make more enjoyable the life of its citizens—should rest always in the splendid isolation of that remote temple or palace erected for them.

Museum Objects May Be Lent

Art museums frequently borrow collections of objects and show them temporarily. Why do they not more often reverse the process?

More than 20 years ago, a self-constituted committee of women established in Massachusetts what was in effect a library art league. With the aid of the libraries which joined the league, they brought together a large number of interesting collections, chiefly of pictures of many kinds and dealing with many subjects, which traveled about and were shown at one library after another. For many years the University of the State of New York has been sending out from Albany collections of pictures to be exhibited in the libraries of the state and in other proper institutions.

Groups of museums, notably the group now operating under the direction of the Federation of Arts, have long been borrowing and successively showing collections of paintings, engravings, pottery, bronzes, and other objects. The Newark Library has prepared or arranged several exhibits of art and handicraft which have been shown in a total of more than 100 American cities. The American Museum of Natural History lends annually thousands of specially prepared exhibits to the schools of New York and vicinity. The Commercial Museums of Philadelphia prepare collections for the schools of the whole state of Pennsylvania. In St. Louis, an educational museum—geographical, scientific, and industrial, maintained by the board of education—lends many thousands of objects and collections each year to the schools of the city. In Germany, there go forth each year from a central bureau in Hagen many carefully prepared exhibitions of objects of art and handicraft gathered from the best workshops in the empire; and the South Kensington museum has been lending objects to towns and cities in Great Britain for many years.

In spite of all these good examples of the possibilities for helpfulness which lie in loan collections shown for brief periods in each of a score of cities or in each of a hundred schools of the same city, the habit of lending subjects from and by museums of art is almost unknown in this country.

Even the youngest and most modest of museums—unless it is of the purely mortuary type, housed in a temple, complete in all its appointments, installed for all time according to the museum laws of its founders and hastening to its destined end of disuse—even such a museum has objects which would find a hitherto useless life crowned with good works were they lent freely to schools, libraries, art schools, civic centers, and whatnot in the town to which they belong.

Museums of science are sending their exhibits to their patrons, old and young. It is quite evident that art museums will soon follow their example.

The art museums are just now greatly concerned over the question of how they shall make themselves of value to the young people of their respective communities. It is plain enough that it is impossible in a large city for the young people to make the journey to the central museum times enough to gain more than the most fleeting of impressions. They have not the money for car fares, they must go in crowds and teachers must accompany the crowds, and school time for this is lacking, and if they were to go times enough to get any enduring lessons from their visits, they would crowd the central building to the doors.

Why not take the museum to the young people? Public branches can serve the adults; and collections, groups, single objects, and photographs and other pictures can easily be placed in school houses, and surely soon will be.

Do We Need Museums at All?

I have ventured to mention the great department stores in the same sentence with museums of art. No sooner is the comparison made than other suggestive comparisons come to mind. The dealer in paintings has his art gallery, always convenient, open to all without charge, with exhibitions constantly changing. Dealers in works of art in general seem to approach even nearer to the museum ideal. Then on the industrial side we find that every factory and workshop is a museum in action, and, if it produces beautiful objects, is a living exhibit of arts and crafts.

Stores are each year more attractive and more informing; each year factories are more humanely and rationally managed, are more inviting and more informing, and are more freely open to interested visitors under reasonable restrictions. Each year the printing press produces better and cheaper illustrations of artworks of every kind, with a descriptive letter press which grows each year not only more ample but also more direct and simple. And each year the cinema reproduces for us more faithfully the activities of men in all lines of work and in all countries and makes it easier for us all to understand what books and journals try to tell us through text and pictures.

This question then arises: Does a world which is supplied by mere trade and industry with convenient storehouses of the world's products old and new, the best as well as the poorest, with industrial exhibits in factories of every kind, and with pictures and texts of amazing beauty and suggestiveness—does a world having all these things need the art museum at all?

The Museum as the Public's Friend and Guide

The question just asked answers itself at once, of course. Save for the very young, the opportunities for self-education offered by the street, the store, the factory, the movie, and the all-pervasive page of print are quite ample. Any boy or girl who will can gain an excellent education without the ministration of the school. But, on the whole, in spite of its manifest deficiencies, it seems wise to maintain the school and promote education through it.

Just so with those refinements of human nature—those betterments of manner and feeling, which I have ventured to name as good things which art museums exist to promote—these refinements may be attained by any, save the very young, who will attend thereto and will diligently use, to that end, the materials always at hand in dress, architecture, shop window, nature, and the ever-present picture and printed page. But in spite of the infinity of ever-present opportunity for everyone's education in the refinement of life and the enrichment of the leisure hour, it has seemed wise to establish and maintain the museum of art.

I have tried to show that this museum has been so absorbed in one aspect of its work that it has left untouched its more important and pressing duties. It has built itself an elaborate and costly home, beautiful after the fashion of its time and the taste of its community. In this home it has gathered the rare, the curious, the beautiful, and always, when possible, the unique and costly. So doing it has paid its debt to history and archaeology, has gained for its city a certain passing and rather meretricious distinction, and has given a select few an opportunity to pursue their study of fashion in taste, in ornament, and in technique.

Now seems to come the demand that the museum serve its people in the task of helping them to appreciate the high importance of manner, to hold by the laws of simplicity and restraint, and to broaden their sympathies and multiply their interests.

A Plan for a New Museum: The Kind of Museum It Will Profit a City to Maintain

Introduction

I read a paper on "Increasing Usefulness of Museums" at the meeting of the American Association of Museums, May 1916, in Washington, D.C., and it was printed in the proceedings of that association.

Although a few of the suggestions and criticisms here set forth were presented in that paper, this book is more than a revision of it. I have rewritten it and added to it further suggestions of my own and others from the museum literature of the past three years.

It is now much less a prophecy and much more a record than it was when it was read in first draft to a group of museum workers. The suggestion that museums should be of definite value to the communities which maintain them is now quite generally accepted, and is being worked out in practice as rapidly, perhaps, as the indifference of the public, the conservatism of trustees, and the incubus of expertness will permit.

This is the fourth of a series of small volumes on museums that I have written in recent years, volumes that I must frankly admit are little more than essays. I have published them at my own expense, partly to please myself and partly because I found they were not acceptable to publishers of either books or journals. Elsewhere I have given a brief statement of how they came to be written.

In May 1919, I read a paper to the trustees of the Newark Museum Association, which was afterwards published as a pamphlet with the title "The New Relations of Museums and Industries: The Story of the First Ten Years of a Group of Experimental Museums." In an appendix to this paper was included a brief summary of the activities of the Newark Museum. This summary tries to make emphatic my feeling that all museum work is today experimental and should be frankly regarded as such, even by those who are developing and managing our largest and richest museums. A glance at a

---

The New Museum Series, no. 4. Woodstock, Vt.: The Elm Tree Press, 1920.

"Summary" in that pamphlet will show that we have here in Newark, in a very modest way, made trial of many of the forms of activity mentioned in this volume. This fact does not prove that those forms of activity are fundamentally good; it does show that they can be carried out, and, by so much, shows that my mention of them, and of others akin to them, is based on more than imagination.

A Record and a Prophecy

It is easy for a museum to get objects; it is hard for a museum to get brains. The objects are seen, talked about, wondered at, and bring praise to those who give them and prestige to those who choose them for purchase. The brains are not seen, are chiefly in the heads of hirelings, produce results slowly, and the results produced are seen only by those with a gift for education or with training and experience in it. But objects do not make a "museum"; they merely form a "collection."

What is true of museum objects—rare, wonder-producing, and pride-evoking objects—is true also of museum buildings. It is easy to get them, much easier than to get museum brains. They are large, monumental, obtrusive, make impressive photographs, help to give cities plausible reasons for existence, furnish to donors a refined publicity for unselfish expenditures, and endow laborious trustees with a sense of duty done and with the immortality of bronze tablets. But a building of the kind that is usually constructed to house a museum is not in itself a museum; it is almost always a storehouse for "collections."

Probably no more useless public institution, useless relatively to its cost, was ever devised than that popular ideal: the classical building of a museum of art, filled with rare and costly objects. And it adds to its inutility a certain power for harm. To its community it gives a specious promise of artistic regeneration, and it permits those who visit it to put on certain integuments of culture which, although they do not conceal aesthetic nakedness, inhibit the free exercise of both intellect and sensibility.

What I mean is this: Museums, and especially art museums, are social conventions or community fashions. When a city puts on a museum it puts it on in obedience to the dictates of municipal fashion; it erects a museum building in accordance with current architectural fashion; and it places in the building objects selected after the fashion of art museums. These municipal, architectural, and museum-object fashions are becoming out of date. Conformity to them is not useful but moderately harmful and gives to conformists the notion that they are doing something which in fact they are not doing.

To conform to all these things is easy, as is all conformity. To get brains into museums is difficult, because brains object to mere conformity; brains criticize fashions and promote those unusual activities which are so painful, after the universal laws of neophobia, to almost all good citizens and especially to prominent and wealthy ones.

If, now, museums are to be of greater use to the world, here are the things that museum brains must fight against: fashionable museum buildings, fashionable museum collections, and fashionable treatment of collections.

And here are the things they must fight for: the making of such collections; and the construction of such buildings; and the employment of persons of such skill; and the granting to those persons such powers and liberties as will compel the collections, the buildings, and the staffs all to work together for the pleasure, the education, and the profit of their respective communities.

In the kind of conflict here indicated—brains and ideas against the inborn tendency of good citizens to prefer the old ways—the better manner of conducting the campaign is plainly that of seeming retreat, accompanied by the construction of new and better things in the peace and quiet of the rear. That is to say, the advocates of the type of museum described in this volume must work for the most part in the obscurity and gloom of the old-fashioned museum temple, and there must awaken the embalmed bodies of the sacred "collections" and put them at useful tasks. Then, when the cohorts of the ancient, honorable, and ignorant finally penetrate the lines of the intelligent and reach the rearguard, they will find there, already constructed and in use, institutions so well adapted to obvious needs that they will adopt them at once and call them their own creations and the very realizations of the ideals for which they so long have fought!

That which common sense dictates as the proper course for propagandists of the new museum is precisely the course which they are following. Here and there are men and women, relatively few but in the total a goodly number, who are constructing institutions of a usefulness so great that they are paying in some cases fair returns on their cost, even though burdened with the handicap of being called museums.

Three museum studies have been made by Paul M. Rea, who is the director of the Museum of Charleston, S.C., and secretary of the American Association of Museums, and appeared in the annual reports of the U.S. Commission of Education for 1913, 1914, and 1915. These very valuable studies are quite discouraging if one looks only at results as set down in cold figures. They are quite cheering if one reads between their lines and considers them with an eye to the future.

The study of the educational work of museums made in 1914 by Miss Louise Connolly, educational expert of the Newark, N.J., museums, is of necessity more optimistic, being frankly an effort at construction rather than a description of conditions. The recent annual reports of the American Association of Museums can give even the most depressed of museum revolutionists much encouragement, for they show that the one ever-present desire of many museum workers is to discover and exploit new avenues of definite usefulness.

I shall try to suggest this rapid increase in the usefulness of museums by drawing, from the latter day writings, reports of those forms of museum activities in which progressive museum workers take the most pride, making the museums in which they appear more widely and more definitely useful to their respective communities. These varied forms of activity I shall unite in one imaginary museum, which, as I shall try to suggest, has for its community a certain definite and clearly understood value. In thus depicting, in rough and incomplete outline, an institution of excellence and effectiveness as yet unattained, I add to it certain features and put upon it certain peculiarities born of my own imagination. Only thus, it seems, can I give the vision a certain needed fullness.

Those things which the new museum will not do, and the kind of institution which it will distinctly not be, must be indicated chiefly by exclusion. It is not needful to begin by saying that the ideal institute of visual instruction will not be thus and so. One negation, however, seems essential: It is that the new museum is not a museum of a certain kind. It is not of fine art, or applied art; or of all sciences, or of any special science; or of industry or commerce; or of pedagogy or technology; or of hygiene or religion. Carefully selected and laboriously identified, completely labeled, fitly installed, and safely housed collections of objects in each of the fields mentioned, and in many others, are needed now, and now and always will have their select, high, and usually narrow range of usefulness. But basic to all the projects I here set forth is the statement that either these must no longer be called museums, but "collections"; or a new name must be discovered—such a name I suggest in "institute of visual instruction"—and applied to those creations whose usefulness is wide, direct, obvious, and in fair degree measurable. And that word measurable leads to one more remark prefatory.

All public institutions (and museums are not exceptions to this rule) should give returns for their cost; and those returns should be in good degree positive, definite, visible, measurable. The goodness of a museum is not in direct ratio to the cost of its building and the upkeep thereof, or to the rarity, auction value, or money cost of its collections. A museum is good only insofar as it is of use.

It is easy to evade the importance of this obvious fact by airy talk of the uplift value of architectural façades in the classic manner; of priceless antiquities; of paintings by masters; and of ancient porcelains, jades, and lacquers; to say nothing of replicas and habitats of whales, Indians, and mastodons. But the evasion does not serve. Common sense demands that a publicly supported institution do something for its supporters, and that some part at least of what it does be capable of clear description and downright valuation.

The museum project I present is assumed to be part of and to be supported by one of our large, ugly, industrious, and rich American cities of mixed population. I select this special environment for many quite obvious reasons, but chiefly because a museum of the type I shall describe can in the environment suggested find a maximum of usefulness.

The main building is near the center of the daily movement of the citizens. It ought not to be necessary to say that an institution which is supported partly or wholly by taxation—and is thus supported that it may give, and because it is supported does in fact give, pleasure and profit to all citizens—should stand where all citizens can most easily reach it. But again and again the plea is made for the choice of a certain museum site that it is, or in time will be, near the "center of population." It is difficult, apparently, for the old-fashioned museum mind to grasp the fact that "center of population" and "center of daily movement of population" are not one and the same.

The reasons usually given for placing a museum in an isolated building, preferably in a park, and for causing it to be designed in the classic manner, all with the general spiritual uplift of the passing citizen in view, have heretofore quite universally won over our museum trustees. That the usefulness of an institution which is primarily intended to be visited is directly proportioned to the number of its visitors, and that this number is directly proportioned to its accessibility—these are facts that have found a very difficult entrance to the museum mind.

The building's narrow and modestly decorated entrance fronts on a side street, just off a main artery of travel.

It is 16 stories high, with an area of about 10,000 square feet on each floor, giving a total of 169,000 above the basement. It is constructed in the ordinary modern, fireproof, brick-steel-and-concrete manner.

The general floor plan need not be described, as it must in good measure conform to the land purchased for it. The lighting problem is solved largely by electricity, though windows are abundant, especially in workrooms.

The entrance hall, a stairway of moderate grandeur, cloakroom, toilets, shipping rooms, and several small halls of wonders and several lecture rooms occupy most of the first floor. The halls of wonder contain a few oil paintings, sculptures, and curios such as every museum of art is supposed to possess; and a few of the habitat groups, large skeletons, and curiosities of nature which convention bids us look for in a museum of science. If these were not on view in a convenient place and near the entrance, they would be earnestly and persistently sought for by visitors until they were found. By putting them near the entrance, and by giving the entrance just a touch of grandeur, all visitors who have the conventional museum expectancy enjoy at once the agreeable reactions they look for, and are fit to proceed further in a quiet and receptive mind—or to withdraw from the building! Many of these objects, or others akin to them, are found again where needed to teach this, that, and the other lesson, according to the museum's general scheme of instruction.

Always among the objects shown in these halls of wonders are some which are recent acquisitions, some which cost a great deal of money, some which enjoy provenances of astonishing lengths and of aristocratic flavor, and several which are the only ones in the world, or at least in this country.

The modesty of the entrance hall is compensated for in part by the presence in it of a panel of glass mosaic, very unusual, very expensive, very elaborately made, very old, very historical, and distinctly a museum piece.

The suggestions in the last paragraphs are not intended to be satirical or merely humorous. The traditional conception of a museum is very deeply set in the minds of our people, rich and poor, ignorant and cultivated. A museum which did not conform in some degree to this traditional conception would hardly win the approval of the voters as something worth adding to the city's equipment; and, when in operation, would not for years win the approval of the common people who must vote for its income or its treasures. Nor are the suggestions in this paragraph merely supported by an appeal to popular though mistaken conventions. There is a certain value to a community in the knowledge that it is living up to the traditions of its kind. Indeed, if money were abundant, either from gifts or from appropriations of unexpected size, some of it could quite properly be spent in giving a museum building more room, and in making it more ornate than I have suggested. The chief points in the museum conception I am here setting forth are that it must be central and useful. It quite clearly follows, then, that it must, unless its income is very large, be simple and tall and not greatly supplied with objects of high cost.

The floors on which are found the other things to be mentioned need not be specific. For all objects and activities there is abundant space. Many are moved from time to time, as the development of the museum's activities and as changes in museum method dictate.

I do not attempt to say with any degree of definiteness what kind of a structure and what arrangement of rooms an active, growing institute of visual instruction needs. No one knows. We have not, as I have said, even demonstrated that the best of museums is worth the money it costs. We can, on the contrary, almost prove that the conventional, "gazing," "art-gallery" type of museum does not give such returns in pleasure or betterment of any kind as justify its existence, even though it gives good ocular evidence of its city's power of indulgence in conspicuous waste. We are trying to find a type of museum which demonstrably pays its community fair interest on its investment. As to its housing, we can only be sure as yet of two things: first, that like any institution dependent on public use for adequate returns for founding and upkeep, it must be where its supporting public can most easily and most cheaply reach it—that is, it must be near the center of daily movement of population; and, second, that it must have all the floor space the money to be put into it will give. This floor space can be gained today, under modern city conditions, near a city's center only by making the building tall. Following on these two self-evident propositions come the facts, based on our ignorance of the future of museums, that this floor space must not be definitely assigned to definite purposes, but must be capable, having the fewest possible permanent partitions, of rearrangement almost to the last degree.

What the building may contain and what are the activities which may center in it must be told in outline only. To those familiar with modern museum work the items which follow will almost automatically expand themselves.

The staff, which is adequate for the work the objects named and the activities suggested may require, is larger, relative to size of building and cost of collections, and more highly paid, than it is in any existing museum of equal floor space. The large salary roll is compensated for in part by a very moderate expenditure for objects, by dues paid by certain classes of students, by payments for certain definite commercial and industrial services rendered, and, if admission is charged on special days or to special exhibits, by entrance fees. Moreover, the obvious and the definitely proven usefulness of the museum does, in due course, reconcile its supporters to its cost.

The quality of the staff and the special talents and the experience and skill of its members are indicated by the statements which follow of the things they are expected to do. For much of the more important work of the institute, most museum workers of conventional experience and training will not be fitted. For this work it will be necessary to engage persons whose opinions of what a museum should be are quite loosely held, and whose susceptibility to new ideas and powers of initiation are quite marked. More is said on this subject later.

Of paintings there are many, chiefly recent American, but with an abundance of copies of old masterpieces. A few are shown in the building; some are lent to schools; some are placed in windows of stores; some are in libraries and branch libraries; and some are in museum branches. Most are without frames, and for storage are slipped into shallow boxes of uniform size which stand on end on racks like books on a shelf. For showing these there is a collection of extremely simple frames of many sizes. The museum acquires a minimum number of those products of aesthetic aberration—

elaborate gold frames.

As already stated, a few examples from the collection of paintings are on view in one or more galleries, except when the galleries are needed for other purposes.

One painting at least is almost always in view in a small special room. Visitors to this room are expected to be seated in chairs provided for the purpose and to study the painting for some time. As an aid to such study, a leaflet descriptive of the painting and explanatory of its assumed excellences is given to all who wish it.

A like use is made of many of the paintings which are lent, they being suitably placed, lighted, and accompanied by seats. In the center of the city and in parts of the city where the poorer citizens have their homes, advantage is taken of opportunities to engage vacant stores, small halls, and even rooms in private houses. In each of these a good painting is set up for a week or a month, and the place is opened, with an intelligent person in charge, for an hour or two each day and evening.

This plan of showing single paintings is followed not because paintings have a very high value as promoters of happiness, as teachers of facts, as aids to forming good habits, or as founts of inspiration; but because this is the period of the oil painting, because some knowledge of the history of its development and some acquaintance with the most prized examples is good mental baggage, and, particularly, because by this plan the average lover of painted pictures gets more out of them than he does in any other way.

The "Stories of Paintings" that are printed for distribution at these "one painting" exhibits are usually illustrated with a picture of the painting, sometimes in color. Some of these leaflets, written with special reference to the purpose, are used as reading texts in schools, and, when possible, the painting which the leaflet thus describes is placed for a time where the class which is reading the leaflet can see and study it.

A plan almost identical with this is followed in the use of bronzes, large and small, copies and originals; of plaster casts; of prints, including especially those in color; of reproductions of paintings in color, both the expensive and the cheap; of wood carving; of brocades; and of many other kinds of museum objects. In the case of the smaller and less story-full objects, more than one article is sometimes shown at a time, though the very special value of a careful and undistracted study of one thing is never forgotten.

The sculptures include many American bronzes, with others of all countries and all times, the latter being in most cases inexpensive copies. Most of these are usually stored, or lent, or are on exhibition in other places. There is no grand sculpture hall of plaster casts, though there is at least one room in which may be aroused the peculiar aesthetic emotion to be experienced in the presence of a congruous group of marble sculpture. Some casts are colored in the ancient manner. Some of the larger pieces are set up for a few months in schools, and in other places as noted in detail under paintings. Small casts for the use of students are many in number and lent freely. Large use is made of plaster copies in small size of important sculptures. Groups of these, skillfully arranged and properly lighted, are found particularly useful for work outside the building.

Such of the objects of applied or decorative arts as are purchased are largely copies. The acquisition in this field, even by gift, of ancient, rare, and costly originals which have a very high market value and involve great labor in handling and great care for preservation, is not encouraged, especially if with them goes the condition that they be constantly shown. Even if they are always on view, such things take up much valuable space, while the labor of handling and storing them and showing them occasionally is, in view of their value and fragility, very great. As is indicated under other items, the products of American workers are especially sought in this field, the products of individual artisans with private shops and of employees in large establishments being both regarded as quite honorable.

The collection of prints is large but not very expensive. Valuable prints are accepted as gifts, but few are purchased. No large permanent collection is always in view.

A constant effort is made to humanize the print. As a mere story-picture, the print, in the form of a reproduction of a pencil, pen, or wash drawing, is everywhere present and has a universal appeal. It is difficult to discover the reason why the print proper, the first-hand product of a man of genius and of exquisite skill, is entirely without interest to all save a very small part of even the more educated and experienced. Our museum tries to change this state of things. Good prints are lent, accompanied by notes descriptive of origin, character, and points of special interest. As in the descriptive leaflets on single paintings or pieces of sculpture, these print-leaflets often dwell much on the print's content, its mere story, and pass from that to the reasons for its appeal to students. And all this is frequently accompanied by illustrations and by objects which help to make clear the methods by which any given print was produced.

In connection with the remarks on paintings and prints and inexpensive copies thereof, it is proper to consider that fashion of the time which gives a very high value to originals in every field of art, handicraft, and design. A copy of a great painting, for example, even though it be so perfect that at a distance of a few feet not one person in 10,000 can tell that it is a copy, is looked upon as a dangerous foe of art and as an almost blasphemous tour-de-force. Still lower in the scale of being are photo-mechanical reproductions of paintings and prints, and pictures in color and black and white of textiles, laces, wood carvings, and other objects, even though these convey to the intelligent observer a very correct impression of the design, color, and technique of the originals.

The fashion is very injurious, for, being set and followed by the elect in the art work—wealthy collectors, dealers, museum experts, and critics—it is naturally followed by the commonalty, inhibits their powers of observation and comparison, and leads them to feel that if they do not look upon "originals" they can make little or no progress in their education in art. It does more than this: It tends to prevent the would-be designer from making full use of the countless admirable pictures of artworks of every period and country which lie open to his hands. In Paris is an art museum containing no objects of art whatsoever. It is merely a collection of pictures wide in its range and classed by objects depicted and by the period and country from which the originals come. Our museums would do well to copy this artless plan. Whether they do or not, the plan is being in measure forced upon us by the printing press, as is noted later.

Of paintings, sculptures, and other objects in the field of the fine arts, so called, the museum finds it wise, as already noted, to secure, but chiefly by gift, a few honorific originals—originals, that is, of high market value, greatly esteemed by collectors and connoisseurs, and giving to the institution a certain distinction. In the present state of art appreciation, these objects gain newspaper notice, attract an occasional student, and stimulate an occasional donor to add other like objects to them.

A like policy is pursued as to objects in the applied art field.

But it is not forgotten that the chief reason why the authorities of our projected museum secure and label and set into view any given object is not to evoke wonder in the casual observer, or to arouse the admiration and pride of fellow citizens or the astonishment and envy of citizens of other cities.

In the field of art, where the discussion for the moment finds us, our institute secures and displays and describes and lends objects in the hope that they may produce certain rather definite effects on those who see them, handle them, study them, and in any manner make use of them. It hopes that these objects will increase the local interest in the art of adapting objects to their specific useful purposes, in the ornamentation of useful objects, in the history of developments and changes in that ornamentation, in current methods of ornamentation, in the transfer with agreeable modifications of old schemes of ornament to useful objects made today (especially, of course, to machine-made objects), and, in general, in plans to increase the efforts of designers and decorators of today to give to the useful objects of the life of today an interest and charm peculiarly their own.

The remarks made on the museum's collection of pictures are, in large part, particularly pertinent to the objects in the applied art group. It is, of course, very true that to look upon an ancient chest of wood with elaborate carvings and with hinges, handles, and locking devices cunningly wrought in iron, arouses a keen interest in the observer who is informed as to its age, its origin, and history, its present great market value and the high esteem in which it is held by those who are careful students of such things. This emotion is accentuated if the observer learns that the chest is unique and that it has been acquired through the generosity of a wealthy collector of things akin to it.

It is clear that such of the emotions aroused by the sight of the ancient chest as may lead to the use of it as the basis of construction or decoration in any field of production are emotions which will be almost, if not quite, as fully aroused by a careful copy of it or a measured drawing of it, or a photograph of it, or of all of these presentments combined, as by the original itself. It is not the wonder, astonishment, pride of quasi possession, or authorized admiration of the chest that will make it useful to the observer or to his fellows through the activities it will induce in him. The thing that makes the chest worthwhile is the use of it, and nearly all of this use can come as well from good pictorial presentments of the chest as from the chest itself.

Before leaving the chest and its decoration, it is proper to call attention to the fact that chest rarities in our museums, and kindred originals of old-time decorative effects in wood, metal, and leather, have not as yet affected that modern descendant of the chest, the traveling trunk. If museums were the active agents in elevating the taste and the productive skill of their respective communities which they bravely try to think they are, they would have long since attempted, and attempted with no small success, to arouse such an interest in the skillful adornment of the common trunk as would have led to efforts to give it charm as well as strength and endurance. But alas! Under present museum conventions, trustees and directors and curators are amply content if they secure and expensively install an old, rare, and costly chest, which attracts the gaze and evokes the wonder of the casual visitor and the envy of the occasional expert.

The collection of things made in the city which supports the museum consists of a selection, constantly changing through rejections and renewals. Of some of these an important exhibit is held each year. These annual exhibits of local products are not large, but are carefully selected and arranged and labeled with special reference to these points:

1) Making the city known to itself, and especially to its young people.
2) Presenting one of the city's activities in an attractive, interesting, and advertising manner to non-residents.

3) Encouraging improvements in manufacturing methods.
4) Presenting a modern industry in a comprehensive and enlightening manner to pupils in the schools.

The exhibit of New Jersey textiles made recently by the Newark museums cost—including materials, labels, arrangement, and work—less than $800; it brought to the museum many gifts and received 50,000 visits.

These local industries displays are quite frankly commercial. They illustrate each year the best the city can produce in the line selected. They are accompanied by or preceded by or followed by exhibits of goods in the same line from other countries and from other periods. The objects shown are selected not with reference to their money value, but almost solely with reference to their suggestive value to local manufacturers and their teaching value to old and young.

It is difficult to attach too much importance to the exploitation by a museum of the products of its own community. On the art side of its work, a museum is supposed to be of help in improving the taste of its constituents and in increasing their interest in, and their powers of discrimination concerning, the objects they daily see and use. Now, good taste and keen interest in the pots and pans of daily life do not emerge from the awed contemplation of unfamiliar objects enshrined in the cases of a public institution, as has just been illustrated in the case of the ancient chest and the great American trunk.

But, leaving aside for the present the subject of improvement in adaptation to purpose and of technical skill in production, it is obvious that in almost every industry—from farming to the making of shoes and through the whole gamut of manufacturing—there are to be found a few workers who delight to add to what they make or help to make a very definite bit of what to them is beautification, adornment, or art. It is this delight in a surplus of finish, a vague something beyond the needful, that is the very foundation and origin of all the arts of decoration in every field. This desire to add this surplus has been found in every country and in all times, from the savage and his paddle to the costumes on the avenues of our modern cities, and this desire has moved those possessed by it to definite and widely approved decorative accomplishment wherever and whenever their fellow citizens have been interested in that decorative accomplishment and have been willing to pay reasonable sums to secure it.

The conclusion is that a museum of art, supported by a community, should encourage the movements toward the beautification of its products which that community discloses. A generous encouragement, one commensurate with the tremendous importance of the development of decorative power, would include far more than the exhibits of local industries already alluded to.

One form of such encouragement could be, for example, the careful selection and purchase by a museum of examples of what experts call the best, and also of what experience has shown to be the most popular, of decorated objects of utility made by manufacturers in the city which supports the museum. The purchases should include, in some cases, objects from producers in all parts of the country and if possible from foreign makers as well. These should be displayed with ancient originals or copies or pictures of originals of kindred objects, or objects bearing kindred decorations, and they should be accompanied by labels and leaflets suggesting how certain types of decoration have developed, and where and when; and why certain of those shown in the work of today are likely to meet with popular approval for a long time; and why others promise to be only ephemeral fashions. More than this as to the "art" value of specific types of decoration it would be dangerous to say, but much could be said on other aspects of the subject that would be of interest to manufacturer, artisan, mechanic, salesman, advertiser, and the buying public; would help them to a clearer conception of what makes decoration more or less enduring; and would lead them to see that the decoration made by their fellows today is the decoration that chiefly concerns them and is the decoration which they can, by agreeable conscious effort, help to improve.

If it be said that such forms of museum activity as are here suggested would be very expensive, the reply can be made that the price paid for one rare painting, or one rare old bronze, or one year's excavations in Northern China would finance much of the work of encouraging and developing native decorations for several years. And to say this is not equivalent to saying that the painting, the sculpture, and the excavations alluded to should be neglected. The zeal of the rich for the acquisition of the honorific in art will assure us that ample care and thought and money will be given to these things. But the same prevailing fashion in the display of art zeal which condemns the rich to the acquisition of the old and rare and costly almost completely inhibits their taking an interest in and contributing to the patronage of the designs and decorations of their own country and their own time. One of the newest museums of art has aptly illustrated the remarks just made. Its opening was celebrated by the display of a large collection of rare and costly objects, and of these objects was published a very beautiful illustrated catalogue. The articles and pictures this catalogue described were not, with perhaps a very few exceptions, made in the city of which the museum is a part, or in this country, and they did not bear any direct relation to the daily life or the daily activities of anyone in the museum's city, which is one of the most progressive, prosperous, and intensely industrial in America.

This is typical. A museum of art is not thought of as the chief patron and encourager of the arts of its community, but primarily as a storehouse of expensive curios. Of course the administrators of the typical art museum of today hope and believe that its rarities and curios, all genuine and therefore elevating to the community, can be used to stimulate an interest in great and good art. But building and contents are alike remote from the community's pots and pans and can affect the latter's advancement very slowly and very slightly.

In support of these statements I would call attention to the proceedings of the Royal Society of Arts in London, October 28, 1918. The meeting of that date was given up to discussion of "The Promotion of Industrial Art." Two schemes were submitted: one formulated by the Royal Society, the other by the Board of Trade. The two originated independently but proved to be complementary and were expected to work in close cooperation. Hon. W. A. L. Fisher, president of the (National) Board of Education, was chairman. In opening the meeting he said that the project under discussion had the approval of the Board of Education as well of the Royal Society and the Board of Trade. Its purpose is, he said, "to lift our national industries on to an altogether higher line of aesthetic achievement, by affording encouragement to our designers to obtain first-hand acquaintance with the medium in which they work, and, by the formation of a permanent Exhibition of British Industrialist Art, which shall not only offer a stimulus to our craftsmen and designers, but also enable us to obtain a conspectus of the state of contemporary art at any given period of time. One of the schemes before us today is a scheme for the establishment of a British Institute of Industrial Art. The Board of Trade, in conjunction with the Board of Education, and with the advice of representative members of the Royal Society of Arts, the Arts and Crafts Exhibition Society, the Art Workers' Guild, the Design and Industries Association, and various persons and organizations connected with manufacture and commerce, have framed a scheme for a British Institute of Industrial Art, and it is proposed that this institute should be incorporated, under the joint auspices of the Board of Trade, as the department dealing with industry, and of the Board of Education, as the authority controlling the Victoria and Albert Museum. The methods by which it is proposed that our objects should be achieved are first of all the establishment of a permanent exhibition in London of modern British works selected as reaching a high standard of artistic craftsmanship and manufacture."

It is not necessary to quote further, for I wish merely to show that the most important educational bodies in England are today of the opinion I am trying to set forth in this volume: that under current methods, museums do not fulfill one of their primary functions, if not the most important of all their functions, that of teaching. They are now, for the most part, mere collections, mere gazing museums, producing only slight effect on the development of industrial art, that is, on the application of decoration to useful objects. So entirely have museums of the old type failed to be of definite educational value that when it is asked in London how the "national industries can be lifted to a higher level of artistic achievement," the answer is found not by turning to existing museums, but by proceeding to the erection of a new museum of the definitely useful, teaching type which I am here trying to describe.

✦

The artisans and other members of the museum staff who mount birds, animals, insects, and other objects and make habitats and other groups are in many cases so placed that visitors can see them at work. Visiting painters, designers, and craftsmen are usually compelled to work in the exhibition rooms where they can be seen by all who are interested in their procedures. General museum workers are also presented as object lessons. To them are added occasional exhibits of bench workers, artisans, and craftsmen, and of sculptors and modelers, painters, engravers, wood carvers, designers, and artists in all fields, engaged for the specific purpose of being seen in the practice of their several callings. I am aware that our institution does not find it easy to discover persons in these many fields who are ready and willing to work under observation of a general public. But they can be found.

If the cost of doing the things of many kinds which I have noted is offered as an obstacle thereto, the answer is ready. Our new museum does not devote large sections of its annual income, sums ranging from $10,000 to $100,000, to the purchase of single objects like rare paintings. Notorious and costly rarities are given by the rich, or not acquired at all. The institution we are considering is trying to arouse an interest in all the refinements of life, and especially in the refining of the most common objects of daily use—the pots and pans of the commonalty already alluded to. This it is trying to do on what we call the art side of human activities. And it is equally interested in the task of arousing interest in the sciences, in the material history of the community—in the modest meaning of that phrase—and in all the industries by which we live and thrive.

Returning for a moment to the special displays of single objects or small groups of objects which have been briefly alluded to, it should be noted that activity of this kind is all quite distinctly educational. It is not found difficult, indeed, to connect some of it closely with the work of the schools and even to include it in the definitely required work of the curriculum, and to give teachers an opportunity to acquire merit in its supervision. In certain high school courses in history, literature, and art, for example, the observation and study of paintings, sculptures, and architectural pictures, with the aid of proper leaflets, guidance by teachers, and suggestions from museum assistants, can be made to form an essential part of the work of a given year or half year.

Add to the objects of these three kinds the many others that a general museum of the type I am describing—well settled as it is in the habit of sending out for special service almost anything it possesses—has gathered into its halls and storerooms, and it is easy to see how our institute becomes an active ally of all the city's educational institutions.

It displays, for example, in rented rooms, in libraries, in welfare departments of great industrial establishments, in the rooms provided by institutional churches, in schoolhouses, and many other places, a series of models of the habitations of men; bird and animal habitat groups; charts and maps descriptive of the development of mankind; and like documents on climate, products, and geology; and it adds to these some of its own workers and installers of museum material, and workers in certain fundamental crafts like pottery-making and weaving. By this last it is obviously suggested that our new institute uses not only its objects—all save those that are in fact both rare and of definite historical value—but also its activities in extending its teaching power through branches and other avenues of distribution to every part of the city and to all its citizens.

If it be said that a publicly supported art museum cannot commercialize itself by the acquisition and display of commodities currently offered for sale, I would first admit that the matter must be handled with common sense. Then I would reply that all museums of art enter the field of commerce when they borrow and display, as all do, the products of painters, sculptors, and art-and-craft workers. A painter works and wishes to sell his products. No one has yet shown us that he and his colleagues in sculpture and handwork are more noble, more sincere, more worthy of special privileges than are those who design and produce the output of our factories; or that they are, through the peculiar nature or quality of their productions, endued with any special sanctity which makes their desire to sell their goods exempt from the taint of commercialism. It is well to patronize our artists, commonly so called, to examine their wares, and to buy them if they are good. Indeed, no small part of this book is devoted to an argument in favor of this very thing. But the argument also goes to show, and I think unanswerably, that a museum of art is under the same obligation to patronize the maker of pots and pans that it is to patronize the painter.

And to all this I would add the statement that commerce is not sinful. It exudes no virulent poison which is harmful to the elevated souls of art museum trustees, administrators, and visitors.

This also should be noted that even as I write these lines I receive notice of the second exhibit in the Metropolitan Museum of Art in New York of "commercial" products. The taint of sordidness is not removed from these products by the fact that they are in some degree based on objects—rare, old, and costly objects—which the museum has long housed. The fact is, of course, that they never were tainted at all, and that if their presence in a museum can assist that museum in its proper task of improving our commercial products and of refining and broadening the taste of its community, then they are quite as much at home in the museum as is the rarest, oldest, and costliest object it possesses.

As I write I receive also a notice of an exhibit of "Art in Everyday Life" to be held in the Buffalo Art Gallery. This museum has long been a stronghold of fine art, and it is significant of the changing view of the functions that museums are taking on, that here, at last, applied arts of many kinds are to be shown and are to compete for prizes and are to be offered for sale! Perhaps the absence of the machine in the factors that produce the objects here to be shown is held to sanctify those objects and make them proper associates of old paintings and other fine art things. Yet surely not, for a loom is a machine, even though moved by the hand, and so, on second thoughts, is a hammer! No, the useful arts, that is, useful things somewhat adorned, have come to the Buffalo gallery, and it cannot be long before there will come to the same place and to every other active, useful museum, these same useful objects, made, and adorned as made, by mere machines for mere purposes of sale to persons who will merely use them, enjoy them, and thank the manufacturers for making them.

✦

Our museum contains many objects illustrating such fundamental industries, whether followed in the city or not, as have greatly influenced the development of civilization. These include products in clay, glass, wood, wool and other fibers, leather, metal and other materials, and also foods and medicines.

They are shown to illustrate these among many other things:

1) The historic development of the industries which produce them; and the relations of those industries to the development of social conditions.
2) The processes by which such objects are made today, with the science and skill involved.
3) The art qualities found in such objects, in both past and present times.

In doing this last, the collection exalts the maker of pictures above the maker of mugs only when the former shows more genius and skill than the latter. One of the wider purposes of our museum is to make life better worth living, not by adding luster to riches and creating pleasurable reactions in the avowedly aesthetic, but by encouraging all to discover possibilities of agreeable emotions in the contemplation of common things.

The objects in this group are in many cases the same as those in the groups described in discussing applied arts and things made in the city, and, as our description indicates, many of the objects found in all these groups are used for several purposes.

That part of our institute's work now under consideration has to do with the history and technique of industries. No museum can hope to be, by assembling machines to illustrate every step of productive processes, a complete object lesson in these topics. But the subject can be illuminated and made attractive by pictures of machines in several stages of development, by a few of the earliest types of machines used in fundamental industries, and by examples of products of handwork, and of machines from those from the earliest to those of the latest type.

The habitat groups are usually rather small, and many of them are in miniature. They include birds, animals, insects, plants, and human beings. A few selected ones are always on view and are well arranged to be shown to groups of schoolchildren. Many of the less important, less complicated, and less expensive groups, small and easily moved, are placed in museum branches, in windows of stores, and in branch libraries and houses as needed—all in the manner described in the discussion of the use made of paintings and sculptures.

In a few of our largest and richest museums, habitat groups of full size and of the utmost accuracy will continue to be made and will furnish endless pleasure and much visual instruction to thousands. But the more modest institutions like the one we are projecting will find amply sufficient for its purposes groups of modest dimensions. In many cases they may be very small. The majority of them are to be viewed from one side only, being in small cases with the background carried out in drawings and paintings. These are so constructed and cased that they can be easily transported.

In the consideration of the utility of all this work in the habitat field, several questions arise, some of which it will be part of our institute's activities to try to answer.

For example, this is the era of pictures. The quantity of pictures presented every day to the eyes of the average person, old or young, is enormous and increases constantly. Not only does the quantity increase, the quality steadily improves.

What are the effects of this increasing flood of pictures on the individual brain? Does it hasten brain development? Does it make easier the acquisition of knowledge without lessening those powers of planning, adjusting, and generalizing by which acquired knowledge is made of definite value to life? Does it tend to modify those habits of observation and analysis which are acquired through other mental activities than that of picture gazing? Does it make it necessary for us to change our current methods of education?

These and many other questions are waiting to be answered. If our institute of visual instruction can, while it pursues its work along the lines suggested by our schools, by our conventional museums, and by the new museum methods which are being widely approved and are here and there put in practice—if it can carry on work which will test rather definitely some of the effects of picture-using, it may thereby add a little to our much-needed knowledge on this subject.

The picture assails us everywhere. It not only brings to us a certain kind of knowledge of every aspect of nature and of every form of human life and activity, it is also producing for us representations, those of each day more nearly accurate than those of the day before, of products of human hands in every field, including the so-called field of art. Add to the picture the moving picture, and we have, awaiting our eyes and the visual centers of our brains, the very movements of nature herself, the operations set on foot by man, and man's daily activities. And again the question is, what are all these worth to us? Are they to prove altogether helpful or in some degree harmful? And again the answer is that no one knows. Nor does anyone know the values that may lie behind the use of the picture in museum work.

I am dwelling long on this subject of pictures because I wish to present to museum workers not only the unanswered questions already presented, but also certain others that lie in this same field of visual instruction.

Museums have thus far collected and displayed chiefly objects and not pictures of objects, save those pictures and photographs thereof, which are possessed each of certain peculiar qualities given it by the brain and hand of one certain person, together with photographers of art objects as such. These objects, including those in the graphic arts field, are supposed to have a special value by reason of their power to arouse in the observer certain helpful reactions. These reactions are not easily defined, but are assumed to exist and to be of value. It is commonly supposed that they help the observer to understand life, to be more interested in the adornment of himself, his home, and all things with which he comes in contact, and, especially, to be more susceptible to improvement in his tastes, to take a deeper interest in life, and to patronize more generously those who give themselves to the task of sweetening human society. This is, I admit, a very vague presentment of the assumed beneficial effect of a sight of an Egyptian tomb or of a Greek vase of approved excellence and unquestioned authenticity; yet surely it is less vague than are most statements of the great and good influences of a gazing museum.

Let me make it clear that I do not deny that objects which time has tried, which have given pleasure to many, which continue to give pleasure to those of wide experience in the field of art, so called, and are by those same persons pronounced good—that I do not deny that such objects are worthy of safekeeping, high esteem, and even of a certain veneration. But I do hold concerning them that they should be looked upon, first of all, as marks of the possession of high skill, refinement of perception, and of keen sensibility by those who made them, and only secondarily as aids to the development of like skill, like refinement of perception, and like sensibility in those who gaze upon them. In a word, they are stigmata of civility and not the causes thereof. They should be studied and not worshipped. They should be preserved that they may help us, not that they may amaze and confound us. And, above all, we should study them with the purpose of learning from them, and in the hope that we may learn from them not the secret of their making but the factors that united to bring them forth. Thus studying them, in relation to their time, their country, their purpose, and the position which those who made them occupied in relation to the society in which they lived and of which they were an essential and foreordained part, we shall learn, even though not closely and completely, how we may so adjust our own social mechanism as to cause to come forth from among us also men and women who can produce for us as great and helpful and pleasure-giving stigmata of our own civility as are the greatest artworks the world has in its inheritance.

If these conclusions are sound, it follows that the thing needed today to provoke art among us is not so much great and richly housed collections of rare and costly objects as a widespread interest in the products of the men and women of our own times. It is to the products of living men and women, not to those of men and women long since dead, that we must look for the art of our day. And, that good things may come from these, we must help them, sympathize with them, understand the influences which our present social, economical, and industrial order brings to bear upon them; and place their products frankly before us to be measured as things born of these days, and not of other times, other incentives, other conditions, and other needs.

✦

As to science collections in the visual instruction institute which I am outlining, many of these are made with special reference, first, to the science work in the schools, and next, to the interests of local groups of scientific men—collectors, students, and industrial experts. They are quite largely arranged as needed. Those which serve the schools are in large part collected and set up by young people in accordance with instructions given by museum workers skilled in such matters; and those serving groups of scientists are closely correlated with the work of these groups and are in many cases supplied by them.

Supplementing the collection of objects is a large collection of pictures in color, forming part of the picture collection mentioned later, carefully labeled and arranged, and including diagrams, charts, and maps.

The general science collections cover in outline most of the subjects that are fully treated in large museums devoted to science only. Long series of rocks, minerals, insects, fish, birds, and animals are chiefly supplied, as already noted, by local scientific men. These are arranged and stored and made as easily accessible as those who contribute them may desire.

Short series of such things as building stone; useful and commonly used minerals and semi-precious stones used in the arts; plants of medicinal and general economic value for the drugs, fibers, dyes, woods, fruits, etc., which they furnish; insects notably harmful and beneficial—these are made from duplicates of the science collection proper, are assembled on cards or in small boxes, are fully labeled, and are accompanied with leaflet or pamphlet stories. These, like small groups of industrial products, local and other, are lent to schools in large numbers, and a few of them are always on display in the main building or branches for their own general interest and to call attention to the character of the whole lending collection.

The wide range of objects in this science field; the great importance of the interest that may be aroused for them in young people; the value to young people of practicing, even for a short time, the arts of the collector; the help that young people can give in adding to the collections of their own local museum, and the increase in interest in that museum which is gained by one who makes even modest contributions to it—all these make it plain that the young people of the community should be encouraged to collect, first for ourselves, and next for their museum.

Several museums like the one I am projecting have been very successful in their attempts to discover among their visitors boys and girls who are interested in the museum itself or in groups of objects that the museum wishes to add to its scheme. The method of finding these young museum aids is usually that of giving a person of modest scientific knowledge, of keen interest in natural history in general, of strong sympathy with activities of curious and inquiring children, and of experience in the art of teaching, the task of drawing them to the museum and then holding their interest in it. She watches the young visitors; explains things to them; asks questions; suggests that groups come to be instructed in the arts of collecting, arranging, mounting, and labeling; takes with them a few short walks; and leads the more active spirits up to the idea of forming clubs of their own. Our institute finds this process slow and modest in results, but it also finds that out of it all comes a wider and deeper interest among young people, even among those who are not active members of any group; that a few of the more intensely interested collectors add no small sum of useful objects to the museum in the course of a year; and that the deeper interest aroused among the young extends itself quite naturally to the elders.

The proper source of all this work is, of course, the public schools. But a full and rigid curriculum leaves little time as yet for the discovery and development by teachers of the kinds of special interest in a few of their pupils which the junior museum we have been describing carries on. The institute, of course, always keeps in mind the school, the teacher, the course of study, and the very strong influence and guidance which the school management can give in all work of this kind. Consequently it reports its efforts and its successes to the school authorities; on every possible occasion secures the sympathy and cooperation of teachers; and finds it possible to pass on to teachers much of the work which it initiated.

Our institute has a collection already alluded to of about a million pictures of paintings, sculptures, architecture, and, chiefly, of decorated objects of daily use. It is classified by objects, schools, periods, etc. These are used by students in the building and are lent freely for home, studio, school, and factory use. They form one of the most valuable assets of the whole institution.

Purposely repeating myself, I ask again this question: "Whatever may be the purpose of the museum of the old type or of the new, how is the method of attaining that purpose affected by the coming of the picture?" Surely those methods of adding to the richness and fullness of life and of enhancing its finer forms of activity—which were proper to a time when the picture was a thing painfully wrought by the hand of an engraver, and therefore imperfect as a presentation of the object pictured and slow and costly as well—cannot be entirely proper now, when we are supplied by scores of skillfully employed processes with countless pictures of all things under the heavens; and pictures, too, which every day approach more closely to precision in every detail and give us even the very movements of nature herself.

But the coming of the picture is not the only thing which is making it necessary to change museum method. The development of industrial processes, the growth of transportation facilities, and the increase of wealth have brought into being the modern city; and this modern city spreads before the eyes of every one of its inhabitants, through its countless merchants, every conceivable kind of product. In their galleries and stores may be seen and, one may almost say, must be seen even by the casual shopper and passerby, almost every kind of thing that the museum gathers, labels, and displays. The merchant, moreover, permits a personal investigation of his gatherings which extends even to a touch and a handling that are forbidden by the museum management. Add to these wares of the merchant the life of the streets, the moving picture of its endless and infinitely varied activities, the countless productive processes of the factories open to almost any interested visitor, and the wonderful background of architecture, and we of our cities have set before us, and daily filling our vision, a museum-city far richer in every respect than any city-museum can ever be.

And it should be noted, in speaking of objects displayed by merchants and of those displayed by museums, that the latter are looked at largely as a matter of duty, and largely as a part of an ungrateful self-educational process; while the former are looked at as part of the very life of the day, as possible possessions, and are considered deeply as to quality and as to fitness for certain specific purposes. In a word, a visitor goes to a museum to gaze as a duty, with some hope of uplift; but to a store to enjoy, to compare, and to study in sheer delight.

The picture, the moving picture, the modern city, and the great and ever-changing exhibitions of merchants and manufacturers—these have all come into our lives in vast quantity and infinite variety since the management methods of the conventional museum were developed and adopted. And to these factors should be added the public school.

What changes in museum management do these new social forces call for? It is no doubt as yet impossible to give to this question a definite answer. And it is because no definite answer is as yet possible, and because it is nevertheless so obvious that fundamental changes in museums are demanded by these new social factors, that I have ventured to prepare and publish this group of suggestions concerning the museum of the future. That the suggestions will all prove to be good it would be absurd to assume. But they and many other and better ones should be made and studied and tested. Only by a constant testing of new methods and new schemes can the museum of the present justify its existence. A cursory glance at today's world of picture, print, shop, factory, school, and city streets makes it seem almost needless.

One addition to museum work of wide scope and almost endless variety seems to be clearly essential (though that it will make museums so definitely useful as to assure their continuance no one can say), and that addition is teaching—expert, carefully directed teaching. It is to this addition that this essay continuously and persistently returns. The objects the museum gathers and displays and also the new flood of pictures; the moving pictures; and shops, factories, schools, city streets, and nature herself—all these may form part of the new museum's equipment.

To the mere sight of these things, it seems clear there should be added instruction concerning them by print, by more pictures, and by the skillful teacher. A brief examination of the recent reports, bulletins, and other publications of our museums makes it clear that most of them have vaguely recognized the vast importance of this new factor, and are devoting to its application a very modest portion of their incomes. This essay is in a measure an appeal to museum promoters and managers to reduce materially the sums spent on the acquisition, installation, and display of rare and curious and costly objects, and to spend the money thus saved on a series of carefully conducted, minutely reported, and humbly studied experiments in museum teaching.

✦

The main buildings of our public museum and our public library are both near the city's travel center, and are therefore near one another. The library of the museum is, in fact, a branch of the public library from which it receives a daily delivery of books and other material needed in its work. It is quite full in all the subjects which the collections cover—for example, pedagogy, occupations, trades, fine arts, technique of museum management, making of collections, and installation of exhibits. It has, of course, the museum literature of recent years, both books and journals, including the late publications of scores of museums of all kinds. It also includes an ample collection of dictionaries and encyclopedias, and the best and latest standard books on art, pure and applied, and the sciences. The collection of a million pictures already alluded to, including many thousand photographs, supplements the books in countless ways. Museum libraries do not, with few exceptions, lend their books, or their photographs, or other pictures. This custom reduces their value to a minimum. It would be difficult to find a point of time in the life of any visitor who has shown a lively interest in some of the museum's collections, when a book or a package of pictures, or both, bearing on the visitor's line of special interest, would be as useful to him and as productive in him of thoughts and feelings useful to his community, as when he has just been examining the collections which attract him. Consequently, this is the occasion on which we are most eager to hand to him any book or picture he finds he wants to read or study. The non-lending habit in this field is a mere fashion, of course, with very little save precedent to support it.

Stereopticons and moving pictures are possessed in large numbers and of a character appropriate to the museum's work. Several rooms of various sizes can be adapted to their use. Slides, films, and lanterns are used in branches and are lent for educational purposes. The use of the moving picture as an educational tool has not yet been sufficiently studied to give definite conclusions. Its possibilities are probably very great. The museum joins in the effort to discover how it can be used to the greatest advantage.

For visitors of a certain quality—those, for example, who understand what they hear better than what they read, and for certain large groups of visitors—the phonograph is used to give short explanatory talks. The machine, when set in motion, repeats an interesting story concerning a special exhibit and then automatically sets itself for a repetition. An attendant handles it in some cases, usually an attendant not sufficiently skilled to give the talk himself. In some cases the machine is set in motion by visitors by dropping in a coin or a blank furnished at the desk for the purpose. Thus far this use of the phonograph is not more than a promising experiment. Mr. F. J. Urquhart of the *Sunday Call of Newark* was the first person to suggest this plan, to our knowledge. This was several years ago. Others have since had the same idea, and it has been tested in a few cases.

✦

The whole museum is in itself an institution for encouraging the use, not only of objects in its possession, but also of the natural and man-made features of the city and its immediate surroundings.

It is the duty of certain members of the staff to know the city, and particularly to know of the persons, objects, processes, civic and educational enterprises, and of the social groups and the educational work, that may find the museum helpful; or that can be of service to those who come to the museum for advice, information, or assistance. These members of the staff form a department of cooperation; they see to it that the museum and city are always working together at all possible points.

It is the habit of the city to turn simultaneously to library and museum when information is wanted. A local railroad magnate or automobile manufacturer, asked by a board of trade or a Sunday school class to speak on transportation, naturally calls up the museum and requests a room for a few days in which small models and pictures, slides, etc., of carriages, ships, and the like may be placed; and then asks the library to send appropriate books and material on transportation to that room. He uses the room and its contents for the hours it takes him to collect his data.

It is the custom of the museum to send to the parks of the neighborhood some of its moveable collections which illustrate the phenomena then and there visible. And the park managers send to the museum many specimens illustrating natural phenomena. All art, industry, and science schools use the museum and its collections just so far as falls short of interfering with their more democratic use by the city's laymen. And their first impulse, when producing or acquiring anything capable of use in visual instruction, is to duplicate it or share it with the museum. These correlations tend to prevent unnecessary duplication of collections.

One department of the museum contains lists, pictures, and reproductions of notable art, science, and industrial features of the city—the visual information as to its political, religious, philanthropic, and civic institutions. In architecture, mentioned only to illustrate the statement just made, much use is made of the architecture of the city itself. This is studied, described, characterized, and used as the basis of work, both in the school department and in the illumination of the general public.

Those in charge of the parks, public gardens, and shade-trees of the city have helped to make the science or the nature-study part of the museum's work more effective in many ways.

They supply samples of wood and branches from trees of many kinds. These show bark, selections of wood, habits of branching, form of buds, and, in the proper season, the leaves, blossoms, and fruit of so many trees and shrubs as the museum needs. In late winter they furnish branches of many kinds which are placed in water in the museum until they send out leaves or blossoms. In summer they permit the museum, under proper restrictions, to gather flowers of all kinds, and these, added to the wildflowers, form in the museum a procession of blooms and fruit.

In the larger parks, they have erected, in consultation with representatives of the museum and the schools, several buildings which are adjuncts to both schools and museums. These buildings are used by the park's plant experts as centers for labeling trees, shrubs, and flowers, and for the work of fighting plant diseases and noxious insects. At certain specified hours will be found here during all summer and on mild days in winter a member of the park staff or a skilled teacher from the schools or the museum ready to conduct a teacher and her class on a tour of the park, all as previously arranged. In the building, which is in part a small nature laboratory, is a lecture or study room holding about 60 persons, and a large room in which collections of objects, brought in by park authorities or by visiting groups under the former's specific directions, are sorted and discarded or arranged, mounted, and labeled. The best examples are reserved for the permanent exhibit of the park's material, and others are taken to the museum for school work.

Of the work of these small, park-study-museums, much more could be said. It is enough, perhaps, to add that they have helped to give the nature study or science work of the schools for the first time a definite and substantial value.

Of other work growing out of this cooperation among schools, parks, and museums, it is well to mention the small geographic forms—rivers, falls, lakes, deltas, etc., made by the park authorities in the parks, under school and museum guidance—and also the opportunities which the parks offer for the study of the elements of geology.

The problem of cooperation among all schools and teachers, the museum, and all the staff of the parks management, has been recently solved by the employment of an expert in science teaching who has general supervision of the whole affair.

In addition to the work with that greatest of all museums—the people of the city, their products, and their daily activities, and the material part of the city itself—the department of cooperation is engaged in extending the museum's field. Artists, designers, manufacturers, sellers, exporters and importers, engineers, chemists, and scientific groups and individuals are asked to give help in widening the museum's activities and in adding to its collections. The schools are studied with special care, and every possible avenue of usefulness to them is sought. Other museums in the vicinity are asked to help.

The working force of the museum is made up of persons who like to do things and wish to learn how to do them better; that is, they are all student workers. Experts are not employed as experts, but as workers whose experience and knowledge enable them to tell some of their associates how some of the work they wish to do can best be done. Those statements merely suggest the general attitude which members of the staff are encouraged to hold toward one another and toward the museum's needs. For new members to the junior staff, a simple course of reading, study, inspection, and work is laid out, varying somewhat for each one.

The activities of the whole institution are divided into departments under semi-independent heads or chiefs only so far as the demands for easy and effective work make such division quite imperative. The department method of administration is very agreeable to most workers, and especially to those who through it gain, as heads, dominion over a certain field of work and authority over subordinates. This fact, and the fact that the "expert" is especially desirous of having his own special field in which he may supervise and direct (both facts flowing from well-recognized tendencies in human nature) make it almost imperative that departmentation be tolerated to some extent. But it divides a working force, as its very name indicates, into groups. These, very naturally, tend to hold themselves apart from one another and desire to establish between each other solid walls of distinction.

In place of this cleavage into groups by and through differences in work, in kinds of knowledge and expertness, and in varieties of likings and feelings, the staff is directed chiefly by through-and-through supervision. Great care is taken to find for each worker the kind of work for which she is, by native bent and by training and experience, best fitted. Every effort is then made to keep clearly in each worker's mind the fact that all that she does is part of a common product—the museum's output in influence for the community's happiness and profit. An expert is encouraged to make the most of what lies within his field, that he may produce a semi-detached product not as a witness to his skill and learning, but as an added somewhat to the whole museum's armamentum.

By repressing quasi-independent groups, and by guiding all work largely by through-and-through supervision, we eliminate as far as possible the feeling that one's immediate task is an end in itself and not a means to a far more important end. At the same time we succeed in fair degree in leading the museum staff to look upon itself as a body of students without teachers, and not as groups of pupils each under a master. And the whole institution presents itself to the public as a collection of objects which a group of student-workers is trying so to administer as to make it accessible, enjoyable, and useful.

The several units of the staff work together as learners. The teaching and the pupilage states of mind are inhibited as far as this is humanly possible, and the inquiring visitor usually finds at once that he is addressing a learner, like himself, and not an adept, self-isolated by his consummate intellectual excellencies, or an expert conspicuously and inhospitably hallmarked.

To the staff as learners are joined as closely and as frequently as possible teachers from the schools of the city, especially in the study of the art of visual instruction. My belief that little is yet known concerning this art has already been expressed. Here it is mentioned again only to call attention to the fact that every opportunity is taken to make experiments, to note results, and to urge teachers to do the same as they borrow and use in their schoolrooms objects from the museum.

✦

The workshops include the places in which museum work is done, from the receipt, examination, recording, photographing, and cleaning and repairing of some ancient, rare, beautiful, and costly gift like an early textile, to the making of a simple case to hold a few geological specimens for lending. The shops are not rooms, save for a few types of work, but spaces to which the public have access. Separated from workers only by railings, visitors can see the work that goes to the making of an active, teaching institution. Here boys and girls note how the artisan, mechanic, or craftsman treats the museum's rare material and brings it into form for use in visual instruction.

Child and man alike are somewhat moved to interest, appreciation, clear understanding, and development of their powers by reading of a thing or process; they are still more moved by seeing the actual thing or process and learning of it through the ear; still more by handling and hearing and asking questions and receiving replies; and most of all by trying, under skillful guidance, to produce the thing or to repeat the process.

The museum, therefore, is a workshop of education in which objects are handled, descriptions are given, questions are asked and answered, and, as far as possible, visitors are moved to attempt, chiefly in school or at home, to produce objects of interest to themselves or of instructional value to the community.

Many children in the city are led by what they read and hear and see, in school and museum, to make and install exhibits for museum and school use, from models of kites and birdhouses, to life histories of birds and insects. What they create is used in the museum itself, in its branches, in the schools, in cooperating museums, and especially in and by the state's central museum, which never has enough of the simple and less expensive exhibits of natural history in all its phases—from harmful insects to forest preservation—to meet the ever-increasing demand therefor from all over the state.

✦

Branches and the lending of objects have already been discussed, but the great importance of these two lines of development and activity are so important as to make repetition thereon almost essential.

One central museum can be of slight benefit to all the people of a large city—since not all can easily and quickly reach it—unless it extends its work in the two ways already alluded to: by lending objects and by establishing branch museums. Our museum, as repeatedly stated, lends its objects freely. Particularly does it make use, for lending purposes, of its vast collection of pictures. It lends also objects in the field of applied art, these being chiefly either inexpensive originals or inexpensive copies of rare originals; and it even lends paintings, casts of sculpture, and bronzes to schools and individuals under proper conditions. Indeed, the loans range from a fossil wanted by a lecturer to complete what he shows at a talk, to a doll wanted by a dramatic club as a model for costume effects; from a vase for a still life group wanted by an invalid who paints in her bedroom, to an entire case illustrating textile history for the employees of a silk mill; or to an entire hall of pictures wanted by the museum of a neighboring village for its spring exhibition.

The branches are in some cases little more than rooms, like stores, fronting on the street, at the street level, in business parts of the city. Some are in buildings of their own. Others are in factories, stores, schools, settlements, clubs, and churches. They are decorated and finished in accordance with the uses made of them. Some contain, at times, little more than a few chairs set before one or two paintings or sculptures, which are so placed and lighted that they can be seen, day or evening, with the maximum of pleasure and the minimum of fatigue. With these are very full labels, in large type, supplemented by descriptive leaflets which bring the objects described into direct relation with daily life and encourage thought and study. Some are distributing centers with a museum assistant in charge who is able not only to discover the needs of teachers but also to assist borrowers in the art of using to the best advantage.

No one of the branches is all the time a showroom, though any one of them may be little more than a showroom, as indicated above, for a brief period now and again. Every branch aims to be a complete teaching museum, and is as far as possible fitted to the character of its neighborhood and to the degree of education and the occupations of its residents.

✦

As our museum is itself a school in which all members of the staff are both students and teachers—having, as the latter, only such authority to teach as their learning and experience gives them, and, as the former, every incentive to learn without the compulsion of pupilhood—it is plain that the opportunities for studentship which may be offered to outsiders are limited only by space and the absorptive power of the whole organization. Student workers are admitted on examination. The examination tests applicants for habits of industry; for serious intent; for accuracy; for thorough grounding in such education as is found a necessary equipment for helpfulness in the several lines of museum work in which assistance is needed, from carpentry to archaeology; for definiteness of aim; and for manners and good repute.

Visiting students who come in for independent study are welcome up to the limit of space and the proper supervision of books and objects used.

The museum makes arrangements for lectures or class work by members of its staff; but only as such may be requested by groups of students who give reasonable assurance of definiteness of purpose, are confessedly of that quality of mind which finds it impossible to learn by studying, and are willing frankly to admit that they are in the pupil stage of their development. Of such classes a rigid system of records is kept that the museum may be assured that the time its assistants give to teaching, in either the class or the lecture manner, is not wasted on mental sponges or on those temporarily possessed by a fad.

In a word, the museum is a place for students and workers—for those who wish to work hard at studying. As such a place it may be called a school, in the usual sense of that word, of designing, of drawing, of art, of science, of museum method of any other subject, only as it is made so by those studying within its walls, or outside its walls with the help of loans from its collections. These students form themselves into groups; certify the museum as to their seriousness and their fitness; ask for and receive members of the staff—and even, on occasion, persons who are not members—as guides, fellow students, student workers, or "professors"; and proceed to go seriously at the acquisition of that for which they have united.

An explanation and an excuse, if they are needed, of the apparent formlessness of this manner of schooling within the museum are found in the ever-present and never-forgotten fact that the museum is the assistant to and the handmaiden of all the formal educational activity of the whole city. It is an "institute of visual instruction." This means that it is far more than a storehouse of objects which may be used in object teaching, for it is an object-teaching school itself. But the city's educational activities, from the kindergartens through to the local university, are all of the conventional teacher and pupil type, of course. And the museum finds it, thus far, unwise to attempt to add to this huge body of classroom work—to the improvement of which, by the use of its materials, it devotes much of its energies—by the development within itself of "courses," thus necessarily duplicating work which is being done in the schools.

Though the museum withholds itself from the field of formal instruction so far as its character as an institute of visual instruction permits, the very nature of its collections, and of the labels, leaflets, guides, and handbooks that go with them, compel it to act continually as a teacher. The mere process of setting up an object to be looked at, giving it a label, and putting it in a certain sequential relation with objects, is pedagogic; that is, it aims to interest and to instruct. The museum teaches, therefore, in its main building and wherever any of its objects go. But its work is not of the classroom. It gives talks or lectures, singly or in series, to groups of children or adults, with other than definite pedagogic aims always in mind. It seeks through them to gain a certain needed publicity or popularity; to discovery by and through them if its methods of installation and its notes and labels are well fitted for their purposes; and to persuade teachers to use museum objects in classroom work by showing them some of the ways in which such objects can be used.

It is true that most museums are better equipped financially, by reason of limitations set on their incomes, for the purchase of rarities of high market value than they are for carrying on the kinds of work I have outlined. But this unfortunate condition is not permanent and in many museums is rapidly being removed. Trustees and donors begin to see that money which could be used for active work, with definite educational results in view, should not be surrendered to the purchase of very expensive objects,

objects to which a few point with pride and on which a few gaze with that improper self-satisfaction which is bought at the cost of museum fatigue.

The phrase "improper self-satisfaction" requires explanation. I have had ample opportunity to learn that one who criticizes any aspect of an institution whose general character is so well established in public opinion as is that of the conventional museum of art, is at once, by most persons, assumed to be critical of that institution in its entirety. If I venture to say that a public-supported museum should be of definite use to its community, and that by the mere display to a few random visitors of costly works of art in its galleries it is not of definite use, I am at once charged with saying that no community should make for itself a collection of the world's art treasures. This manner of condemnation and of summary dismissal of the innovator is universal and inevitable. But it is, in fact, as unjust and unintelligent an opinion as is that which leads one to call him a blasphemer who speaks disrespectfully of the architecture of a cathedral. The fact is that I believe that a community—and by that word I mean any fairly prosperous town or city in this country—can well afford to collect, and ought to collect, beautiful objects, far more of them and far more expensive ones than any city has yet gathered for itself; it ought to house them permanently, beautifully, and in such a manner as to keep them from all possible harm. Every town and every city almost without exception can afford to do this, and, as I said, ought to do this. But when it does this it ought to clearly understand precisely what it is doing; and if it does not thus clearly understand what it is doing, then it ought to be told; and the persons whose peculiar duty it is thus to inform it are not lay preachers of museum gospel like myself, but museum persons, museum workers, and experts in the art and science of museum management. The thing a city is doing when it thus collects beautiful things and beautifully and carefully houses them is just that and nothing more. It is putting the rich products of its purchasing power into a storage warehouse. It is not making those products of effective use, save to a very small degree, in adding to the pleasure, the general enlightenment, the physical well-being, and the industrial power of its citizens.

If this is denied, let us look for a moment at the facts. Our richest museums of the general storage warehouse type receive in a year a total of visits equal to, say, 10 percent of the permanent population of their respective cities. Subtract from this total the visits of transients and all visits after the first of residents, and there remains, of the visits of residents for instruction, enlightenment, and inspiration a few thousands only. Of these thousands a few hundred attend one or more lectures, which are to them in most cases mere titillations of their intellects via their own auditory centers, having no relation to their mental development or to their trades, vocations, or professions. And of these few thousands, a still smaller number are conducted in groups through the museum and thus acquire a few fragments of information concerning a few exhibits.

The buildings and collections forming the material presentments of these museums are of slight cost relatively to the wealth of their respective cities; but of high cost when considered as the underlying planks of the foundations of educational institutions, and as such planks their product in definite influence on their respective communities is, as shown by figures I have roughly estimated, most lamentably slight. In fact, they are so slight as to make seem quite reasonable the statement I have elsewhere made to the effect that no other public educational institutions give so little return for the money spent on them as do art museums.

Now, we desire beauty. We are by nature as artistic as was ever any people. We wish to learn. We wish all things that we produce to have that indefinable somewhat which would give them unmistakable and permanent charm. And to us come the wealthy, and our mayors, and our aldermen, and tell us that they have noted our desire for the beautification of life, and that they will help us to achieve it. Therefore, they build us a temple of art in a remote corner, and put into its stately but wearisome halls long files of costly products of the past; and make it all so pretentious, so cold, and so unsympathetic that we do not visit it at all! And then by the power of wealth, of high cost, of great age, and of expertness, they so obfuscate us that we believe that what we see in their temple is very art of very art, and that it is to be seen nowhere else; and that our effort to make beautiful our own modest homes are pitiful and laughable. Consider, now, a museum's possibilities in promoting the quest for that form of broadening our daily life which we call beautification.

In its city are thousands of shops, factories, stores, and homes. In these are hundreds and thousands of workers; and do not forget that those who manage and those who labor in the homes are as truly workers as are those in the factories. Assume for a moment that the wealthy citizens and the governors of the city are willing and eager to spend their own and the public's funds in an effort to make more agreeable, more beautiful, more enduringly satisfying, the products of the factories and the tools of domestic life. Thereupon, in the center of the city, they set up what they are pleased to call a museum, and they place in this museum, as workers, a group of men and women who are sensitive to the appeal of beauty; are persistent students of beauty, down to its most modest appearance in the decoration of a broom handle; are skilled in the arts of presentation and appeal; and believe that most of their fellows are glad to learn, but that they learn best who are least conscious of being taught. This staff of workers surveys the city and its life and industries. It discovers what it produces and what it uses; and things produced by it and the things used by it are by the museum staff gathered in typical examples into the museum. By these are placed examples, from other cities and other times, of kindred things, sometimes originals, sometimes copies—and often merely pictures of them. It arranges these for display and labels them freely and describes them in leaflets, and, on occasion, sends groups of them to schools, factories, and storerooms in all parts of the city. And it says to the citizens, "Come and see. We think you will find that, as a result of such a study and daily use of what we can show you in your museum or as we can help you to make in your homes and factories, your products will sell better and at higher prices, your homes will give you more pleasure, your knowledge and sympathy with the peoples of other lands and other times will be broader and deeper, and you will get more enjoyment out of every working hour."

And that, briefly, is the text upon which I have tried to construct this little volume.

IV. Museums and Community

Increasing the Usefulness of Museums

It is easy for a museum to get objects; it is hard for a museum to get brains. The objects are seen, talked about, wondered at, bring praise to those who give them and prestige to those who choose them for purchase. The brains are not seen, are chiefly in the heads of mere hirelings, produce results slowly, and the results produced are seen only by those with a gift for education or with training and experience in it.

What is true of museum objects—rare, wonder-producing, and pride-evoking objects—is true also of museum buildings. It is easy to get them, much easier than to get museum brains. They are large, monumental, shiny, obtrusive, make impressive photographs, help to give cities plausible reasons for existence, furnish to donors a refined publicity for unselfish expenditures, and endow laborious trustees with a sense of duty done and with the immortality of a bronze inscription.

Probably no more useless public institution was ever devised than that popular ideal, the classical building of a museum of art, filled with rare and costly objects. And it adds to its inutility a certain power for harm. To its community it gives a specious promise of artistic regeneration, and it permits those who visit it to put on certain integuments of culture which, although they do not conceal esthetic nakedness, inhibit the free exercise of both intellect and sensibility.

What I mean is this: Museums, and especially art museums, are social conventions or community fashions. When a city puts on a museum it puts it on in obedience to the dictates of municipal fashion; it erects a museum building in accordance with current architectural fashion; and it places in the building objects selected after the fashions of art museums. These municipal, architectural, and museum-object fashions are becoming out-of-date. Conformity to them is not useful, but is moderately harmful, giving conformists the notion that they are doing something which in fact they are not doing.

Proceedings of the American Association of Museums 10 (1916).

If, now, museums are to be of greater use to the world, here are the things that museum brains must fight against: fashionable museum buildings, fashionable museum collections, and fashionable treatment of collections.

In the kind of conflict here indicated—brains in ideas against the inborn tendency of good citizens to prefer the old way—the better manner of conducting the campaign is plainly that of a seeming retreat, accompanied by the construction of new and better things in the peace and quiet of the rear. Then, when the cohorts of the ancient, honorable, and ignorant finally penetrate the lines of the intelligent and reach the rearguard, they will find there, already constructed and in use, institutions so well adapted to obvious needs that they will adopt them at once, and call them their own creations and the very realizations of the ideals for which they so long have fought.

That which common sense dictates as the proper course for protagonists of the new museum is precisely the course which they are following. Here and there you find men and women, relatively few but in the total a goodly number, who are constructing institutions of a usefulness so great that they are paying in some cases fair returns on their cost, even though burdened with the handicap of being called museums. Mr. Rea's museum studies of recent years are most discouraging if you set down results in cold figures; but quite cheering if you read them with an eye to the future. Miss Connolly's study is more optimistic, of necessity so, being an effort at construction rather than a description of conditions. The recent annual reports of this association can give even the most depressed of museum revolutionists much encouragement, for they prove that the one ever-present desire of museum workers is to discover and exploit new avenues of definite usefulness.

I shall try to suggest this rapid increase in the utility of museums by drawing, from latter-day writings, reports of those forms of museum activities in which progressive museum workers take the most pride, which are most approved by their associates, and which are plainly making museums in which they appear more widely and more definitely useful to their respective communities. These varied forms of activity I shall unite in one imaginary museum, which, as I shall try to suggest, is so valuable an asset to its community as to make it seem that its title "museum," already a misnomer, should be changed to "institute of visual instruction." And thus depicting, in rough and incomplete outline, an institution of an excellence and effectiveness as yet quite unattained, I must add to it certain features and put upon it certain peculiarities born of my own imagination. Only thus, it seems, can I give the vision a certain needed strength and fullness. In thus adding, to what I find in actual practice, possibilities that are mere ejects of myself, I shall, as I am well aware, give you a project of which no one of you will entirely approve. But, after all, you are not asking of me something

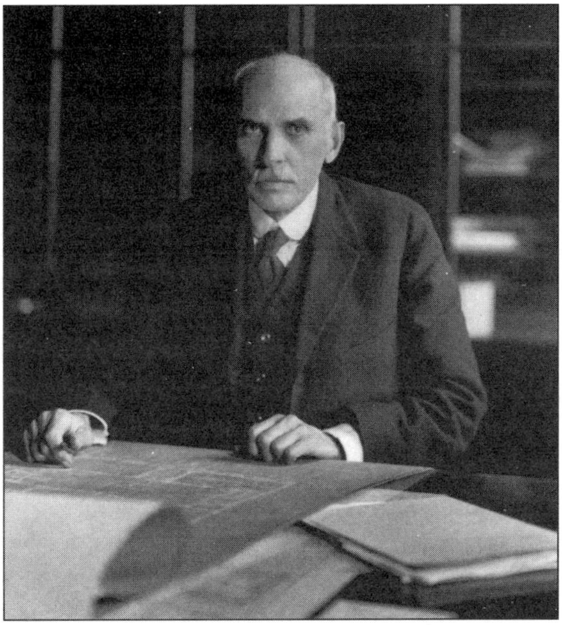

John Cotton Dana at work on plans for the new museum.

to which you can all give assent; but something which may strengthen your faith in your own work and—though this is asking too much of a non-expert—something which may move you to pursue your present tasks with added zeal and to venture upon new lines with proper courage.

Those things which the new museum will not do, and the kind of institution which it distinctly will not be, must be indicated chiefly by exclusion. It is not needful to begin by saying that the ideal institute of visual instruction will not be thus and so. One negation, however, seems essential; it is, that the new museum is not a museum of a certain kind. It is not of fine art or applied art; nor of pedagogy or technology, nor of hygiene or religion. Carefully selected and laboriously identified, completely labeled, fitly installed, and safely housed collections of objects in all the fields mentioned, and in subdivisions of those fields and in many others not mentioned, are needed now, and have now and always will have their select, high, and usually narrow range of usefulness. But basic to all the project I shall briefly set before you is the statement that either these must no longer be called museums, but collections; or a new name must be discovered and adopted, such as I have roughly suggested in the phrase "institute of visual instruction," for those creations whose usefulness is wide, direct, obvious, and in fair degree measurable.

And that word measurable leads to one more remark prefatory.

All public institutions, and museums are no exceptions, should give returns for their cost, and those returns should be in good degree positive, definite, visible, measurable. The goodness of the museum is not in direct ratio to the cost of its building and the upkeep thereof, nor to the rarity, auction-value, or money cost of its collections. A museum is good only in so far as it is of use. It is easy to evade the importance of this obvious fact by airy talk of the uplift value of architectural façades in the classic manner, of priceless antiques, of paintings by masters, and of ancient porcelains, jades, and lacquers, to say nothing of replicas of whales, Indians, and mastodons. But the evasion does not serve. Common sense demands that a publicly supported institution do something for its supporters, and that some part at least of what it does be capable of clear description and downright valuation.

The museum project I present is in one of our large, ugly, industrious, and rich American cities of mixed population.

Its museum is near the center of the daily movement of its citizens. The narrow and modestly decorated entrance fronts on a side street just off a main artery of travel. The building itself is 16 stories high, with an area of about 10,000 square feet on each floor, giving a total of 160,000 above the basement. It is built in the ordinary modern, fireproof, brick-steel-and-concrete, loft-building manner, at 25 cents per cubic foot, and cost, with the land, complete with decorations, furniture, and cases, about $1 million.

The main structure is a parallelogram, about 60 by 160 feet. The lighting problem is solved by electricity, though windows are abundant, especially in workrooms.

The entrance hall, a stairway of moderate grandeur, cloak rooms, toilets, shipping rooms, several small halls of wonders, and several lecture rooms occupy the first floors. The halls of wonders contain a few examples of the oil paintings, sculptures, and curios which every museum of art is supposed to possess, and a few of the habitat groups, large skeletons, and curiosities of nature which convention bids us look for in a museum of science. If these were not on view in a convenient place and near the entrance, they would be earnestly and persistently sought by visitors until they were found. By putting them near the entrance and by giving the entrance just a touch of grandeur, all visitors who have the conventional museum expectancy enjoy at once the agreeable reactions they look for, and are fit to proceed further with a quiet and receptive mind. Many of these objects, or others akin to them, are found again where needed to teach this, that, and the other lesson. The modesty of the entrance hall is compensated for in part by the presence in it of a panel of glass mosaic, very unusual, very expensive, very laboriously made, very old, very historical, and distinctly a museum piece. Always among the objects shown in these halls of wonders are some which are recent acquisitions, some which cost a great deal of money, some which enjoy provenances of astounding length and of aristocratic flavor, and several which are the only ones in the world, or at least in this country.

The floors on which are found the other things to be mentioned need not be specified. For all of them there is abundant space. Many of them are moved from time to time, as the development of the museum's activity and as changes in museum method dictate.

I can tell what the building contains and what are the activities which center in it in the briefest manner only. To those familiar with museum work the items on the list which follows will almost automatically expand themselves.

Our projected institute contains the following:

1) A staff adequate for the work which the objects named and the activities suggested may require. The staff is larger, relatively to size of building and cost of collections, and more highly paid, than it is in any existing museum of equal floor space.
2) Paintings, many of them, chiefly recent American, but with an abundance of copies of old masterpieces. A few are shown in the building; some are lent to schools; some are placed in windows of stores; some are in libraries and branch libraries; and some are in the museum's branches.
3) Sculptures, including many American bronzes and others of all countries and all times, the latter being in most cases inexpensive copies. Most of these are usually stored, or lent, or are on exhibition in other places. There is no grand sculpture hall of plaster casts; though there is at least one room in which the peculiar esthetic emotion to be experienced in the presence of a congruous group of marble sculpture is produced.
4) Prints, a large collection, but not necessarily an expensive one. Valuable prints are accepted as gifts, but few are purchased. No large permanent collection is always on view.
5) A collection of about a million pictures of paintings, sculptures, architecture, and, chiefly, of decorated objects of daily use. It is classified by objects, schools, periods, etc. These are used by students in the building and are lent freely for home, studio, school, and factory use. They form one of the most valuable assets of the whole institution.
6) Collections of metal and wood work, textiles, etc. Such of these as were purchased are largely copies. The acquisition, even by gift, of originals which have a very high market value and involve great labor in handling and great care for preservation is not encouraged.
7) A selection, constantly changing through rejections and renewals, of things made in the city. Of some of these an important exhibit is held each year.

These local industries displays are quite frankly commercial. They illustrate each year the best the city can produce in the line selected. They are accompanied by or preceded by or followed by exhibits of goods in the same line from other countries and from other periods.

8) Many objects illustrating such fundamental industries, whether followed in the city or not, as have greatly influenced the development of civilization: objects of clay and glass, textiles, leather, metal objects, jewelry, wood, and foods.
These objects are shown from three standpoints: the historic development of the industries involved in its relation to the development of the social conditions influencing and influenced by them; the processes by which such objects are made today, with the science and skill involved; the art qualities inhering in such objects, in both past and present times.

9) Habitat groups, usually rather small. Many of them are in miniature. They include birds, animals, insects, and men. A few selected ones are always on view, and well arranged to be shown to groups of school children. Many of the less important and less complicated groups, small and easily moved, are placed in museum branches, in windows of stores, and in branch libraries and school houses as needed.

10) Science collections. These are made with special reference, first, to the science work in the schools, and next, to the interests of local groups of scientists. They are quite largely arranged as needed.

11) A library, for reference and lending use.

12) Lanterns, lantern-slides, stereomotorgraphs, moving picture films, all of a character appropriate to the museum's work, with moving picture machines and rooms in which all can be shown to small audiences.

13) A department of cooperation. The whole museum is in itself an institution for encouraging the use, not only of objects in its possession, but also of natural and man-made features of the city and its immediate surroundings. It is the habit of the city to turn simultaneously to library and museum when information is wanted. It is the custom of the museum to send to the parks of the neighborhood some of its movable collections, which illustrate the phenomena then and there visible. And the park managers send to the museum many specimens illustrating natural phenomena. All art, industry, and science schools use the museum and its collections just so far as falls short of interfering with their more democratic use by the city's laymen. And their first impulse, when producing or acquiring any thing capable of use in visual instruction, is to duplicate it or share it with the museum. These correlations tend to prevent unnecessary duplication of collections. One department of the museum contains lists, pictures, and

reproductions of notable art, science, and industrial features of the city, and visual information as to its political, religious, philanthropic, and civic institutions.

14) With this department goes another, which gives its time chiefly to instructing teachers and others in the art of visual instruction, including the preparation of labels and of descriptive leaflets.

15) Workshops. These include the places in which museum work is done, from the receipt examination, recording, photographing, cleaning, etc., of some ancient, rare, beautiful, and costly gift like an early textile, to the making of a simple case to hold a few geological specimens for lending. The shops are not rooms, save for a few types of work, but spaces in one or more rooms to which the public has access. Separated from the workers only by railings, visitors can see the handwork that goes to the making of an active, teaching institution. Here boys and girls note how artisan, mechanic, or craftsman treat the museum's rare material and bring it into proper form for effective use in visual instruction. Child and man alike are somewhat moved to interest, appreciation, clear understanding, and development of their powers by reading of a thing or process; more by reading and at the same time seeing a picture of thing or process; still more again by seeing the actual thing or process and learning of it through the ear; still more by handling and hearing and asking questions and receiving replies; and most of all by trying, under skillful guidance, to produce the thing or to repeat the process.

16. Branches. One central museum can be of slight benefit to all the people of a large city, since not all can easily and quickly reach it, unless it extends its work in two ways: by lending objects, and by establishing branch museums.

The branches are nearly all little more than rooms, like stores, fronting on the street, at the street level, in the business parts of the city. One is in a build ing of its own. Others are in factories, stores, schools, settlements, clubs, and churches. They are decorated and finished in accordance with the uses made of them. Every branch aims to be a complete teaching museum, and is, so far as possible, fitted to the character of its neighborhood, that is, to the degree of education and the occupations of its residents.

17. A school. This had been in active operation as a school for many years before the museum opened. As it grew slowly, and chiefly on its own initiative, it had adapted itself admirably to the demands of such young people of the community as wished to work in the field of applied art, or who, being already engaged in offices and shops, wished to improve themselves by definite and formal instruction. It is now open both day and evening and follows, as income permits, the development of the best schools of fine and applied art in the country.

The museum teaches daily in its main building and its branches and wherever the objects it lends may go. The influence it has on a community is difficult to measure. We can put our fingers on results no more than we can say of a drop of water in the Gulf of Mexico that it is the result of a shower in South Dakota. Emotions sink into the soul; actions seep out at other levels of time and circumstances. All we can do is to plant and water; somebody else will sit in the shade.

It will be said that it is impossible for a museum in any city to secure funds for the purchase of efficient brains with which to carry out a program that even approximates the one here roughly outlined. But large museum incomes are spent today in the acquisition of expensive treasures, to which a few point with pride, on which a few gaze with that improper self-satisfaction, which is bought at the cost of museum fatigue.

This paper is based on the belief that the conditions which led to these expenditures are past; and that the primary duty of those same institutions is to justify their existence by becoming effective agencies in the intellectual, esthetic, industrial, and moral progress of their respective communities. If they do not do this they should resign themselves to the acceptance for all time of the fact that they are mere museums. Then, in their respective communities, should arise new institutions, fitted to satisfy the needs of these days—institutes of visual instruction.

The New Relations of Museums and Industries: The Story of the First Ten Years of a Group of Experimental Museums

Note of Explanation

Ten years ago the government of Newark said, in answer to an inquiry from a group of citizens which included the trustees of the public library, that if the inquirers would cause to be formed a proper corporation to receive same, they would appropriate $10,000 for the purchase of a collection of Japanese and Chinese art objects then on exhibition in the library. The suggested corporation was formed, with a charter including this declaration of purpose: ". . . to establish in the City of Newark, New Jersey, a museum for the reception and exhibition of articles of art, science, history and technology, and for the encouragement of the study of the arts and sciences. . . ."

The association is engaged in activities so varied and has collected so wide a range of material that it might appropriately be called an association of museums and not a museum association.

The following outline of the ideas in accordance with which I have managed the affairs of the association for 10 years was read to the members of the museum association at their annual meeting on May 29, 1919.

Museums and Industries

If you use the word "art" in talk with the average person of intelligence, that person is almost sure to think at once of paintings. If the word is "museum," the thought is almost surely of a gallery of these same paintings. If by chance the word "art" is so used as to make plain the fact that reference is not thereby had to oil paintings, you will find that it calls up in the minds of most hearers of intelligence the thought of objects that are probably old, are almost certainly unique or rare, and are indubitably costly.

This tendency to think of art and museums in terms of paintings in oil on canvas with gilt frames, or of objects which are old, rare, and costly, is quite as unfortunate as it is universal. It is unfortunate for many reasons. Some of these reasons I shall try to suggest, and shall at the same time try once more to show why I have been glad to give my time and thought to the development in this city of a museum of a certain rather definite kind, which I call "new"—and to no other.

Since this association was formed 10 years ago, certain ideas that had been expressed by a few rather bold and inquiring spirits, but had not received general approval by friends of museums, have come to be accepted by good authorities as cardinal principles of museum management. They are lived up to in actual administration by very few museum directors, partly because of the great burden of conservatism under which most museums are obliged to live; but they have produced quite definite results on the museum conceptions of active and observant laymen by almost compelling the adoption of new museum methods, and by calling forth new museum-like enterprises with specific activities quite impossible to the older forms of museums.

Of these undertakings, inspired by modern notions of the powers and duties of a museum, I will mention only a few.

In England, long before the war closed, men keen for the welfare of their country laid plans for the betterment of her industries. In October last, even before the armistice came, these plans were brought out and definite steps taken for their accomplishment. The British Royal Society of Arts, an ancient and powerful body, held a conference with the National Board of Trade, a most important factor in the government of Great Britain. The conference was presided over by Mr. H. A. L. Fisher, then president of the National Board of Education. To this conference were brought the plans which had been prepared independently by the two conferring bodies. These plans were found to be so alike in aims and methods that they were easily merged into one. This plan is, briefly, to establish a "British Institute of Industrial Art, with the object of raising and maintaining the standard of design and workmanship" (and note that here mere workmanship is put on a level with design) "of works of industrial art produced by British designers, craftsmen, and manufacturers, and of stimulating the demand" (note that demand is to be stimulated as well as design and workmanship) "for such works as reach a high standard of excellence."

This institute will be incorporated under the joint auspices of the Board of Trade, as the national department dealing with all industries, and the Board of Education, as the authority controlling not only the schools but also the Victoria and Albert Museum, that vast collection of the world's best products of former days in the field of applied design, commonly alluded to as "South Kensington."

The Central School of Arts and Crafts of the London County Council, the National Amalgamated Union of Shop Assistants, the Imperial College of Science and Technology, the National Physical Laboratory, the Art Workers' Guild, the Home Arts and Industries Association, and other like bodies have expressed their approval of the scheme and their desire to help it to complete fulfillment.

The methods by which this new institute for the betterment of Great Britain's manufactured products proposes to attain its purposes are these:

Set up a permanent exhibition in London of the current products of British factories and shops, selecting the best in design and workmanship, together with kindred products from other countries, both modern and ancient.

Make a selling agency part of this exhibit.

Establish a fund for the purchase for the state of objects of outstanding merit shown in the exhibits of the institute.

Through the institute bring designers, workers (meaning men who carry out through and with modern machinery the suggestions of designers) and manufacturers and distributors into close touch with one another.

Set up special exhibits and cause them to travel through the whole country.

Make use, through constant and persistent cooperation, of all existing organizations and agencies devoted to the improvement of design and workmanship in Great Britain.

✦

That is a very brief outline of a great and moving enterprise. The enthusiasm which the enterprise has called forth on all sides is indicative of the existence in England of widespread and deep conviction that its industrial output must be notably improved in design and quality if it is to compete successfully in the world's markets.

Note that what this group of wise men purpose to establish through their institute is a museum. Note, also, that they find it necessary to establish a museum, although they have already in London two of the world's greatest museums, the British and the South Kensington. And note, once more, that the reason they do not turn to either of these museums as the central point of their activities is plainly because neither of them is connected closely with British manufacturing interests; neither of them shows the designers, the bench-workers, the machine-tenders, the manufacturers, or the distributors what they are all doing, what their competitors are doing, what the world is doing, in their several lines; and neither of them is, in any proper sense of the word, an industrial, a commercial, or a teaching institution.

The reasons why these existing museums are not in touch with modern industry and do not teach lie largely in the facts to which I called attention in beginning this paper—that intelligent and influential persons today think of museums in terms of oil paintings or of rare, old, and costly objects, and not in terms of service. Behind this conventionalized museum concept, made up chiefly of paint, antiquity, and price, lies an interesting story, the story of the origin and modern development of the museum idea, too long to be here set forth.

The first point in my argument is reached when I have shown, as I have, that if moving spirits in a great modern nation seek for help in the betterment of their industries through the medium of a museum-like institution, they find that none of the established museums has shown itself, by its acquisitions or its activities, ready to do the museum-like work which they find needs to be done.

At the risk of being unduly personal, I shall try to apply the lesson of this British New Museum movement to our own local situation.

I interrupt the argument here to mention three facts:

Designers, artists, workers, manufacturers, and distributors of goods of Germany formed an association some 10 years ago for promoting good design and good workmanship, and for the diffusion, through all parts of the empire, of knowledge to each line of industry of the progress made by the best men in that industry. This, you see, anticipated by a decade the plans now being formulated for like work in England.

Through a wealthy patron of the arts living in Hagen in the heart of the great industrial district of the lower Rhine, this association was able to secure—thanks to the influence of the art patron of Hagen and his close touch with the association just mentioned—a very admirable exhibit of the products of German applied art in many lines, the first exhibit of its kind ever brought to this country. It was shown here, and later in six other large cities.

This association asked the Metropolitan Museum of New York if it wished to show this exhibit. The reply came that the Metropolitan did not find it advisable to show these objects of applied art, partly because it could not run the risk of coming thus into close contact with anything commercial. This was only eight years ago. And you should note that in a time as near to us as is even 1911, the thought I am developing of the necessity of making our public museums of definite industrial value was still alien to our most important museum.

In 1917 and 1918, and again in the current year, the Metropolitan has held exhibits of purely commercial products. These products have been admitted under the very admirably conceived condition that they be made from designs which were themselves taken direct—with any desired modifications—from objects already in the museum's collection. That is, our greatest American museum now commits itself definitely to the policy of helping industry in its search for those factors in manufacture which are now seen to be so essential to England—better design and better workmanship.

These facts show that England is late, though we hope not too late, in following the lead of its great competitor; that our association was doing sound pioneer work for the museums of this country when it brought over here and showed certain distinctly commercial products of Germany; and that the vision I had of a museum of definite industrial value to our community was after all only a few years ahead of actualities as entered upon by our greatest of museums of art.

It is proper here to note that we have in the Commercial Museum of Philadelphia an institution which has for many years in its special field of commerce anticipated some of the work that England hopes to do through its proposed institute. It has not only—by its collections and its service of a corps of experts—been of immense value in promoting foreign commerce; it has also, through its very valuable traveling school collections, helped to make of more interest and value much of the teaching work in scores and hundreds of Pennsylvania schools.

The opinions I am expressing in this paper are confirmed also by the recent action of the Cleveland Art Museum. This museum opened not long ago with a very expensive loan exhibition of works of art—including the inevitable paintings and other rare, old, and costly objects—not one of which can be said to have borne any helpful relations to the varied and wonderful industrial activities of the city which the museum was founded to serve. Today this same museum begins to collect objects—not, I fear, made in Cleveland, as they would in that case be neither rare nor old—but objects "related" to objects made in Cleveland, and acquired with the avowed hope that they will prove helpful to the Cleveland designer and mechanic.

I am confirmed again in my opinions by a recent decision of the Art Museum of Buffalo, which has in recent years found large sums with which to defray the cost of very elaborate and very expensive exhibits of paintings and sculpture, to open its doors to the products of American arts and crafts—meaning thereby the products of private, individual workmen. This action is surely a step toward admitting the work of those designers and mechanics of our great shops, who design with their brains and produce with their hands, but as yet are anathema to most museum directors and trustees because they bring forth their handiwork through mere machines!

The management of the American Museum of Natural History has from the very first foreshadowed the aims and activities of the proposed British institute in the field of industries; for it has always taught, has always advertised, and has always been an institution of service, as well as of research and acquisition.

✦

Our town is industrial; its products find in the main an easy market in our own country. But as peace conditions come upon us, Newark products will surely feel a little more keenly than ever before the pressure of competition from European and Asiatic manufacturers. Also, we must expect a somewhat more strenuous competition from other American cities. These facts alone would be abundant reasons for making an effort to improve—as is all of Great Britain—the design and the workmanship in our own shops. To these facts we can add the fact that our city has in recent years begun to think of herself and her development, and now quite definitely desires to be considered as good a city as any, and to be such in fact. This growth in municipal pride, this increase in a proper local patriotism, should alone lead us to wish to put on foot a movement for developing better designers and better workmen, similar to that which Great Britain is promoting through the institute I have described.

Let me here add that arguments much like those just noted led us, here in Newark several years ago, to do certain things for the improvement of design and workmanship. Those things include, in part, the making of three new high schools, the increase of attention paid to our evening drawing school, the building up of vocational schools for boys and girls, the use of vocational guidance, the opening of county vocational schools, and the development of our Technical School. These are all helpful to the end we are having in mind, and though our city, in spite of them, is not where it should be in education, in design, industrial design, they point to a public opinion which will surely continue to demand better and broader work for the improvement of our industrial products.

Turn, now, to the very modest efforts of this association and to the thoughts which led up to it and to the conclusions in accordance with which I have tried to guide its development, and you will see wherein lies the lesson it may draw from the industrial-betterment plans that are taking form in England.

About 13 years ago, I presented to the Board of Trade the suggestion that that body help to establish here a "Museum of Local Industries." I was made chairman of a committee on the subject, and with the assistance of Miss L. Connolly, then a supervisor in our schools, proceeded so far in investigation and plan as to be able to present to the Board of Trade a definite suggestion of certain tentative steps. The cost of these preliminary steps was to be from $150 to $300. The Board of Trade directors were not able to see how this would help the city and declined to appropriate the money needed.

Our plans were for gathering at a central point certain products of Newark factories, so installed as to be easily seen and understood, with supplementary exhibits put up in convenient form for travel from schoolroom to schoolroom throughout the city. As the purpose of the whole scheme was educational, we inevitably tied it up to and looked upon it as a modest aid to our public school work.

Had this museum of Newark products and processes—a museum of Newark's position in design and workmanship precisely in line with that now projected by the wise and progressive men of Great Britain—had this museum once come into being, it would almost inevitably have been taken up into or have itself taken over by the "Monsignor Doane Museum of Industrial Arts," which I later urged the Committee on the Doane Memorial to establish instead of buying with the funds contributed for that memorial a quite inferior bronze statue by a rather inferior sculptor.

When this association was founded 10 years ago, I soon discovered that though its initial $10,000 given by the city was used to buy a collection of objects which were chiefly in the applied arts field (were models, that is to say, for all students of design and workmanship), the thoughts aroused by our name—"Museum Association"—in the men chiefly concerned in its promotion were, as my opening remarks indicated they would be, almost solely of oil paintings and of old, rare, and costly objects.

I had then studied museums for some 10 years. I knew that to spend our very limited funds on paintings and on rare and high-priced objects would merely lead us to construct here—in a purely industrial city—one more of those useless, wearisome, dead-alive gazing collections of which the whole community would soon tire.

I thought I knew then—and no end of modifications of museum and educational practice since then have helped me to what I fear has been to some an almost unpleasant assurance that I was right in my thinking—I was sure then that this city could be helped in its educational and industrial life by an active, teaching museum; and certain aspects of the museum that it was my ambition then to work for were quite identical with those of "the Institute of Visual Instruction in the Arts of Design and the Refinements of Workmanship" which England now proceeds to establish.

A little later I was again able to confer often with Miss Louise Connolly, and as I had taken from her certain of my ideas about making for Newark a useful institution instead of a gazing gallery, I asked her to go again over all obtainable museum literature, and then to visit a long list of museums and schools and to give me her conclusions thereupon. Those conclusions, found in part in her reports of study and visits, and in part in definite suggestions for a museum for Newark, were duly published.

Circumstances connected with their publication obliged me then to say that, as my study of museums compelled me to feel that I could give of my time and energy only to the construction of a museum that promised to be active and useful to our city, I would have to withdraw from the museum's work if my own projects, as reflected in Miss Connolly's report, were not found worthy of acceptance.

I rehearse this episode only to make clearer to you the fact that it has not been easy to insist that this organization should move toward a museum giving rather definite values to its promoters and upholders—our fellow taxpayers—in attractiveness and in helpfulness to industry and education, and should not move toward a mere group of galleries of paintings and costly curios.

In our attempt to make this association both attractive and definitely useful, we have made it broader in its range of activities than museums generally are. Knowing that the average person of intelligence has been compelled by current opinion to look, first of all, in a museum of art for oil paintings, we have, by purchase and by gift, acquired these until our collection of them numbers more than 60. Next after paintings, convention demands of a museum of art that it possess sculptures, and our acquisitions in this line include plaster copies of antiques and bronzes, many of the latter being of the best quality. Next after paintings and sculptures, museum precedent and popular feeling insist that we have the old and rare and costly in objects of applied art; and in this line, largely through gifts, we have come into the possession of things that fairly well meet these requirements.

If I seem to you to imply that all these paintings, sculptures, and objects of age and value have been acquired against my judgment and advice, then I give you quite the wrong impression. A city as big and rich and as increasingly conscious of itself as is ours ought to feel that it is not properly advanced, in comparison with other cities, if it has not a few treasures in the field of art, and they of the highest type and beautifully housed. And I expect to live to see Newark properly advance herself in this regard. Indeed, by far the greater part of the many exhibits we have set up in these 10 years have been distinctly artistic, in the old museum meaning of the word.

What I am trying to convey to you is a clear impression of my very strong conviction, based now on more than 20 years of study of the subject of museums and 17 years' study of our own city, that with our limited income and our limited quarters we should give much of our time and energy to testing acquisitions and methods, by and through which we can project for our city an institution of definite and measurable value; and of measurable value particularly—this being very manifestly an industrial city—in the improvement of design and workmanship in our industries.

Because I felt that we should construct for ourselves here a useful museum, I suggested a museum of our industries to the Board of Trade 13 years ago; urged a Doane Memorial Museum of Applied Arts 11 years ago; have acquired applied art objects as our modest fund permitted; and have brought out such exhibits as those of modern German applied arts, and of the clay products and the textiles of New Jersey.

The best of museums, no matter how diligently it tries to be attractive and useful, is quite minor in its influence compared with the schools. We have tried to adjust ourselves to this fact. We have known that what we can do in the teaching line with young people should be looked on as experimental. If we are successful in discovering a few boys and girls who are born to become students, collectors, and organizers in any field whatever of sciences, art, society, or industry—and we have been remarkably successful herein, in view of our limits of income, space, equipment, and staff—then we can do little more. The schools, we have a right to assume, will take advantage of our modest discoveries and pursue them. This assumption applies also to such success as we have had in meeting the calls of teachers for objects that they can use in their classrooms to make more attractive, more easily understood, and more impressive the topics their textbooks expound. We lend, of objects gathered for this purpose, several thousand each year. With our present income we cannot extend this work. I am sure we ought to extend it and to be granted ample appropriation for that purpose. A school museum can be far more effectively and far more economically maintained as a part of a general museum of art, science, and industry than as an independent institution.

When one of the museums in Philadelphia—following herein the old museum idea of the supreme importance of the rare and costly—can spend $60,000 on a single vase, the cost to this city of a good school museum of daily interest and use to thousands of our young people seems quite negligible.

I speak of these matters at some length because I wish to make clear the wide range of our own activities, modest as they are, and to suggest that, when you do finally achieve a great and worthy museum building for Newark, it should be not merely a palace of art and a quiet and retired home of pure science. It should contain treasures, of course—our city cannot afford not to own such and rejoice in the ownership—but it should provide liberal space for setting forth the real Newark, and that means the Newark of great industries. It should promote the keenest possible interest in the products of those industries in young people, and it should give room, money, and service to those methods of making those products in a large way by Great Britain. It should give ample room to display and use—to use in education and also in expounding the raw materials of industry to managers and workers and in helping the students of all the sciences—such a collection of scientifically gathered, arranged, and labeled objects as we already have in our Disbrow collections. It should afford ample room for school collections and for their study by teachers and for their transport to and from schools as needed. And it should tell the story of the life of man, in his age-long rise from cave-dweller to city-dweller, in a manner to attract—by picture, map, model, tool, and implement—both old and young, and to serve as a supplement and explanation to every student of society and to every reader of history.

I am trying to give the impression that in the 10 years of my very cheerfully given services to this association, I have been working for a vision and a very large vision, not for a moment to be confounded with the conventional vision of a museum of art for the momentary delectation of the passerby.

I have tried to show you that this vision has been the product of things seen and known and not of the mere idle imaginings of a summer day. And I have tried to suggest that this vision, which could be made real here and only to that very, very modest degree which the narrow limits of our income, our space, and our own understandings permitted, has been seen by many in recent years, and is soon, in many of its more important factors, to be put to the test of actual practice by some of the ablest men of our day.

This test will, if it is successful, go far toward removing from the minds of the average intelligent citizen—man or woman—that tendency to which I have so often alluded, that tendency to think forever of museums in terms of oil paintings and old, rare, and costly objects. As this tendency weakens, so will strengthen the tendency to think of an association like this as devoted to the task of constructing here an institution of great power for pleasure, for instruction, and for industrial betterment; as devoted, in a word, not to acquisition and conservation, but to service.

Appendix

The preceding paper—which is in some degree an apology for my last 10 years of museum activities—was read at the annual meeting of the Newark Museum Association on May 29, 1919. The notes which follow make clearer its meaning to the few who may read it who are not familiar with the association's work.

In the paper itself it is perhaps not made plain that a very large part of our activities had been experimental; that is to say, we have done many things the definite value of which had not been determined by the practice of the other older and larger museums. We have, as I think my paper intimates, frankly begun certain forms of activity which, we were well aware, could not be carried on to definite conclusions by us, but which it seemed wise to open up for consideration by modest experiments. These statements apply especially to certain publications, like the "Stories of the Sculptures," the "Habitations of Man," the "Stories of the Prints," the "Stories of Clay and of Textiles," and the pamphlet on snow paintings.

The experimental character of our work is suggested also by our Junior Museum Club, with its "Junior Museum News," which we can promote and guide to a limited extent only; by our exhibits of modern German applied art, of New Jersey clay products, of New Jersey textiles, of the Republic of Colombia, of the colonial kitchen, and of the study of birds.

Our city has no museums. It was clear to us from the first that it would in due time come into possession of museums. Our question was, what kinds of museums should they be? To this question the literature of the subject gave no answer and did not even try to give one. Nearly all that has been written on museums begins with the quite unwarranted assumptions that museum types are fixed; that the pressing questions concerning them are questions of verification, acquisition, conservation, and installation; and that when a city decides to give to itself such of the stigmata of culture as accompany museum ownership, it must acquire, first, an ornate and expensive building and then fit that building as well as its constructive features permit to the assumed needs of a museum of one of the well-known types.

Our movements in developing our very modest institution were not guided by these assumptions, and for several reasons. The reasons were, first, those that have been suggested by the paper that precedes these notes; next, the limitation of our income—$142,000 in 10 years; next, the narrowness of our quarters, they being a few rooms in a public library building; next, the presence by our side of a public library, with the accompanying feeling that we were almost a component part of that library; next, the acquisition of a large, rich, and growing collection of objects in several departments of the field of science; and next, and most important of all, the knowledge that we were supported by, and were in duty bound, to try to be of direct value and service to a city of industries, a city singularly void of those institutions and objects which mark most cities of 400,000, and a city which has at its doors and of easy access the institutions and objects of delight and education of the greatest metropolis in the world.

Facing these facts, and keeping always in mind the idea of service for the pleasure and advantage of our chiefest patron—the people of Newark—we have done what we could; we have frankly experimented; we have acted much as if we were a laboratory of museumology for a great city. Fortune has favored us in the fact that our staff of workers has been almost a part of the larger staff of a public library, and that its members have never known how to spare themselves when the museum's interests were concerned.

Libraries and Museums

How Museums Came to Be So Deadly Dull (May 15, 1921) Museums of art are not made to fill a present need. They are made in obedience to an ancient fashion. The fashion grew up several centuries ago among kings, princes, and other masters of men and wealth. Early museums were not made by the common people to supply a want which they felt; and when these common people found that they had, through taxes, money held in common and at their own disposal through their elected servants, they decided to use some of it to buy museums for themselves. Unfortunately, no one was at hand to tell them that they would get no pleasure or profit out of the kinds of museums which kings, princes, and other masters of people and wealth had constructed; and so, being ruled by precedent or fashion, as were also their rich donors, their important citizen-trustees, and their architects, they voted for, or silently approved, spending public money for the old kinds of museums. They cared more to be in the fashion than they did to get something useful and enjoyable.

That is only part of the story. The mastery of people and wealth by a few came on down to modern days. Most of us prefer mastery by another to the irksome task of mastering, and being responsible for, ourselves. The supermen who held and still hold the mastery of men and things inherited the fashion of their predecessors—kings, princes, and others; therefore, they copied the old style of museum even when it was their purpose to make it for the people and not for themselves alone.

Museums of science were made of a stupefying dullness to the common man, because those who inspired and directed their construction and management were natural-history enthusiasts and scientists who loved to observe, collect, name, label, and arrange for themselves; but never gave time, study, and thought to the problem of making the objects which interested them inviting and profitable to the average intelligent person. Also, they gave no heed to children, being satisfied with the conventional thought that as the children have schools they need nothing more.

That story of the way deadly dull museums have come to be part of our accepted social equipment is in broad outline only.

One important factor in the process of making them deadly dull has been already hinted at—the stupidity of the rich who knew one type of museum only—the remote, unvisited, and melancholy temple to the dead gods of art and science. This stupidity was the basis of much insistence by givers, and by complaisant trustees of their gifts and, alas! by architects, that the buildings given should be patterned after ancient, dark, and uninviting temples to gods, or fortified palaces of princes, also dark.

Another factor that helps make museums of art body wearying and soul stupefying is the exaltation of the oil painting. To tell whence and how came this exaltation would be too long a story here. It is enough to say that during all our museum-of-art development, those at the forefront in that development—rich donors, well-to-do and unimaginative trustees—have assumed that the one thing essential to a museum is a long series of oil paintings in elaborate gilded frames, hung in sky-lighted rooms. Though many visit these long series of pretty, colored pictures and enjoy them as they do our colored Sunday supplements, they do so because they think they ought; and they find those visits wearying to body, brain, and eyes; and they carry away from them a minimum of suggestion for making daily life more entertaining and houses, homes, dress, and domestic equipment more attractive and enjoyable.

What I mean is this: that the oil painting seems not to help in any discernible degree to make us more interested or intelligent in the application of decoration to daily life; but that the worship of it does seem to help to increase the number and size of soul-and-body-tiring galleries of pictures.

Among the obstacles to the development of museums which shall daily add to the agreeable reactions of all members of the community which supports them, and at the same time be helpful in broadening and enriching life through the educational work they do, is the all-pervading convention concerning the character and location of museum buildings. This has already been touched on, but needs another word of explanation.

As kings and princes passed away, or became little more than conventions, some of the palaces they had occupied were taken over by the new government and were turned into museums. This set the fashion of making museum buildings low, usually one story and a basement only, and of Greek or Renaissance style.

The ideal museum building today, constructed in conformity with the precedent just noted and with the fashion that other precedents have set, is made to look as if it were of one story, with a basement; has skylighted rooms in the roof; is located at such a distance from the center of its city as to discourage visits; is grand and uninviting to the common people and within is elegantly embarrassing to most visitors.

If these preceding brief notes are in the main correct, then they sufficiently explain the average museum's unpopularity. To them should be added a further word as to the lack of friendly and helpful relation between the contents of museums and the daily life of the people who maintain them.

Art, as represented by a museum of art, is thought of by museum enthusiasts and by the country at large as peculiar to itself, remote from daily life and quite unrelated to chairs, linoleum, wallpaper, bonnets, shoes, and tableware as used by the world outside. This potent convention as to the isolation of art-in-a-museum from all other things has been recently aptly illustrated by the remarks of a museum enthusiast in a talk on art appreciation. The assumptions the writer made were that a knowledge of art and an appreciation of it could be gained only be seeing real art, and that as real art can be seen by the non-wealthy only within the walls of a museum of art, a person who has grown up in a western town or village cannot have either art knowledge or art appreciation.

It would be difficult to add to the impression that remark makes on the thoughtful by discussion of it.

The foregoing brief mention of some of the factors that have made museums remote, unvisited, and melancholy needs modification, of course. Especially does it need mention of the fact that in the past 10 or 15 years much has been done in not a few museums to redeem themselves from the charge of being unused and unattractive. Space does not permit me to note here specific cases. If it is found possible to add other informal papers to this one, the modern movement for making museums attractive and helpful to the commonalty will be described in them at some length.

II. The Functions of a Museum (June 15, 1921)

To librarians, when speaking of museums, it should first be said that to be interested in museums after the modern manner is to be interested in visual instruction. Just what is meant by this phrase it is not easy to say. The methods, the tools, and the results of teaching with the aid of objects and pictures are being studied as never before. The movie would have compelled such study if the modern museum idea had not. For the purposes of this discussion it is enough to say that the old type of museum was almost useless as an educational tool, educational here being used in its popular meaning. The educational inutility of museums of the old type would still remain even were they greatly visited by both old and young, and they are not.

Hence the question which confronts one who [considers] museums is not how to make them more attractive—that can be done, as experiments have shown, by the skillful use of free ice cream and free music. The question is, how can they be made so useful, so helpful toward happiness, intelligence, and general well-being, that all save those of quite the lowest mentality will be moved to use them.

It is impossible to bring to a museum in any community so many interested visitors as to make the aid it gives to those visitors in making them happier and more intelligent citizens an adequate return for the cost of building, contents, and maintenance. A study of its finances and of its report on its visitors of our largest and richest museum, located in our largest city, will be sufficient proof of the truth of that statement. A few students can and do visit museums each year for definite and useful ends. The relatively small attendance of them, however, is chiefly made up of casuals; and even if they gain from their visits reactions of extraordinary aesthetic value or enthusiasms for popular science of extraordinary range and depth, those reactions are adherent to so small a part of the whole citizenship as to make them almost negligible, and they are entirely negligible if one attempts to set them over against the museum's cost as an adequate return therefor.

Space is here lacking for further argument against the old doctrine that a museum, like beauty, is its own excuse for being; and in favor of the new doctrine that all institutions supported from the public purse, including museums, should show returns for their cost which are definite and in fair degree measurable. The conclusion is, briefly, that no museum can pay for its upkeep through the good it does its visitors.

If library enthusiasts here interrupt to say that the facts and conclusion which have just been roughly outlined can be applied to libraries established for reference use only, this comment may be made in return: that the use of books in a reference library is in most cases far different from the use made of objects in a "reference museum," and that the development of printing in the last half century has given us conditions under which the old type of reference library is in much the same position as is the old type of museum; and that nearly all of the world's reference libraries would be far more useful than they are now did they lend freely or place in branches, or both, about 75 percent of their books and journals.

The museum that is chiefly under view in these notes is the museum which frankly admits that its value to visitors is quite slight, being a value realized by few and decidedly minute to most of the few, and finds its excuse for being chiefly in four forms of activity, to wit: It lends its objects for use in school, studio, shop, or home; it places its objects, often in moveable groups, in branch museums; it publishes things of use to its community, things based on the museum's objects and activities, yet not

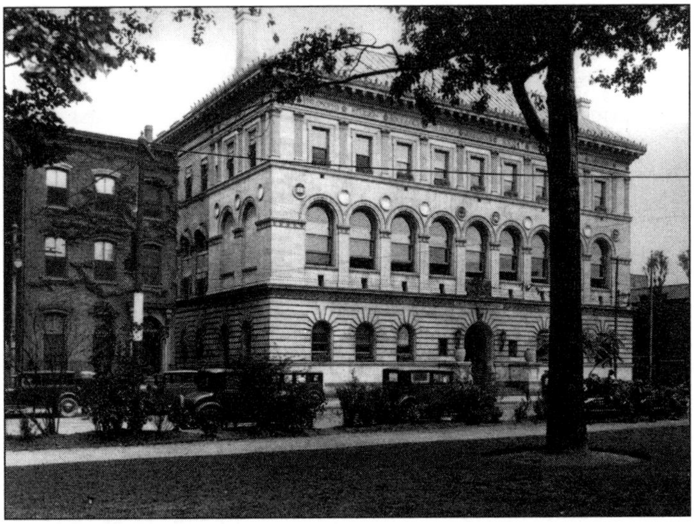

The Newark Free Public Library, the first home of The Newark Museum.

demanding of one who gets profit and pleasure from them a visit to the museum itself; and it teaches many, not merely through casual gazing at its objects, but with those objects as illustrations of spoken and written treatises.

It is now obvious that . . . a public library is in many respects well equipped to do the fundamental things in modern museum making; and that a public library is a good and proper place in which to lay the foundations of a museum. The librarian is friendly to students who come to his collection of books; he lends books freely; he puts books in branches, including in this term every group of books that goes out to a certain spot and there eagerly seeks for ways of usefulness; and he publishes useful things, so far as funds and imagination permit.

It is worthwhile to note here the fact that most of the movements toward museum beginnings that have been set up in libraries have had the earmark of the modern library and consequently of the modern museum. Objects and collections gathered in libraries have been selected, where that was possible, not with a mind set on cost, rarity, and age; but on immediate value as a tool in teaching. And again, the collections of pictures which libraries make and lend are in fact collections of museum objects. One very important museum consists of pictures only. Many museums have picture collections, but are in most cases far behind libraries in that they do not lend them.

A library, then, is a good place in which to lay a museum's foundations, or, to put it in better phrase, in which to begin a modern museum's pleasure-giving and helpful activities. In later papers it may prove possible to suggest definite methods, furniture, and devices for modest museum beginnings.

The museums of the future, especially those in industrial cities and smaller towns, will not be each of a definite kind. That statement does not say and does not imply that collections of objects in many specific fields will not continue to be made, and if wisely administered, will not be useful and even essential tools in the development of knowledge in the fields they severally represent.

The meaning of the statement—that the coming museum will be, in most communities, not of one specific kind but of all kinds—will perhaps be made fairly clear by what follows.

The new museum wishes to be useful to its community from the very first day of its existence. It finds in the public school system of its community demand for the most modest objects it can collect. It proceeds at once to make itself a helpful adjunct to that system, thus following that fundamental law of social economy which insists that existing organs be utilized to the utmost in the development of new ones. To fill the demands for objects useful in schoolrooms it must go into fields of art, science, industry, and history. [In] so doing it forms collections which make it at once not a museum of a certain fixed type, but a group of museums of all types.

Looking about for other fields of usefulness it finds that in its community is a wish to see and to make use of industrial products, old and modern, local and foreign; a wish that is in most communities far stronger than that for seeing and enjoying paintings and sculptures. It begins, therefore, to collect examples of the city's own products, and forms thus an industrial and commercial museum such as England is now developing through some of its most important industrial and educational organizations.

And so it proceeds, gathering and making available for study such things as it finds its constituents can enjoy and can use and are eager thus to do.

The new museum, then, is not a museum of art, or science, or industry, or history, or of any other type of field; it is such a wide-ranging collection of material as careful observation and controlled experiment indicate are useful and pleasure-giving to the community which supports it.

These remarks have, it is hoped, cleared the ground for the statement that just as a librarian selects for purchase for a library for the public the books that will be to that public most acceptable and most useful and most used, so the director of a museum of the new type collects for his community not what convention and fashion say a museum should contain, but what a study of the tastes, industries, and pastimes of the community suggest as best fitted to fill that community's wishes.

It follows, once more, that a good librarian is eminently well fitted to be a museum founder.

III. First Steps Toward Museum Founding (September 1, 1921)

What has thus far been said should make it clear that I feel that the usefulness of museums to the general public may be frankly questioned. I have tried to show that utility is a museum's only excuse for being; that a test of its utility lies in its use; and I have hinted that its use as a collection of objects which are available in "visual instruction" has not been proved to be of great value. Hence, why museums at all?

To all this the retort can be made that only a . . . dull or narrow and bigoted mind cannot see the profit to the world, in the long run, of the collection, identification, and safe storage of the tools and adornments of human life, and of a like treatment of all objects [within] the realm of science—meaning here well nigh everything that man can touch and see. To this retort comes the reply that I am speaking of museums for the average person, old and young; and freely and gladly admit that all the "storage" and all the "gazing" museums in existence find a certain slight degree of usefulness today and will ultimately find more thereof. The argument for the establishment of general collections of objects—so chosen, so described, so intelligently presented by curators, so freely lent, and so open to study so as to be obviously useful and obviously pleasure-giving—this argument may be confused by vague allusions to the general uplift given by the exterior and content of a gallery of fine art, and to the high value to students of the marvelous regiments of objects in a museum of science, and to the high duty of the men of today to collect for the men of tomorrow all that they can gather of records of the past. But the confusion thus produced does not go beyond confusion of mind and does not affect the argument. Indeed I present, strictly speaking, no argument at all. I make merely the statement that a new type of museum is here and now in process of development; that it finds the cause of its existence in the fact that museums of the old type do not render the service which those of the new type purpose to render; that it denies neither the propriety nor the value—in the long run—of museums of the manner now dominant, and admits that its coming may irritate the advocates and workers in many of the existing museums; and will probably lead to an insistent demand that these latter change some of their ways.

I dwell so long on making it clear that we should turn some at least of our thoughts and our energies to a new kind of museum, and on making it clear that in so doing we are not forgetful of the good things that may be said of the old museums, because of the existence of an ancient, stupid, and unjust custom of charging the advocates of the new with a wholesale condemnation of the old. As an abstract proposition we are all ready to agree that progress involves change and, conversely, that where there is no change there is no progress. But in real life change is usually accompanied by pain in our minds, or in our sensibilities, or in both, and the proponent of change is usually condemned as a cause of that pain.

If the subject of museums is of interest to you, then you have already examined casually the museums of your town; but if you purpose to use your library, and your position as a library worker, as aids in local museum development, then you should proceed to examine them critically. You should visit them; examine their contents and their methods of administration, their finances, their annual cost to your city, and what the return is for that cost in influence on the lives of citizens, old and young.

I assume that you know something of the use of objects and pictures in the practice of teaching. You find about a thousand times as many visits are paid to movies in your town in a year as are paid to your museums. Your movies practice visual instruction; your local museums may vaguely wish to practice it, but succeed in doing little more than giving to a few, on rare occasions, opportunities for idle gazing. A few inquiries will probably show you that new methods will not be seriously considered by your museums. Let us assume that you ask if you can put slips into your books on art and science referring to objects in your museums and saying that old and young will be conducted over them and shown the things each may wish particularly to see; that you ask for objects to display in your library; that you ask that readers, notably teachers, having borrowed books from your library to aid them in their work, may borrow from the museums objects which will make their classroom work more instructive and more interesting. To all these queries the answer will be, in most cases, no.

Your interest in visual aids to education continues, and you find that the literature of the subject is interesting, and leads you to the conclusion that the use of such aids is well worthwhile. I have hinted that, in my opinion, the value of these aids has not been thoroughly demonstrated; but that very fact makes me the more keen to see the subject more widely studied and visual aids more used. Only by use and observation can the question of value be answered.

You probably have already a collection of pictures from which many borrow examples for a score of uses. That teachers use them freely is indicative of their utility to them in their present stage of pedagogic knowledge. That designers, movie men, newspaper men, decorators, architects, and others use them is ample evidence that they are useful to the community at large, even though their utility in educational work is not yet definitely proven.

If you have a collection of pictures which you do not lend, then you have in your library the foundation of a museum of the old type. It is still more definitely of the old type if the pictures are under glass, can be examined only with a certain quantum of back and neck twisting and of eye-strain, can be seen only up to 5 p.m., and only by walking carefully a goodly distance on hard and polished floors, and only by prolonged standing—comfortable seats not being of the essence of gazing museums.

If your pictures may be freely handled, may be examined and used by the student or the pleasure-seeker when seated in a chair at a convenient table, and if they may be borrowed in quantity for use at home, or in office, shop, or school, then you have in your library the beginnings of a museum of the new type. All doubts about the value of visual aids as giving pleasure and profit to your community as a whole are nearly forgotten in the presence of the simple fact that they are used, and with evident enjoyment.

Having shown by your success in founding and conducting a museum of pictures that you have already certain of the qualifications of a museum manager, you are perhaps moved to go further and begin a collection of objects. You are convinced that such a collection, directed as are your pictures, will be useful, and you have found that the museums of the neighborhood will not lend objects and do little or nothing to make themselves attractive, pleasure giving, and of influence on the tastes, thoughts, and aims of your community. If you learn these things in no other way, you can almost surely learn them from the one fact that visitors to them are few—few absolutely and also few relatively to the money that has been spent on their foundation and maintenance.

At this period, beware of the benevolent museum founder; especially of him who has made a collection of objects of art and curiosity and wishes to present them to [you] on condition that they be kept forever in certain rooms of their own, that the rooms be always plainly marked with the name of the donor, and that they be always open to the public. Collections and even whole museums, including the buildings that house them, are not uncommon as gifts of well-meaning persons to their respective communities, and are in nearly all cases entirely dead as soon as they are set up. A finished museum is a corpse, and so is a finished collection. In common with all other institutions, a museum to be of any value must grow; and it must do more than that—it must change its objects, their manner of presentment, and its methods of management that it may meet the ever-changing needs of a changing order of society. A librarian is peculiarly well fitted to see the truth of that statement, for he is familiar with the library's recent history and has noted the radical changes it has undergone. A few years ago libraries were as are museums of the old type today, with bound books for adults as almost their [only] objects of collection, and these rarely lent and under many restrictions, with no access to them by their owners save through a catalogue and an attendant, and with the slightest of a clientele. Today we have in our libraries books for all ages, maps, pictures, pamphlets, clippings, records, and movie films. These objects may all be freely handled and examined; all ages and all classes use them; skilled attendants serve as "docents" concerning them to all comers; and they are borrowed under few and simple rules.

Do not, then, think of the museum you may hope to help establish in your library, or with its aid, as something which will ever be complete. Think of it always as a beginning, as an ever-changing series of collections, administered in ever-changing ways.

After what has been said it is not necessary to suggest that your collections be not encumbered with mere curios, objects that derive all their interest from such facts as age, origin, ownership, cost, or former use. A bit of stone may be of value in a museum; but not because it was picked up on Bull Run battlefield, or was once in the pocket of Abe Lincoln, or cost the owner a million dollars. Among the friends of the museum enterprise which I assume you are seriously contemplating will be a few who will offer you curios of the kind just suggested. It may be wise to accept them in most cases, but not to pay for them with promises of their display or eternal preservation.

If your thoughts go so far as to the formation of a museum organization, let this wait until you have still further examined the field. Just as the teachers of the city are the persons most ready to exalt your position as librarian by a commendable use of your books; so are they the persons most inclined to approve of the idea of a local museum, with a quality of service like that of the library, and to make good use of it.

At a meeting of teachers, then, with the approval of the superintendent of schools, you may well present in rough outline a scheme for a museum. If you put first the fact that it will collect objects to lend to teachers as aids in schoolwork—the objects to be examined and lent just as are the library's books and pictures—you may then well add that the museum shall be, so you hope, adapted as it grows to the needs and wishes of the whole community, including the arts, fine and applied, the sciences, trades and manufactures, commerce and society.

In a Changing World, Should Museums Change?

The words "Changing World" refer to more inventions, discoveries, and habits than time permits to be mentioned. A few of them are the telephone, gas engine, motor car, inflated tire, airplane, radio, railroad, steam engine, steamships, photography, transmission of electric power, electric light, typewriter, cheap postage, trolley car, movie, rapid printing, type casting, typesetting, lithography, offset printing, color printing, zinc etching, half-tone, paper making, advertising, psychology, steel, stainless steel, automatic machinery, manipulation of metals, department store, shop windows, public free schools, state universities, endowments for promoting well-being.

These are taken at random. A few go back a hundred years; most of them fall within the last 50. Art museum conventions that seem still to be nearly all-potent were quite well established more than a hundred years ago.

If it is even approximately correct to say that our life has been notably affected by the inventions and discoveries of recent decades, while the art museum is in temper and conduct much what it was in 1800, the question in the title of this paper is answered in the affirmative, is it not? Or was the art museum born to perfection and still so remains?

But established institutions change reluctantly and slowly. Opponents of changes in such institutions find it hard to act on the fact that all progress is change. They are hypnotized by the sight of present good qualities, and cannot visualize better ones. Most of us being conservative by birth and training are uncomfortable in the presence of a new idea.

The museum is an established institution. In its present form it seems to have

---

Paper presented at the annual meeting of the American Association of Museums, New York, N.Y., May 19, 1926. Published in The Museum (The Newark Museum Association), September 1926, and Publications of the American Association of Museums, New Series 1, 1926.

begun in Renaissance times. On its art side it retains, as I have said, its earliest form and quality. It aims its influence at the cultured few, just as it did in its beginnings when a culture which made refinement of any kind understandable was quite rare. It stresses the oil painting and the gilt frame, the former having the weight of a religious origin and the latter largely the natural outcome of the love in ignorant wealth of conspicuous waste. It has established a cult of the museum piece, which may be the product of great technical skill, of long labor, and of a creative temper; and must be rare, expensive because desired by the wealthy, and of toothsome age.

The home of the art museum is, in both location and character, as definitely determined by precedent as are its contents. The building, its contents, and traditions draw to themselves for a staff persons friendly to the traditions and easily brought into full harmony with them. Hence the art museum idea is little moved to modification by forces within itself, and seems not to know of others. Hence it is rather a thankless task to suggest that art museums be modified in aim or method.

In Newark we have a museum—only in small part a museum of art. It is but just open, and on its art side particularly it does as yet little more than present itself to its visitors as a modest gazing museum of the old type. I am quite sure that your director, Dr. Richards, in asking me to talk to you today, hoped that I would tell you something of what this Newark Museum may have produced in the way of newness. I cannot do that. In fact, I am confident that no museum, even a new one, and even one with five-fold our Newark building and ten-fold our funds, could not, even after many months of practice, declare with truth that it had solved the problem of making itself a definitely effective factor for more wisdom and happiness in its community, and a factor at all commensurate in its effectiveness with its cost. Hence I deal here in hopes, not in proud facts. Our Newark free public schools cost us more than $8.5 million in a year. Our Newark Museum, with a scant third of all its space and labor devoted to art, costs $100,000—a little more than a tenth of 1 percent of what the schools cost. You can count what the schools do, if only by noting how many children each year are taught to read, cipher, and act somewhat like human beings. Of the influence of the Newark Museum you can as yet say nothing and—here is the point of this brief paper—you can as yet put your finger on extremely little of effect wrought by any art museum.

Perhaps the art museum performs its wonders of amelioration in ways as mysterious as are those of God in our ancient hymn. But my faith has long been and still is that if art museum authorities will look carefully upon the changes that have taken place in human society and its component units in the past 50 years, and then will open their eyes to the fact that their own special organism has continued in its old aims and methods during those same 50 years, they would see that changes are called

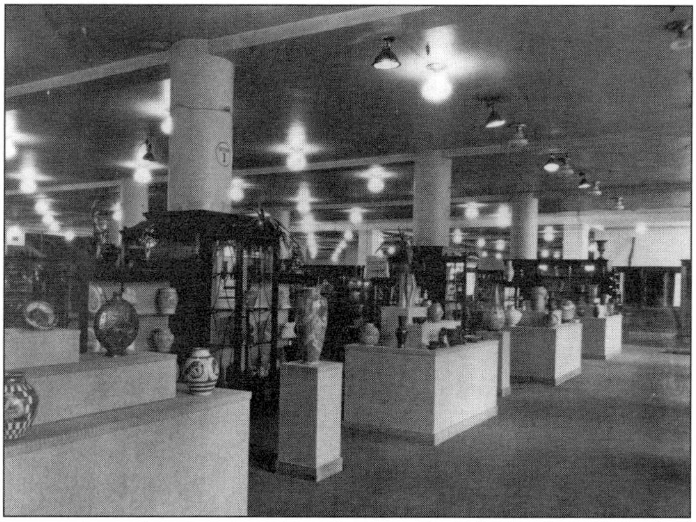

The International Exhibition of Ceramic Art at the Bamberger Department Store, 1929.

for; they would even be able to see what are some of the changes that new conditions and new mores demand; and they would appeal to their masters and supporters—the public they were established to please and enlighten—to bestow on them funds for the special and definite purpose of making their institutions definitely useful parts of the social organism.

The art museum regnant shares with other accepted institutions the power of making a critic of any of its doings seem guilty of condemning all of its doings. Hence I once more try to avoid being entirely misunderstood and charged with hostility to all of the art museum's works by saying that to save the ancient and rare product of high technical skill and unusual taste is an admirable thing and a thing that should be done more freely by all our cities than it is now. But, as I have suggested, the trustees and staff of an institution which does this saving seems compelled, by the character of its work in the field of preservation, to close its mind almost utterly to the far more important task of teaching, and especially of encouraging taste, and interest in the growth and refinement of that taste.

It almost inevitably develops this theory and lives up to it: that real art can be found only in the forms and decorations of the objects it has collected, and that good taste can be evolved only by and through contact with these objects. Of a young woman coming for the first time to New York from a western state, it was said by an art museum enthusiast that, until she came to New York, she had never seen any art. A spokesman for an art museum has often said that in that museum only were truly good designs. The fact is that good art is wherever the interested and intelligent open their eyes and find color, form, line, and light and shade—and it is never anywhere else. The task of those who wish to promote interest in art is to incite man to a greater and more intelligent interest in what he sees. Insofar as the whole vocabulary of art and all the nomenclature of emotions used by art critics and enthusiasts are held in leash by those who believe that a museum piece is the world's only art object, by so much is made impossible the habit of seeing art in daily life and of gaining practice in criticism of it and enjoyment of it.

Art is not in a museum save in relatively unimportant quantity. Art is where it is seen and not merely where self-constituted experts have placed it.

✦

The coming of the department store is one of the many changes I have noted. Its use points at changes in museums. Here is the erroneous assumption—long so widely accepted as to have become almost a gospel—that to train the eye and mind in art, one must see the world's masterpieces. From this comes this result: that of the millions who daily visit the shops and gaze into the shop windows of New York, not one in a hundred thousand realizes for a moment that he or she is seeing art, learning of design, color harmony, and whatnot. Of course, we know better. Like that hand that rounded Peter's dome, these millions of shoppers are building their own art content better than they know!

And what, then, should the art museum do? To answer that is not now my job. If within a city is a building in which is a collection of rare or costly or old and, by-the-experts-declared-to-be the best of art, and if this building is open to the public at reasonable hours, and if it is generally believed, as it at present always is, that a visit to it brings one inevitably into touch with real art, and if it is an accepted dogma in that city, as it is in all cities, that visual contact with those objects gives one almost the only opportunity the city affords to take a step toward really knowing art and being truly artistic, and if now the people of that city pay at least 10,000 visits to department stores and fine special shops to one that they pay to the building in question—this seems to follow: that if the officials in and of that building really believe that what is commonly said of the quality and aesthetic potency of the objects in their charge is true, they should change some of the tenets of their faith, and perhaps even go so far as to change their methods.

The Newark Museum is an experiment, and a small, inexpensive, and simple one. It tries, alas!, to be popular. It is probably not so flatly condemned for trying as it would be if it succeeded. Its effort at popularity is not along any one line. It is not an art museum, but in the art field it would like to popularize art—and that means many things. Here is an illustration of one of the many kinds of things it would like to do: Put up a little shrine-like alcove, or call it a shallow box, say, 20 inches high, 8 inches deep, and 10 inches wide, open on one side and lined with cloth of a dull color but of high reflective power. On a tiny pedestal within the box place a plain drinking glass, costing perhaps 15 cents, half filled with clear water from the tap. Behind it put a card, saying, "Is it a work of art? The glass surely is; the water is a natural product, like a landscape; look carefully at line and mass, at the gleams and reflections on the glass, on the water within, on the water's surface, on the color gathered from the textile—and perhaps what you are looking at will cease, for a moment, to be merely water in a cheap tumbler, and come to be an exquisitely beautiful thing. If you thus see it, is it then a work of art?"

The point aimed at this is: If you look at an object and feel that it is, to you as you look at it, beautiful, you have at once an aesthetic reaction, which means that your whole body is a little stimulated, your heart beats a little more vigorously, your breath is a trifle deeper, you are for a moment exalted, and probably have a cleaner and broader view of life. The delight you find in the appearance of the glass of water should tell you that agreeable and healthful and morally improving bodily reactions, due to seeing art, need not be confined to your art-seeing experiences in an art museum. They await you in the presence of almost any object fashioned by human hands, and can be enjoyed by you if you will for a moment put yourself in a receptive mood.

To put it briefly, the Newark Museum would like to put art into daily life—and this, of course, without trying to make the museum-piece entirely worthless!

What has this to do with modern change? Well, chemistry and physics have put a beautiful drinking glass into the hands of the poorest. They have but to look at one that stands on their own simple dinner table to get all the healthful and agreeable incitation which they could acquire did they spend hours in a long journey and a visit to certain glass by Stiegel, in a museum of real art.

Should Museums Be Useful?

Museums are now in the air. New ones are springing up in scores of towns and cities; old ones are acquiring funds and growing swiftly in buildings and treasures; and vast collections of products of invention, engineering, and industry, each with a building to cost millions, are being projected. Many of the present ones can be called successful, if success can be counted in size of buildings, in value of objects, and in dollars of income. A few of them seem to be working slight changes in their communities because a few persons get from them ideas, or incentives to thought, or incentives to study, or new interests, or hobbies, or new sympathies. But the number of persons whose manner of life is influenced by museums is exceedingly small. Even in our largest cities, few visit them; very few in proportion to the totals of permanent and transient population; and of that few by far the greater part make visits that are merely casual or simply responses to the call of duty.

Unfortunately no one seems to know precisely how to improve museums. The friend of the museum as it is, of course, sees no need for change; and the exponent of the new has no successful experiments with which to point his theories. The present limitations of our knowledge of what is the effective museum permit us to say quite emphatically that the best imaginings of museum enthusiasts have not yet set before us a clear picture of a museum of full and rich utility.

The word utility suggests that the better museum that is to come will be more useful than are those of the present type. This word useful, of course, means far more than profitable in dollars and cents. It means influential in moving its community toward greater skill in all the arts of living. "The arts of living" is a phrase that extends its meaning from clean streets to clean air, from knowing the alphabet to a feeling for

---

The Newark Museum Association, 1927.

high poetry, and from pride in one's city to delight in helping it, even at a personal sacrifice, to become a cause for pride.

Assume now that the promoters of a certain museum set themselves to the task of making it useful in the best and broadest sense; here are some of the many difficulties they will meet in their attempt.

We all move in grooves, and if we have seen a few museums, or have merely read about them, we are sure to have formed in our own minds quite a clear picture of what a museum should be. We have adopted a museum mold, so to speak, and we have adopted also the belief that a museum in our town should fit the mold. This general opinion of what a museum should be stands in the way of the development of a museum which does not conform to that opinion.

All of a museum's possible activities, other than those that fall in with old conventions, must be tried out, in spite of indifference or hostility, before their utility can be said to be proven; and it is not easy to discover that a certain form of museum activity is worthwhile, even after it has been tried, since it may please for a time and yet have no enduring value.

These obstacles to the development of a museum that shall fit its community are obviously products of an ever-present opposition to the new; and to fit modern community conditions somewhat of the new is quite essential.

An attempt to answer questions like those which follow may advance us a little toward an answer to the question, How make a museum useful?

a) Why museums at all?

b) Which of their activities do in fact pay for their cost?

c) Of those that do pay, which would be the more profitable in the average city of this country?

In trying to find answers to these questions, certain conclusions come into view, of which here are a few:

Countless changes have put museums of the old type into quite a different relation to their several communities from that which they once occupied. Pictures in books and journals, now found by millions though only by hundreds a few years ago; print on every conceivable subject, and in quantity that in a few decades has grown almost beyond reckoning; vast museums called department stores, which have developed in the last 50 years, where countless objects from all parts of the world are inspected with keen personal interest by millions every day; daily contact with products of the invention and the industry of a scant two generations—these alone make a new environment for the museum and put it into a quite different place in daily life from that which it occupied a few years ago. Indeed, they do themselves make of the

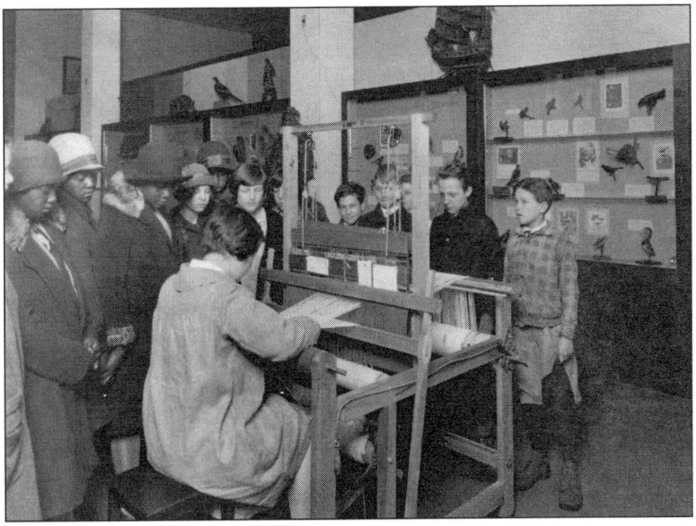

Children learn about weaving at the Newark Museum.

passing show of the world about us a fascinating museum, and one that is before our own eyes every waking moment. Perhaps, then, good reasons are lacking for the existence of most of the institutions of the old type that are still called museums?

Visitors to museums are so few, compared with the vast number of contacts by the whole populace with these new influences, that, in the great majority of cases, their effect on their several communities is even slighter than it used to be, in spite of the vast growth of museum collections and of the great advances made in the arts of housing and presenting those collections. The extension of our contact with pictures, print, and objects that carry to everyone the suggestions and the information that formerly came from museums only has made the world indifferent to the impact on their vision of even the rarest and most costly of the objects, however beautifully installed, that the museum can offer. This obvious fact, of the growth of an indifference to the museum's treasures due to an increase in the interest of the passing show and to the presentation of so much of what a museum offers through print and picture, has been seemingly almost ignored by the conventional museum official. He thinks to regain lost standing in the field of world attractions by adding rarer and more costly objects and by using in presenting them, regardless of cost, countless new devices, arrangements, and settings. He even adds the art of music to the allurements of his objects, as if his institution may properly draw visitors by appeal to their ears, in the expectation that slight aural intoxication will tend to make more welcome and more keenly appreciated a collection of objects which were gathered solely to exalt through the eye. But patronage of museums is not increased by these methods and does not grow, even in due proportion to the size and richness of collections or to the increase in number of possible visitors.

We can go further and say that in spite of the efforts made by museums to hold some of the slight power to attract, which they once enjoyed, their influence wanes. Fashion papers and journals on sports, houses, furniture, gardens, architecture, and whatnot are guides so universally followed that examples set by museum collections have no appreciable influence on public taste or current interests.

The goods displayed in shops of every kind follow in style and character the lead of the journals—and they, of course follow the lead of fashion autocrats—and not the lead of any museum's display of objects.

Some venture to say that the effect of the presence in an art museum of masterpieces in the arts, though subtle, is inevitably great, is deeply penetrating, and is highly influential in the long run. Proof of this statement is lacking. Others continue to insist that the value to artists in any line of creative work, of opportunities to see authentic products by the world's masters of design and craft, is in itself alone a good and sufficient reason for the expenditure of no matter how great sums to secure and properly to house and display these masterpieces. With this statement, though, its truth awaits demonstration, one may be moved somewhat to agree. But one should at the same time insist that, while one of the things for which a community, wishing to disclose to the world its wealth and its deep interest in expensive and ostentatious art productions, quite naturally spends freely on a collection of the world's masterpieces in all fields of art, the harm that such collections may do to the impulse for art production can scarcely be over-rated.

Art production demands, perhaps above all other mental activities, invention—invention that comes out of the social and other conditions of the time in which the invention appears. If, now, a community collects art masterpieces of earlier days, and by the manner of their display and by the ostentatious and fashionable patronage of them by the rich and influential, proceeds to arouse in its several units the faith that they—the old masterpieces—are the last words in all the arts, then does that community thereby paralyze in large measure the inventive power in artists. It tells them, the artists, that the best possible has already been done, and that all they can hope to do is to imitate, copy, or adopt and slightly modify the old. That is, the community in question has developed in its units, by an over-insistence on the value of the old and accepted, the habit of always looking in the art products of their day for likeness to old masterpieces, and has thereby created an atmosphere in which inventive talent, the basis of all art, cannot possibly flourish.

This statement of how museum pieces tend to inhibit art production may be put in this way: Nothing is more harmful to the rise of art impulse into the act of creation than established and accepted standards; and the rare and precious masterpieces of museums are too commonly accepted as standards by the community as a whole and, in consequence, by would-be artists.

The old type of art museums, then, if the statements just made have in them a fair measure of truth, is not helpful in promoting interest in art, study of art, or appreciation of art, and in fact tends to hinder the development of these three movements of the mind. Every prosperous town and city can well afford to maintain a collection of the best examples obtainable of the art objects of other days and other peoples; but these collections should be looked on by the several communities that collect and maintain them not as the last words in the field of art production, not as things to be slavishly worshipped or followed, but as an interesting story of man's efforts through the ages to add something new, attractive, and suggestive to the routine of life.

Communities which have acquired museums of art should remind themselves continually of the fact that a museum is fundamentally an effect and not a cause; is the outcome of interests and desires which have little to do with the discovery and patronage and development of taste, of art talent, and of the creation of beautiful things. A large, well-equipped museum in Athens, 600 B.C., had such a thing there and then existed, filled with what the rich and influential considered to be the masterpieces of earlier peoples in Egypt, Crete, Persia, and other lands, would probably have made quite impossible the flowering in the following two centuries of the Greek art we now admire.

Museums of art now spend large sums on exploration in the field of archaeology; but while it is not easy to have anything but praise for exploration in any and all fields, we find that this exploratory activity is not a part of those activities of a museum that come within the range of the present questionings. The explorations are largely archaeological and ethnological. They disclose to us the development of many forms of art in remote times and in civilizations that have passed; and they tell us with no small degree of detail how one people after another, each working out for itself, in an isolation which we cannot clearly picture and cannot use at all as a condition of our own art development, evolved a method of design somewhat peculiar to itself as a product of its own manners and environment, but always touched by the influence of its own past efforts and by the kindred designs of other peoples with whom it came in contact.

Large and wealthy museums perform a certain educational service in that they develop expertness in some of their curators. In a few cases it may plausibly be said that only by taking advantage of the opportunities which a curator's work affords can a desired expertness in certain fields be acquired. But the expertness is usually that of knowledge, criticism, and comparison and almost never that of production. Of books produced on all aspects of art, so few are the outcome of education by curatorial work in museums as to make the claim that museums develop their workers into useful experts seem not well founded; this in spite of the fact that it is quite a common saying of museums that even though they do not instruct the public, they do at least entertain and improve their curators.

A city should adorn itself. It should not only keep its streets neat and clean, supply itself with good water and construct ample sewers, set up beautiful parks, build plenty of attractive schools, and wear always that air, hospitable to learning, wisdom and art, which has distinguished the world's best cities; it should also take on certain material indications of culture and refinement, such as libraries and museums. Much is to be said in favor of a city's following the good examples of its noblest fellows and putting on the garments of wisdom and refinement, even though it does, in its secret heart, take little thought of them and no pleasure in their content and activities. An attractive museum building is a profitable investment for any city, even if the museum within is asleep, or is merely teaching itself and not helping others, and its outside only is all that stirs civic pride. Here is a good argument, however, not for the establishment in a city of a museum of a certain useful kind, but merely for the erection of a seemly building which shall in its outer aspect have the conventional marks of a museum's home. This home may be useful, even if it be so merely by virtue of its presence as part of the beautification of the city, serving only as a piece of architecture, and not as an active and helpful organism. And, merely as a building, it quite commonly leads collectors to place in it certain of their treasures. So doing, it may be said to serve a second useful purpose; but it still does not exert a direct and persistent influence on the artistic agitations of the members of its community. And again it must not be forgotten that duly venerated museum-pieces, collected and housed by a city, inevitably tend to develop in that city the feeling that it has done well and nobly and generously by art when it has bought and enshrined the art of other days; and, at the same time, tend to check the growth of the feeling that, for the production of art by themselves, they must sympathize with the creative spirit in themselves and patronize eagerly those who display it.

The mention of the presence of a museum building as an incentive to giving brings to mind at once the well-known fact that this incentive leads to actions that are by no means always helpful to the development of a useful museum organism. Many of the gifts that are made to it have little value save in the opinion of the givers. Many have no small value in the auction room; but little or none as part of a living and doing museum. And many, though of great beauty in the opinion of a small group of specialists, cannot make for many years, if ever, any moving appeal to the general public or arouse emotions that lead to good actions. Indeed, one of the obvious hindrances to the growth of a museum's influence in any of the fields in which it is usually supposed to be at work lies in the fact that it is choked by a flood of gifts. The moment a museum is safely and attractively housed, gifts begin to come to it. The larger and richer it is, the more numerous and the more valuable are the gifts it receives. And the more rare and valuable are the objects offered to it, the more insistent is the general opinion that they be accepted. And again, the more valuable the gifts—valuable in the sense of market price—the more essential does it seem that the museum employ experts for their identification, their labeling, their cleaning and repairing, and their installation for public inspection; and also the more essential is it that they have ample space for their display, that they be adequately guarded when on display, that there be suitable vaults or chambers for their storage when not on display, and that they be suitably described in handsome catalogues, and that no pains be spared to have them adequately exploited in the public press.

All these things make heavy calls on the museum's income for maintenance; and that income is almost invariably unable to meet all the demands made upon it. Most museums are poor. No matter how large, important, and valuable are their collections, they find their free income—the income which can be used to meet current expenses —is much too small. Donors have a grievous habit of earmarking their gifts of money for certain definite purposes. Perhaps one of the chief reasons why large museums, rich in collections, fail to put their collections to more active and more effective use in their respective communities is that they have no funds they can employ in developing that use. They are impoverished, so far as concerns funds for the enlargement of the influence of their treasures, by the very profusion itself of those same treasures. And too often trustees are entirely satisfied if the museum in their charge is notorious for what it owns, and are not troubled by the fact that it is not at all esteemed for what it does.

One may admit that a museum's trustees are in duty bound to accept all worthy objects that are offered to them. In the commonly accepted theory of museums is thoroughly embedded the principle already outlined: that good things that come into a museum's possession must be preserved; and quite as thoroughly embedded is the accompanying principle that good things, once they are accepted, must be studied, labeled, catalogued, put into perfect condition, and displayed in a dignified and refined manner. But while these principles are being carried out, the museum ceases to function—in fact in most cases never arrives at the functioning stage of its existence.

From a study of the life histories of museums, one is compelled to conclude that, granted a fairly adequate and wisely located building, a museum can be of highly effective service to its community with a collection of carefully chosen objects costing $10,000 if it has at the same time a staff of workers whose annual payroll is $100,000. If its collection and its payroll be in the reverse of that relation, it cannot hope to rise above the status of a gazing museum of the most lifeless kind.

Objects are silent. They must tell about themselves, their origin, purpose, their relative positions in the development of their kind, and countless other details through labels, guides, and catalogues. Labels, guides, and catalogues can be written to attractive and useful ends only by students of the art of presentation who are in some measure endowed at birth with a touch of this same art. Experts may give the facts, but the expert is rarely found who can so present the facts that the reader is moved to an interest and appreciation by them.

It is not necessary to explain that the museum with a high payroll and few and inexpensive objects will be a museum of brains and not merely a collection of pieces! Brains of a certain specific kind have not been thought to be the prime essentials in a museum's equipment. To this it may be replied that the possession of much special knowledge in any field of art does in itself show that he who possesses that knowledge is a person of brains, which is true enough. But the brains needed for the adequate management of a museum—such management as will cause it to be obviously influential in arousing interests, developing tastes, encouraging learning, and making the units of the community it serves producers of things that have charm as well as utility—must possess far more than expertness in any part of the art field. The brains of the well-equipped museum should include those such as are found in successful commercial, manufacturing, and transportation enterprise. The managing of a museum is primarily a business. It should be in its management as independent of a board of trustees as any successful business is of its board of directors. As a business it should be managed as a unit, as is a business. The manager and his aids, having received from their board of directors general instructions as to the fundamental purpose of their work, and information as to the money available therefor, should proceed to use their imagination and their skill in analysis to discover what is the conduct that will best enable them to arrive at the ends desired.

The usual process of art museum development is far different from that here suggested. A community, having determined to set up for itself a museum of art, at once adopts a set of conventions regarding it. As it is to be an art institution, it must have a home like homes of similar institutions in other cities. The trustees do not even raise the question of the fitness of such a home for a museum of art. They feel that they know instinctively that what has been done heretofore should here and now be done again. With what this home shall be filled is also not a question, for precedent has already settled that point also. Nor is there any doubt as to the character of the site for the home. As it is but a copy of an ancient temple or a ducal palace, it must of course enjoy the seclusion which distance can give it. And they proceed to follow the ancient conventions. Being fearful of using opinions and imaginings of their own or new notions that may be expressed by others, they dare not deviate from the ancient ways. Hence it has come about that few worthy, and usually wealthy, citizens entirely unfamiliar with the whole problem of public education—and with no experience in or knowledge of the difficult task of promoting art interests, of encouraging local talent in design, of leading a community to care for and patronize creative imagination in the field of beautification—guide the founding and the development of museums of art as we see them today. The one thing that has been thought to be sufficient to a museum's existence is the rare and costly object. The delusion has long been held, as already noted, by both wealthy and poor, by both learned and ignorant, by travelers and stay-at-homes, that museum pieces need only to be seen to produce in those who see them a certain elevation of soul, a definite impulse to better living, and a beautiful and helpful broadening of the mind.

Of course, there is not truth in this theory. The French are not leaders in the fine arts and the arts of thought because they have rare, beautiful, and wonder-provoking objects in their museums. They simply are the kind of people who lead in art and thought; and being such, and having been such for several centuries, they naturally possess museums into which they have gathered art and archaeological treasures; and just as naturally they have supplied their country with beautiful monuments by sculptors and architects.

The Italians have lived for several centuries surrounded by the finest products of human genius in the field of art. Since the days when, being inspired in a manner which is past understanding, they produced the treasures of the Renaissance, they have not, by those treasures, been re-inspired.

The formula for producing artists still awaits discovery. The evidence seems ample that no essential part of that formula can be the presence, in rather remote and rarely visited and quite oppressive and almost gloomy buildings of high architectural endeavor, collections of what have come to be referred to as museum objects.

This should be said, lest the comments just made be too grievously misunderstood: The French, having become possessed, out of the gifts of circumstances and time, of a certain genius, proceeded to produce certain objects of beauty in a score of fields, and thereby demonstrated the excellences of their souls. And that is well. And now, the people of this country, the citizens of any city of ours, just as soon as they feel or can be led to think they feel, an urge for the beautiful or an interest in art, should proceed to display some material exponent of that feeling. They should, for example, establish a museum of art and fill it with beautiful things. The psychologists tell us that it is quite as true to say that we are angry because we strike a man as it is to say that we strike a man because we are angry. A city adorns itself with a museum and thereby shows that it is moving toward fine feelings.

The museum and its contained treasures set up by a city are plain demonstrations of that city's growth in grace. But the museum and its museum objects do not, merely by being present, arouse that indefinable movement of the social mind which the French enjoy, and the Italians now lack, and we Americans are taking on very slowly.

Of museums in the science side of life and study, it is not easy to be critical. The science museum which, a few decades ago, found the creations of Mr. Barnum to be quite in the method which they were adopting, has now become an admirable stimulant to learning. The science enthusiast in the museum field is not usually of the belief that if nature's products and methods are set out on proper cases the mere sight of them will not only arouse wonder and awe, but will also equip the observer of them with the power to interpret nature's ways. He does not quite accept the art museum enthusiast's faith that the beauty of accredited art objects enlarges and ennobles the spirit (whatever that phrase may mean) of him who gazes upon them and that therefore his own collections will discover and arouse the spirit of free inquiry.

The science museum collects, identifies, classifies, notes relations, searches for sequences and causes, and arranges things collected, with the student and inquirer in view. But no sooner has this work been done than the teaching motive seems to make itself felt, and the museum adds to its purely preserving and arranging activities such activities as may arouse interest, inquiry, observation, collection, and research, especially in the young. It is safe to assume that the growth in influence on thought, belief, and conduct of museums of science will be very rapid.

The industrial museum has been highly developed in Germany and Austria. Vast buildings have there been filled with objects illustrating the development of appliances of every kind, from knives to airplanes and from wheelbarrows to locomotives. The museum of this type is just now in great favor. The history of invention in this country and of the progress of mechanical engineering are perhaps soon to be concretely illustrated in large and expensive buildings. These projects are most engaging, largely because they will form memorials and exaltations of the forms of activity in which our country most properly takes pride. As a country, we are so rich that the cost of collecting the material for a few national museums illustrative of our industrial progress, and of identifying, labeling, and installing and guarding the same, will be of slight moment. But beyond being somewhat to which we can point with pride as we pass by them, they can not avail much. Most museums of all kinds are too large to produce definite effects on visitors. And vast storehouses of machines and of objects showing the steps in invention by which the machines were reached will surely weary and overwhelm the great majority of visitors. They can with difficulty be used in teaching and inspiring the young. They will be out of date, as far as progress is concerned, even before they are opened.

If it be wise—as it perhaps is—to attempt to make adult Americans more pleased and proud of the mechanical and industrial achievements of their countrymen; and if it be wise, as perhaps it is, to arouse in the young of this country an interest in the doing of all kinds of things, from the driving of a nail with a hammer to the construction of a motor car, then the proper tools with which to attempt these two things are wise and skilled instructors, guides, docents, expositors, or whatever you may call them, placed in a large number of small, easily moved and easily changed and easily renewed and brought-to-date collections of industrial machines and industrial products, chosen with great care from the tens of thousands available as best illustrating certain rather typical activities. A few hundred dollars—given a suitable space for their display—will set up a series of objects, and a few machines that will, at the hands of clever teachers, do more to arouse, in a few weeks, in several thousand young people of a given community, an interest in an occupation, an understanding of its elements, an appreciation of the conquests its promoters have made, a respect for manual labor, and a certain openness of mind toward industry than can the huge museums of the type now proposed.

This last statement seems hardly to need any proof. But it can be proven by calling attention to the ease with which, in narrow space and with limited funds, such subjects as "Clay and Its Products," "Cloth and Its Making and Use," "The Republic of Colombia," and "The People of China" have been made interesting and instructive.

Special museums, such as those of medicine and surgery, the Indian, Spain, need not be here discussed. They are quite distinctly for interested and informed students of their respective subjects, and are not established for the delectation, information, and awakening of the general.

The changes brought about in manner of life, interests, occupations, diversions, and information by inventions and discoveries in the last few decades have as yet produced little change in the general theories on which museums of art, science, and industry are conducted. Museums began, on the art side, as collections of objects brought together and arranged and installed for the pleasure of wealthy and powerful individuals. They were not open to the public. When, in the changes time wrought, they were brought under the ownership and direction of the populace, they retained most of their old features. They were housed in structures which were intended to be stately and were usually repellent or austere or uninviting, or all three, to the commonalty; they were made remote, partly to make it clear that they should be approached with some reverence and visited with a complete suspension of the critical faculty. The art museums were supposed, and are still usually supposed, to be capable of developing in the populace by a few visits a certain susceptibility to environment and a certain permanence of impressions which would cause genuine beauty to be by them thereafter recognized and loved. The supposition has not been verified by experience but is still held.

The science museum began modestly with curiosities, the unusual in nature's productions; went on to the collections of long series of nature's products in special fields, useful to a few specialists; and then slowly added objects, quite as scientific but of more popular interest. In a word, they began as accumulations of things merely curious, went to things so scientific in selection and arrangement as to be of interest only to the expert, and then began to be popularly instructive. They now tend to overwhelm by size of building and quantity of things shown.

Teaching is now common in museums, though it still takes a small part only of the annual cost of maintenance. But it expands rapidly and is so generally accepted as an essential part of a museum's activities that we find quite proper the suggestion of a museum which shall greatly reduce the attention it gives to the casual gazer and shall be frankly an agency for supplying suggestions along definite lines in answer to definite inquiries, or for arousing in casual visitors more than a casual interest in the objects they see.

V.
The Experiment of The Newark Museum

The Newark Science Museum in the Free Public Library

On the fourth floor of the Free Public Library are two long rooms. Each has a floor surface of about 1,400 square feet and well-lighted wall surfaces of about 250 linear feet. When the building was constructed four years ago the trustees placed over the door of one of these rooms the legend "Science Museum," and of the other "Art Museum." The rooms were not then needed by the library proper, and probably will not be for several years to come.

The trustees realized the fact that although Newark does not possess either a science museum or an art museum the time would come in the course of the city's normal development, when both these institutions would be called for. They realized also the fact that the free public library of a city, especially a library as beautifully and as adequately housed as is that of Newark, is, if other means are lacking, a proper place in which to establish the beginnings of public museums of science and art.

The rooms were finished off simply and at moderate cost. As the library produces its own electricity, they are lighted at very slight expense. Although on the fourth floor, they can be reached by elevator. It seemed to the trustees that simply by their presence in the city as fit quarters for such things, they might invite and encourage the beginnings of the two public museums which our city will some day have.

During the four years since the library was opened, these rooms have been used from time to time for various purposes. In one of them, the first meeting called to bring together in one organization all the charitable societies of the city was held, and this single meeting gave to the room a certain dignity. In both of them was once displayed the manual training and sewing work produced by students in all the schools of the city. For other meetings of an educational nature, they have been used many times.

The room on the south side is now opened as a science museum. The first step is thus taken toward the consummation of the thought which the trustees hoped to see

---

The Newark Free Public Library, February 25, 1905.

fulfilled when they dedicated the room to science four years ago.

For many years Dr. W. S. Disbrow, of Newark, has been a tireless collector. He has devoted much of his spare time and thought to botany and mineralogy. For many years he has had in mind the hope that he might be the person to lay the foundation of a science museum in his native city.

Several years ago the board of education furnished about 20 flat-topped glass cases in which Dr. Disbrow installed a portion of his collection of minerals. These cases, at first placed in one of the grade schools, were moved to the corridors of the high school on completion of the new building.

About a year ago the board of education, the trustees of the public library, and Dr. Disbrow, entered into an agreement under which the cases were moved to the south room on the fourth floor of the library, already described, and the specimens were rearranged and freshly labeled. Then more specimens were added, more cases were purchased by the library. To the collections of minerals were added botanical specimens, an interesting collection of Indian relics, portraits of eminent scientists, geological maps of New Jersey, and other appropriate material, and the collection gradually took shape as a science museum, though a very modest one.

The board of education, the board of trustees of the library, and Dr. Disbrow hope that this is the beginning of the science museum that the city of Newark should possess. They do not suppose that the room in which it is now housed will contain it for many years. They do believe that the modest collections here found will be the foundation of a museum which many citizens, old and young, will find interesting, instructive, and a source of pride.

Newark needs a science museum. It does not need one as large as the great museums of New York or Washington; nor does it need a museum for specialists, who must always go to the great cities for their sources; nor does it need a museum of curiosities, freaks, chips from old tomb stones, or fragments of old castles.

The city needs a small, practical museum, made up chiefly of objects illustrating the geology, soil, fauna, and flora of this vicinity; one which shall contain not a large number of specimens in any one class, but a sufficient number of typical ones in many classes to illustrate attractively the science studies in our schools, to interest mechanics and artisans in the materials and objects which they daily handle, and to open the eyes of all who visit it to the beauties, the resources, and the natural wonders of the regions in which they live.

The collections now installed or already in order and awaiting only the cases in which they may be displayed may be briefly summarized as follows:

In geology, specimens showing the rocks, the building stones, both good and

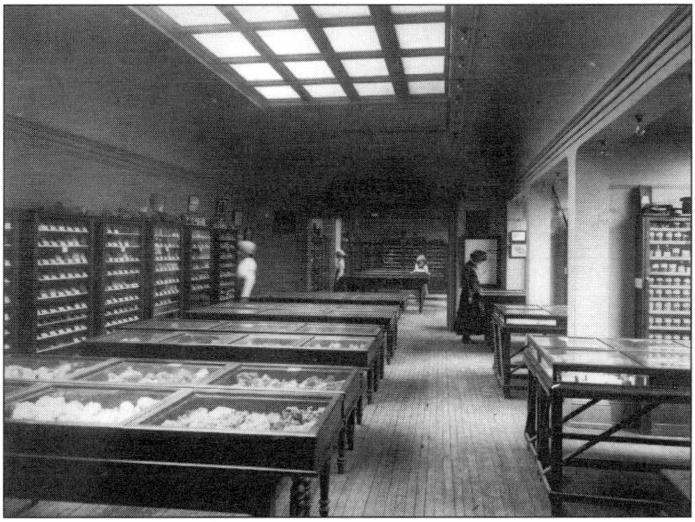

Dr. W. S. Disbrow's collection of natural science objects.

poor, the clays, soils, cement, fossils, etc., of this region. Also specimens illustrating rock formation, decomposition of rocks, and formation of soil.

In botany, there are about 4,000 specimens of plants chiefly of this vicinity, arranged according to the latest botanical rules, especially useful in the study of systematic botany. Also, a large number of specimens illustrating economic botany, including drugs, woods, gums, rosins, foods, and textile fibers.

Maps, charts, and books. All the publications of the New Jersey Geological Survey—and its work is second to none in the country—and of the other scientific departments of the state government are here shown, some of the most interesting being displayed on the walls. The library is well supplied with books bearing on the collections found in the museum, and some of the more attractive of these will be here from time to time displayed.

From duplicates in the science museum, small collections will be made and placed in portable boxes. These will be lent to schools as they are needed and as the supply permits. They will illustrate the deposition of soil, the formation of soil, and the disintegration of rocks, the building stones of this vicinity, the rock formation of this vicinity, and kindred subjects touched on in the geography and science work in the schools. Small traveling collections will also be made from duplicates in other departments of science as well as in mineralogy and geology. These are roughly illustrated by sample boxes already made.

Visitors to the museum at the opening will find that not all specimens are labeled and arranged. This is as it should be. A complete museum is an impossibility. If it is alive, it is always in the making; never quite in order in every part. A growing museum, even though it be small, stimulates the interest from which it gets its growth.

There seems to be no reason for deferring any longer the date of opening. Once open, it will soon be generally known as a public museum of science; it will invite local collectors to add to it; it will grow in general interest as it grows in the number of objects displayed and in the number of subjects it covers, and will give pleasure and profit to many visitors.

An Industrial Exhibit in a Municipal Museum

To show in a bird's-eye view the pottery and brick industries of New Jersey, which in the single year of 1913 turned raw clays into products valued at $19,705,378, the Newark Museum Association recently held for six weeks a "New Jersey Clay Products Industrial Exhibition." This exhibition was the first of its kind to be held in this country by a public, municipally supported museum devoted to art, science, and industry.

An exhibition of an industrial nature usually implies great expenditures of doubtful advertising value, for space and exhibits at huge national and international fairs. Manufacturers have come to balk at the very word. The Newark Museum Association is housed at present with the Newark Free Public Library and has a limited space for display—a limitation, however, which proved a distinct advantage in dealing with an intensive, local, one-industry exhibit.

Manufacturers in all branches of the industry—makers of chinas and porcelains, of decorative pottery, or sanitary ware, of brick and terracotta—were invited to show their products and to cooperate in making an exhibit which should show at a glance what is really meant by the mere statistical statement that New Jersey stands second among all the states in her clay products output. As a result, 42 firms sent carefully selected exhibits.

To this frankly commercial display, the museum added 150 pieces of pottery made in New Jersey prior to 1876, gathered through the cooperation of the women's clubs of the state; a series of eight flat cases of carefully labeled material illustrating the making of pottery and showing materials, casting process, glazing, firing, glazes, methods of making, kinds, and how decorated; an exhibit of clays from the New Jersey Geological Survey; collections showing the experimental and practical work done by students in the Department of Ceramics at Rutgers College and at the School of

The American City 13, no. 1 (July 1915).

Industrial Art in Trenton; exhibits of clay work from the public schools of the state; three cases containing small articles of everyday use made wholly or partly of clay; an exhibit illustrating the use of clay in the filtration of oil; and collections of books on the subject of ceramics and the clay industries. A catalogue in two sections with full notes was compiled. Careful attention was given to every detail of installation and labeling. The regular exhibition cases of plate glass and metal were used wherever possible. The result proved clearly how art and industry may go hand in hand.

To the completed exhibit was added a potter, who for three hours every afternoon, with molds and wheel and small kiln, made pottery for all to see, and explained methods as he worked.

The public response has justified the experiment. The attendance, 25,000 visitors during the six weeks, included manufacturers and builders throughout the state and from New York City, private individuals interested in tiles and fireproofing materials, men interested in South American trade, art potters, and teachers of ceramics and china decorating. Women's clubs, groups of saleswomen from the department stores, and classes of schoolchildren were taken through the exhibit by the museum instructor.

We believe that Newark has shown the value of the specialized exhibit, covering a given industry and frankly commercial as well as scientific, industrial, and artistic in character. We believe that we have also demonstrated how inexpensively museums, cities, or groups of manufactures can get up these exhibits. The world's fair aggregations, where architects, illuminators, and sideshow artists are very prominent and the mere manufacturer is often quite neglected by visitors, do not have the dignity and educational value, nor do they give the rational and helpful publicity which a man today demands in return for his money and effort.

Germany, with her undisputed commercial wisdom and thoroughness, has appreciated the value of the small, intensive exhibition of one industry.

We believe that under modern advertising conditions it would not take much work of this kind to link the name of Trenton, for instance, with the idea of chinas and porcelains in the minds of both the wholesale and retail-buying and the reading public as thoroughly as Limoges has become linked with the same idea. And the same thing would be true of terracotta and the South and Perth Amboy region. Such exhibits should become valuable adjuncts to the "Buy in America" campaign.

Moreover, we are confident it is worthwhile for any state to educate her people to an understanding and appreciation of the state's products. If the people of the state—and we have in mind the young citizen and the citizen-to-be as well as the present potential purchasers—were to gain through such exhibits a clear knowledge and a lively impression of the wide range and the great importance of leading local industries, these industries would profit thereby in many ways. Managers, owners, artists, designers, foremen, and laborers are all stimulated and aided by that sympathy and goodwill of their fellow citizens, old and young, which come from knowledge and appreciation of what they are accomplishing and trying to accomplish. We believe this exhibit has done much to extend the knowledge and appreciation of New Jersey's clay products' industries.

A Small American Museum: Its Efforts Toward Public Utility

Foreword

This report is written in the belief that the varied experiments in museum practice which it briefly outlines may serve as an epitome of much of that educational work which has been taken up in recent years by many museums in America. The museum it describes has all the advantages of youth and of freedom from the embarrassments of precedents and of large and valuable collections. It has the good fortune to be permitted to try many things; and has always had present, in its 12 short years, the challenge to effort presented by a community which is without experience in supporting, using, or visiting museums, and asks only that something of interest and value come forth from this, its new and strange institution.

II. How the Museum Originated

The trustees of the public, tax-supported library of Newark, N.J., an industrial suburb of New York, with a population, 1921, of 420,000, asked the city government in 1909 to buy for $10,000 a collection of Japanese prints and curios, and present it, as a foundation of a public museum, to a quasi-public corporation chartered as the Newark Museum Association. The city government did as asked, and has since then given to the association in annual installments a total of $165,000.

In the 12 years since it was founded, the annual dues of members of the association, now numbering 3,200, amounted to $46,000, and the association acquired, chiefly by gift, about 13,000 objects.

The association was formed, so its charter says, "To establish a museum for the reception and exhibition of articles of art, science, history, and technology, and for the encouragement of the arts and science." These words mean that the association may collect such objects as are found in museums of any kind and may use its objects in almost any manner, and may promote education on almost any subject.

Minerals, plants, economic fibers, roots, seeds, and leaves used in medicine, objects illustrating Indian life, all to a total of several thousand items; and paintings, textiles, bronzes, and objects of many other kinds came to the museum soon after it was established. These helped to fix in the minds of the managers the fact that they were developing not a museum of art, or science, or technology, or history, or any other one type, but a composite of several museums, unified not by a common subject but by a common purpose.

III. Why Composite in Character

It was obvious that Newark ought not to attempt to duplicate or to parallel, save as its own special needs demanded, collections in the great museums of New York City, any one of which can be reached from Newark in less than two hours.

Newark has a wide range of industries. This fact suggested that its museum should include departments of applied art, of technology, of commerce and transportation, as well as of fine art and pure science.

A study of museum literature, of the methods of American museums, and especially of such activities of existing museums as aimed to promote a wider and freer use of museum objects, showed that ancient conventions have museums firmly in hand; that most museums tend to become storehouses, used more to please and educate curators than to entertain and instruct the public; that they are quite averse to change; and that few among them exercise an influence on their respective communities at all commensurate with the cost of founding and maintenance.

It appeared that in a few museums—an increasing number each year—efforts were being made to give definite useful service, by loans, by lectures, by publications, by docents, and by modifications of arrangement and management.

No careful study seems to have been made of what a given community will use, will enjoy, will profit from, and will cheerfully support in the form of a museum. Nearly all museums have either grown haphazard, or in accordance with preconceived ideas of donors, trustees, directors, and curators. The obvious course for a museum association which aimed to create a museum to fit the tastes and needs of its community was to proceed by a series of experiments, with consequent acceptance or rejection of each as helpful or as useless.

Four years after the association was established, the director of its museum printed this statement of what, in his opinion, should be its aim:

"We should try to develop, here in Newark, a group of museums, in the fields of art, science, and industry, of the modern type. Our Newark museums, that is, should be of immediate practical value to Newark citizens, old and young. They should appeal to all of us, to the newer people as well as the older. They should reflect our industries, be stimulating and helpful to our workers, and promote an interest here and elsewhere in the products of our own shops. They should be the handmaidens of our schools, helping to discover among our thousands of young people those tastes and talents which may lead them to such accomplishments as will bring profit, credit, and civility to our city. Our museums should do these things in all the fields they touch: in fine arts, in the applied arts, in industry, in the mere making of honest goods which is in itself a fine art, and in pure and applied science."

IV. Housing, Income: Results Summarized

The museum has been housed in the building of the Newark Public Library, and its space for exhibitions, offices, storage, and shops is less than 7,000 square feet. This fact has compelled it to change exhibits frequently and to close experiments as soon as their success has been fairly well demonstrated.

The total cost of all work done—that is, of all salaries—for 12 years has been about $85,000. Objects and equipment have cost about $65,000; and rent, heat, light, special installations, and publications about $36,000. Total attendance, roughly counted for 100 specific exhibitions up to December 1920, has been about 500,000. Thousands of objects have been shown in the library's corridors and public rooms, where they have had many interested observers among the library's 750,000 yearly visitors.

V. Schools: Other Museums

The public school system is the dominating educational influence of the city. The annual expenditures of the museums have been less than half of 1 percent of that of the schools. The independent educational work of an American museum must be of the slightest value if it is not carried out in close harmony with and in a clear understanding of the local system of public education. The Newark museum consequently engaged in its first years the services of an educational adviser—a person of long and varied experience in public schools and a student of education. Her advice has been of great value. Members of the staff have examined all available material on museum management and have made about 300 visits to museums, often at the association's expense. The educational adviser alone has made more than 100 of these visits of inspection. Firsthand reports of work in other museums, even in those in far western states, have thus come to us.

Many of our observations and conclusions on museum method have appeared in print, in journals, pamphlets, and books.

VI. Wide Range of Exhibits

Limited space has made it impossible to have permanent exhibits, even of paintings and sculptures. This has been fortunate, so we conclude, and has led us to question the value, save in very large museums, of what may be called permanent gazing galleries. We keep most of our collections in a storage warehouse.

Exhibits of small groups of paintings, usually borrowed from American artists, lasting from four to six weeks, have been held every year, often more than one. Moderate success only has met our efforts to popularize these exhibits. They are fairly well attended, but seem to have little influence; to be, in the phrase Lord Sudeley uses in a recent article, of slight "public utility."

Early efforts to persuade local manufacturers to supply us with examples of their products, and of materials showing steps in their processes, were not successful.

VII. A Few Exhibits Described

Hoping to arouse local interest in this method of presenting Newark's industries to Newarkers, and especially to young people, we prepared, in our fifth year, an exhibit of the clay products of New Jersey, a state with a population of over 3 million, which is in large measure a manufacturing suburb of New York and Philadelphia. This occupied about 4,000 square feet of floor space; it was the immediate excuse for compiling and publishing pamphlets on the history and technique of making things of clay, which still find use in our schools; it attracted several thousand visitors; and, especially through the daily presence of a skilled potter who made, baked, and glazed pottery, was intensely interesting to both old and young. Our art classes visited it. Women who had never before taken an interest in fine pottery were led to an intelligent appreciation of it and to a greater domestic use of beautiful things. Children in elementary schools were helped by docents to note carefully what they saw and to find therein what pleased and what displeased them. Even classes of blind children felt and enjoyed qualities of form and texture under the instruction of the same docents, who were volunteer helpers from women's clubs.

In our sixth year we gave a similar exhibit of New Jersey's textile products, which was even more successful than that of clay products. Each of these exhibits was six months in preparation. Both were looked upon with favor by industrialists. With the textile products, as with those of clay, were shown, by samples, steps in manufacturing processes, and, to a moderate extent, processes themselves. In the textile exhibit were to be seen a woman spinning with distaff and spindle, another at a spinning wheel, a crude hand loom, a small Jacquard, copper rolls for printing in colors, and other process illustrations.

VIII: The Art Element in All Exhibits

While many of our exhibitions have been definitely industrial, the art element has been absent from none of them; we have attempted, that is, to touch each of them with that indefinable quality which gives to the simplest of human products grace and charm. For all of them, the posters, circulars, catalogues, letters of invitation, acknowledgments, etc., were designed and printed with such taste and skill as we have or can afford to employ. Color of walls, methods of lighting; character of furniture, mounts, cases, and fittings; manner of arrangement; labels, legends, and explanations, were all studied with a view to making the whole and all of its parts inviting and—if the word is not here too ambitious—beautiful.

IX: Geography and Commerce

The most difficult problem we attacked was the presentation of the resources, products, manners, and customs and geography of the Republic of Colombia, South America. We hope that by this exhibit we showed that it is possible to present in an attractive and informing way, even in a small museum, the salient features of a distant land, and to make it seem, to both young and old, a part of that same wide field of human endeavor, of that same battleground between man and nature, in which the observer lives. Much time and energy were given to this exhibit during an entire year. It had a peculiar value, largely through the wide publicity it gained, in softening the asperities which the relations of our own and Colombia's governments had aroused; and from both governments it received hearty approval.

X. What Other Exhibits Covered

Of the hundred exhibits which have been prepared in the 12 years, many were, of course, quite small and easily installed. Descriptions can be given of a few of the more important only. We have shown, in addition to paintings already mentioned, Greek and Renaissance sculpture in casts; small American and other bronzes; the work of engravers of the first rank; the printing of America's leading printer; a step-by-step description, with many examples, of the designing and making of posters and of advertising in colors; the work of our best photographers, as well as of a local camera club; war and other posters; the applied arts of the American Indian; stencil and batik work; pottery and porcelain; and loan collections of Chinese and Japanese art.

XI. History

Our one historical display had to do with the life of the colonial period of American history. For this we constructed a full-size model of a kitchen of colonial times, the room which, before the invention of stoves, was in most colonial houses the only place warmed in winter, the cooking and dining room, and the center of all family life. With it were displayed domestic utensils in common use 100 and 200 years ago. In our industrial city, where most of the schoolchildren are of foreign birth or parentage, the artistic value of this exhibit was not small. Our country's contribution to art had been chiefly, so far, of that restrained, austere type produced by the Puritan spirit and called colonial. This we here found opportunity to emphasize.

XII. Applied Arts of Germany

From Germany we obtained 10 years ago a large group of objects in the field of the applied arts. This filled all available exhibition space, attracted many visitors, and was shown by request in the museums of six other large cities. We have long tried to secure similar exhibits from France, thus far without success.

XIII. A Civic Problem

The problem of how to get the most help in the development of our country from our millions of immigrants is always in process of solution. We dare to hope that we helped the process locally to a modest degree by holding, five years ago, what we called a "Homelands Exhibition" of textiles contributed by at least 20 of the groups from other countries which our city has attracted to herself.

The materials for this exhibit we secured by asking the pupils in the 16 schools, most of whose pupils, numbering in each 1,000 to 2,000, were foreign-born or children of foreign-born, to bring from their homes to the schools textile articles brought by their parents from their home countries. Museum assistants then went to the schools and selected from the large collections there the articles that seemed best suited for display. In the museum these were installed in our best cases with all the care and skill we could address to the task. Ample labels were provided. Visitors old and young, of at least 20 different nationalities, came by the thousands to see the display. This work led to a still more elaborate exhibition filling a dozen rooms in a huge school building, covering all the household arts, and accompanied in the school's assembly hall by a series of plays, songs, and dances, given by the foreign peoples after their own ways.

Our country is not getting the full value of the heritage in feeling for beauty and skill in crafts which many of her immigrants bring with them, and we believe that these exhibits helped to appreciate that value.

XIV. Educational Work

To all our exhibits we have tried to add certain definite educational work. This includes descriptive labels, forming in some cases complete stories when read in sequence; leaflets and pamphlets, some of which have been used for reading and study in the schools; guides to conduct classes from schools or groups of elders and explain exhibits; attendants competent to talk with knowledge of the exhibits of which they temporarily have charge; and notices to the heads of schools and their teachers of such displays as we think will interest the children in their care.

Our efforts to attain a good measure of public utility have been chiefly in the field of education.

The public library, in whose building the museum is housed, devotes much of its energy and funds, as do all public libraries in this country, to efforts to be attractive and helpful to young people, and, of course, finds that the one open way for these efforts is through the educational system of the city—the public schools. Each year it lends small libraries for home and classroom use to several hundred teachers. It has in its equipment a collection, constantly growing in size, of about 500,000 pictures arranged alphabetically by subject under several thousand headings. We call this a collection of "pictures," meaning thereby to suggest that they are chiefly illustrations of things in the book of daily life; they include, however, thousands of designs in scores of fields, obtained largely by taking apart good books and portfolios, several thousand photographs of famous works of art, and reproductions in color of thousands of great paintings. They are lent for school use to teachers, who make, if they will, their own selections through personal inspections. These picture loans total annually about 75,000.

The library has also about 3,000 prints which present quite well the history of print-making from its earliest days and cover all methods. It is perhaps more a collection for the lay student than for the artist. It is made readily accessible.

Supplementing the collections of "pictures" and of "prints"—and supplementing also, as do both of these, the museum collections—is the library's collection of 2,000 large photogravures and of the best available color prints of some of the world's great paintings. Of these about 500 are mounted, matted, and arranged conveniently for use, just as are the prints. For them the library has on hand a stock of simple frames, glazed and with movable backs. To any applicant who buys one or more of these frames—they are sold at cost—are lent such of the photogravures or color prints as he or she may choose. The borrower keeps the pictures for several months.

XV. Lending Museum Objects

Almost inevitably, the museum, as soon as it was well established, began to lend to teachers objects, just as the library lends books and pictures. It is impossible here to describe the things that are thus lent to make the school studies fuller and more interesting. They number about 4,000 and are constantly added to. Insects, birds, minerals, textiles, sculptures (in plaster), decorative pottery, dolls in the costumes of many countries, objects illustrative of manners and customs of other peoples—these suggest the collection's range. Teachers come to select in person or send requests. Shipments are made twice each week by van. The total lent each year is now about 9,000.

XVI. A Children's Museum

For several years, as long in fact as space therefor could be found in quarters which each month were more crowded, the museum gave up a room to a group of objects and pictures selected, installed, and labeled with special references to the interests of young people. It was, in effect, a children's museum. The person in charge was able to arouse in young visitors—especially in those who were observant and in those who had a native bent for collecting—the wish to form associations or groups. These groups united in a junior museum club, held many interesting meetings, published an occasional journal, brought objects to the museum, and helped to install them and to label them until they formed admirable displays.

Thus we try to supplement what is inevitably the wholesale, standardized work of the schools, in science and art, by looking out for the artistic and scientific interests of variants or "sports" from among whom will come those who shall someday make American art commensurate with American industry.

And the fact that live museum discipline is always freer than even the livest discipline of a library is good for the whole tone of the library atmosphere. Libraries attract readers; museums attract observers and doers. It is good to see non-reading children who have been setting up a case of shells, crowding the desk where books are lent to take out "a book on mussels with plenty of pictures"; and it does a reader of fairy tales no harm to be presented with a museum club button bearing the effigy of the Great God Pan.

XVII. Library Method and Museum Method

The tax-supported group of museums here briefly described is, as has been stated, in the building of a tax-supported library. The librarian of the latter is the director of the former. Naturally, and indeed almost inevitably, the manner in which the library is presented to its owners and users—the residents of the city—was from the first adopted, as far as conditions permitted, as the manner in which the museums should be presented to the same residents. This manner of library management has developed in the past 40 years, beginning with the method of acquisition and seclusion, and gradually changing to the method of acquisition and service. It began with the thought that a library should first of all strive for size, completeness, and for the reverence of the unlettered and the respect of the learned; it grew slowly to the thought that a library should first of all strive to be of immediate practical aid to all of the community that supports it. By adopting this thought, it gained vastly in general esteem and therefor in financial support. Consequently it has enjoyed opportunities for acquisition and enrichment of resource such as would never have been granted to it as an institution chiefly set upon acquisition and seclusion.

It would be easy to enlarge upon this development of the American public library from a closed temple of "wisdom undisturbed" to an open workshop of delight and learning.

It may with much truth be said that museum method is today in this country at about the point of development at which libraries were 40 years ago. Changes, however, are rapidly taking place; and, as has been already frankly said, this paper—descriptive of some of the manners and customs of a young, small, and, in its content, unimportant museum—has as its chief excuse for being the fact that it suggests the rapid development among our museums of the thought that they should first of all be of direct and useful service to those who found and maintain them—the general public. Well nigh all of the many things that are being done in Newark are being done elsewhere.

A Museum of Service

Newark is not and does not claim to be the Columbus of new continents in the museum world. It needed no survey of the city to show that it would be unwise for it to attempt to set up for itself a group of large and costly museums of art, science, and industry. Newark is a manufacturing town of 450,000 people, hardly an hour distant from the museums of art and science, the zoological and botanical gardens, the aquarium, the museums of history, medicine, coins and medals, American Indians, Spain, etc., and from the libraries, laboratories, factories, theaters, colleges, streets, and department stores of New York.

A modest general museum of no specific type, fitted as study and trials might prove to the demands of Newark people, was clearly indicated. That the venture might grow in time into a group of large institutions, each of a well-defined kind, was a possibility which could not well influence its beginnings. All conditions seemed to point to the advisability of developing for Newark a first reader in visual instruction—something that would please, instruct, and provoke to thought and action those who used it, and would serve also as a continuing incentive to the use of the treasures to be seen in the great city near at hand.

Newark's museum is in the city's public library; may be said to be an outgrowth from it; is managed by the librarian and the assistant librarian, and inevitably has taken on the attitude toward the public which has come to be characteristic of library management in the last 30 years. This library attitude may be briefly described as one almost too eager to give pleasure and aid its owners, the general public.

The Newark Library's building, erected in 1900 and planned to suffice for 20 years of growth, for several years gave more floor space than the institution it housed could

---

The Survey: Graphic Number 49, no. 9 (February 1, 1923). Published separately by the Newark Museum Association, April 1929.

use. Its empty rooms were long used for non-library purposes: some as offices of supervisors of public schools, and others for meetings of philanthropic and educational organizations numbering hundreds each year. In some were held exhibitions of many kinds: paintings, posters, bookplates, prints, forestry, geography, schoolwork in the manual arts, Japanese art and Japanese domestic life, and finally a loan exhibit of a collection of objects of Oriental art. This last, being purchased by the city, became the immediate cause of the forming of the present museum association, which took it over as the beginning of its collections. The museum still has quarters in the library, rent free. It has received from the city in its 12 years of existence a little less than $12,000 a year for maintenance.

It is essential to explain here that the library was a museum long before it was conscious of the fact. The trustees of the library have encouraged the addition to its furnishing of paintings, bronzes, lithographs, engravings, pottery, and textiles. In 1901, the library gave to a student of science, an enthusiastic and skillful collector, a large room in which he installed many of his collections; it added to the room from time to time several score of effective but inexpensive cases and storage cabinets, set apart another room for office and library, and found that its modest contribution to the collector's activities resulted in the acquisition in a few years of several thousand carefully chosen and accurately identified and labeled objects. These objects now form in effect the science side of the museum's acquisitions.

About 20 years ago, a generous citizen gave to the library money for the founding of a collection of prints. The collection once established, the trustees of the library permitted additions to be made to it year by year, and now it numbers about 3,000 items, mounted, matted, identified, arranged, and catalogued so that they are easily used. Groups of them have been set up as exhibitions from time to time.

Soon after this print collection was established, the library began to acquire the best available reproductions in black and white and in color of famous paintings, sculpture, and architecture. Of these it now has several thousand, a large number of them mounted and matted in three sizes. Simple, glazed frames with movable backs, made to fit the three sizes of pictures, are sold at cost, and the purchaser selects for his frames, as many as he may purchase, such pictures as he will, and takes them to his home, office, or shop to keep for one month or six.

A collection of large lithographs, numbering now about 2,000, was begun about 20 years ago. Most of these are pasted on stout boards, neatly bound, fitted with eyelets, and lent to teachers for temporary use in schoolrooms. Many of the best, including famous architecture and sculpture as well as landscapes in auto-lithography, were put into substantial frames and are lent to decorate schools, hospitals, and other institutions, usually for a year.

About the same time, the library established a collection of illustrations of all kinds to be lent to teachers. These were at first taken almost wholly from magazines. By slow steps, the collection has grown to about 60,000 pictures, mounted and arranged conveniently under several thousand subjects, with 400,000 others similarly arranged but not mounted. Into it have gone the plates of hundreds of good portfolios and books and, especially, thousands of designs from the best available sources. The collection is open to all inquirers for free handling, and packages from it are lent, often to the number of more than 1,000 in a day.

A small printing plant was early added to the library's equipment and made it possible to give special attention to posters and labels for both library and museum.

✦

The museum in the average American community today is in about the same stage of development in which the public library was a generation ago. It was a closed institution. The public which maintained it was not permitted to touch and examine its books, save the few which might be handed out on duly approved and signed receipts through an opening in a impenetrable barrier. It had the veneration for its books which came down from the 15th century, when printed things were few and costly. It acquired, identified, described, and preserved books and, on rigorous conditions, permitted a few to be seen and a few to be taken home.

A generation ago, a modern library system which should render to students, designers, artists, craftsmen, manufacturers and distributors, teachers, or schoolchildren the varied services now rendered by the public libraries of Newark and other cities was conceived only by a few forecasting minds. Today, a museum that would render similar services still awaits realization.

Words change their meanings and implications as time goes on. The first great museum, that established by Ptolemy I in Alexandria, about 300 B.C., was a library, and not a museum in the sense in which the word is used today, and was open for study, research, lecture, and discussion to all friends of the Muses. The modern public library is in many respects a museum and, in its attitude toward those who own and maintain it, more modern than are most museums. It acquires for use; it prepares for use what it acquires; it invites use; it does not regard wisdom as something which is enhanced by age, rarity, or cost; it is as ready to supply a medicament which may bring relaxation, distraction, and repose to those who are aged, ill, overwrought, or overworked, as it is to supply to the specialist the latest aids to his labors. It invites the old and calls in the young. The one fear that is ever-present to the librarian is that since those who support the library are not using it to its capacity, they are not finding in it what they seek and what they need.

Printed descriptions, plus illustrations easily borrowed and taken home, are far more useful as guides to work, especially in the field of design, than are untouchable objects sealed in glass cases; and the power of the printed page, plus the picture—both of which may be freely lent—to provoke thought, to stir to activity, to give pleasure, and to arouse the critical and appreciative faculty is greater than is that of any object which a museum may display.

This question of what are the best library content and library methods was of course one of the reasons for those extensions of the Newark Library's activities which have just been briefly described. They were largely experiments, and many of them were experiments in that part of the field of recreation and education which is coming to be considered proper ground for the activities of museums. For 12 years now, the same group which had managed a public library for the preceding 10 years has managed also a small museum. The work of both library and museum has been carried on in the same building.

✦

The history of museums and the present accepted methods of administration were studied. It was found that museums are commonly not of much use. Taking the efforts at utility found here and there, the Newark institution definitely decided to be, like the Athenian, rather curious over new things, to try experiments, to be in a small way a laboratory of museum method, and to report, to itself at least, results. Some of the conclusions reached may illustrate the point.

Paintings attract more observers than do other forms of art, either fine or applied. They interest chiefly because of what they tell, because of the stories they suggest, because of the emotions which they arouse through recognition, and because they are pretty. Many observers tend to look upon them as gods and the gallery in which they hang as a sanctuary. From paintings, therefore, little seems to be gained of stimulus to sound labor, or of inspiration to sound morals.

From 10 to 20 paintings on the walls of the library, changed now and then, have presented themselves to all visitors for about 20 years. The library and the museum have together set up, in the same 20 years, for four weeks each, 23 art exhibitions, including a total of 975 different paintings. Not many of these paintings have been masterpieces, but as few of us know a masterpiece when we see it, the lack of them has not been a hindrance to our conclusions as to the effect of such exhibitions.

Sculpture has, of course, less appeal than painting and consequently is of less value to observers. Single pieces properly set and lighted and adequately explained, orally or by printed labels or leaflets, are liked and studied and seem to carry a modest message. A hall of sculpture is a moving and informing thing but seems soon to overwhelm and to make the observers immune to definite suggestions.

Engravings, meaning prints of all kinds, have been shown in groups by the library and museum many times. Like specimens of fine printing, including books produced by the world's best printers, which have also often been shown, they appeal to the native genius of very few; and though it is not impossible to arouse an interest in them in almost any person of intelligence, the task is a long one and cannot even be attempted under the usual museum conditions of today.

From all this one may conclude that the gazing at sculpture and graphic art objects which goes on in most museums of art is mere gazing and little more; and that to expand this little more to something of value to the gazers, and so to the community in general, calls for the new museum methods which are slowly coming into general use. The situation is slightly ameliorated by the introduction of the docent or expounder.

If some of the immortal gods of art—"real museum pieces"—were moved from their holy places—museums—and put in schoolhouses and in library branches in thickly populated centers, and if a few teachers could each year be so taught and so stirred that they would attractively present these transferred great ones to the successive groups of children in their charge, and to adults as well, certain distinguishable results might be secured.

Of curios, meaning objects from other lands and other times, of high technical excellence, not much can be said. Seen in rows in glass cases, they are as speechless as mummies and about as instructive as a row of telegraph poles.

Textiles gain applause from the ladies, but even with them do little to encourage study or ameliorate conduct. Pictures of textiles in black and white and in color, designs for textiles, and bits of inexpensive modern work furnish all the information about pattern and color that is needed by most people. Little textile designing is done in this country, save in a few schools of design.

Pottery and porcelain, like heads and figures in bronze, have seemed to add to the attractiveness of the library during all the 20 years in which they have been used for decoration throughout the building. When placed in cases after the conventional manner, they seem to tire rather than to inspire.

Two exhibitions, one of the clay products and the other of the textile products of

New Jersey, aroused much interest and were certainly more moving than are displays of either textiles or pottery and china in serried ranks of cases after the usual museum manner. Each exhibit showed not only the homely objects of everyday use, but also processes. They showed that the doing of a thing is of greater interest and tends to arouse more thought and action than completed objects, however rare or costly and however exquisitely displayed. This fact did not need demonstration in a museum, of course, being familiar enough to the dullest observer. It did, however, reinforce our conclusion that the museum of the future will, at times at least, permit its visitors to see objects in the process of making, such as a painter painting, an engraver engraving, a potter making and coloring and firing pottery, a weaver weaving, a sculptor modeling, a wood carver carving, a carpenter making things, an illustrator and designer drawing, and skilled workers at their task of cleaning, mending, restoring, identifying, and labeling objects which the museum has acquired.

In history, geography, and the life of man, the Newark Museum has given three modest displays. One told by pictures, objects, and a replica of an old kitchen, of colonial life in this century. It was visited and plainly enjoyed by several thousand, old and young. One covered—of necessity quite thinly—the land, the people, the products, and the problems of the republic of Colombia. It brought our institution to the attention of thousands who had never imagined that a museum might give instruction in the lives, as now lived, of a people of a distant land. One was constructed about a group of objects brought by a missionary from Tibet.

The science collections that have been mentioned are so many, space for their proper display is so small, and the task of selecting a few and reassembling them with proper pictures, charts, maps, legends, and leaflets is so great that little has been done with them. Such ventures as have been made were helpful if only to show that the wonderful work in making science inviting and moving, which not a few large museums are now carrying on, can be repeated with success on a small scale. Weapons; objects illustrative of the life of American Indians; semi-precious stones; coal, its occurrence and extraction—all have been used to good advantage. The shells of several score of mollusks were set forth in a group of flat cases, and entertaining stories, in label form, of the characters and habits of the species shown were brought together in a pamphlet.

Labels, legends, posters, leaflets, catalogues, and descriptive pamphlets have been compiled and published as parts of or as addenda to all exhibits. In total they number tens of thousands, even in 12 short years. The pamphlets alone, including several reports, have numbered about 10 each year. They have been given away; mailed to museums and schools; and sold, as conditions indicated. Our conclusion is that they are absolutely essential if the visual instruction work of a museum is to be of lasting value. This conclusion does not, of course, carry with it the belief that our products were even moderately good. They simply served to satisfy us that printed matter, carefully adapted to the constituency which may read it, and fully illustrated, is indispensable and should be more commonly used.

Most interesting of all activities have been those connected with young people and the schools. The special room for children was the most attractive place in the building to adults as well as to children. It was easy, in connection with it, to cause boy and girl collectors and students to form organizations, conduct meetings, gather objects, and finally to install here their own collections. But it was plain from the first that it is not a proper part of a museum's labors to do more than initiate this kind of work.

Again and again we were reminded that the income of a museum does not permit it to work in the field of formal, direct education save to the slightest extent. Newark's museum has had an annual income of less than $20,000, now employs eight or 10 persons, and is confined in its activities to one building. Newark's public school system has an income of about $6,921,000, employs about 2,250 persons, and does its work in 75 buildings; and for proper comparison these totals should be largely increased for parochial and private schools of all kinds. Similar figures for any city would show that, no matter how large are its museums, they are almost negligible as to their direct teaching power when compared with the schools. It is obvious, then, that museums should put their educational energies into the effort to induce others, notably teachers, to learn how to use the objects they acquire.

One service which conditions of American life seem clearly to require of a museum is that of lending. This fact has been accepted in recent years by a good many museums, notably by those of science, industry, and commerce. It will surely soon be even more widely accepted; and museums of art will set up branches for wider display and will also place objects of many kinds in schools, shops, and hospitals. In Newark, the lending of museum objects to teachers for use in schoolrooms followed inevitably the lending of pictures, illustrations, designs, etc., by the library for the same purpose. The objects lent are mostly small and inexpensive, but they cover an unusually wide range. A van furnished by the board of education delivers and collects three times a week. The work is capable of indefinite extension. It makes of every schoolroom to which material goes a branch of the museum and of every teacher who uses them an admirable docent. As docents or expounders of the lessons the objects may carry, the teacher is all the more eager and interested because he borrows objects for school use of his own free will, and not at the command of his superiors.

This story of the development of one small museum is in fact but an outline of the much longer story of the developments taking place in many museums. The idea that museums should be more serviceable to their respective communities has grown rapidly in recent years, has been fitted to definite ends, and has deeply affected museum management.

A Museum Of, For, and By Newark

Miss Blank wants to know can she have a glacier for tomorrow, please? And, oh yes, a celluloid process, some early Dutch settlers, and a coal mine."

This is the sort of request which children bring daily from their schoolteachers to the Newark Museum. Teachers send slips asking for the "Middle Atlantic states and a crocodile," "The Civil War and China," "Street cleaning apparatus or volcanoes when you have them." Occasionally a little boy strolls in and asks for "bones or a skellington or sump'n like that." These requests are filled from a collection of models and objects in the Lending Department.

The museum has been lending, during the past year, nearly 2,000 individual exhibits a month to Newark schools. Exhibits in the lending collections cover industrial processes from asbestos to zinc, all obtained from Newark factories to enliven and amplify the study of commercial geography and local history; minerals from agate to wood, petrified; objects illustrating the customs of the races of men; insect life, bird life, and countless other subjects.

Local industry exhibits have been displayed at the museum, at the library and its branches and in schools, showing products of the community's activities in factories and workshops, textiles, leather, varnish, celluloid, pottery. They showed not only Newark products, but also like objects from producers in other parts of this country and from foreign makers, all accompanied by labels and leaflets.

Through these exhibits the museum staff has learned to know something about its city: its organizations and individuals and civic and educational enterprises that can be of service to those who come to the museum for advice, information, or assistance—artists, designers, manufacturers, sellers, exporters and importers, engineers, chemists,

The Survey: Graphic Number 55, no. 11 (March 1, 1926).
Published separately by The Newark Museum Association.

and scientific groups. And the staff has before it at all times the ideal of a museum and a city working together at all possible points. The Newark Museum is trying to be a workshop of education, an assistant to all educational activity in the city.

What is the meaning of these deviations from the traditional museum pattern?

When the Newark Museum was born in the Newark Public Library 16 years ago, it looked out upon the life of its city and endeavored to find out what it was to do. In those days Newark was already on the high road of a great commercial expansion. It was developing from a village which commerce and industry had quite overwhelmed, from a village which could not at first believe that it had grown into a town, and in fact into a city, and was unable to adjust its small-town ways to the manners of the city which it had become. The Newark of today has grown into an alert and fully conscious city which has turned joyfully to the task of making itself over anew, of fitting itself to its new needs, and of so adorning itself that it may properly demand of its citizens that they care for it because it is worthy of their care.

The museum from the beginning asked itself the question, "What can I do to help make life in Newark a little more gracious and livable?" We might have answered that question by bringing well-authenticated masterpieces to Newark, an occasional Nicolas Maes, a second-string Tintoretto or Rubens now and then. But Newark is near America's greatest museums of art, history, and science. Newarkers can easily visit the Metropolitan Museum, the Museum of Natural History, and others. For Newark to attempt to compete with these museums in their fields would have been an absurd waste of money. But we saw an opportunity to approach the people of our city in a more intimate way by serving immediate community needs.

Newark is a manufacturing city. We found that it has more than 250 distinct lines of manufacture. These have to do with the things people wear, with articles of personal adornment such as jewelry, with goods used in the household, upholstery, furniture, pottery, and even bathtubs and open plumbing.

It might be said that a museum has very little to do with all this. We have been taught to believe that museums have to do with the past, with artistic, historic, and other objects of great repute and of certain antiquity. Few of us, at the time the Newark Museum began its career, dared say that they found art and beauty in industry, in the products of American factories. But the fact is that it is precisely in industry that the most native and original art expression of America has come. Who in Europe or Asia or Africa or Australia cares for American paintings? for American sculpture? But who that counts himself civilized, in any continent, has not heard of American bathtubs, of American automobiles, and of a thousand other contrivances produced by American manufacturing skill?

"What's an automobile or a bathtub to do with art?" you ask at once.

The answer is "much, if not everything." Leaving aside the representative and purely expressive elements in art, one finds that the thing most pervasively associated with art through all ages has been beauty. Now beauty is a very elusive thing, but sifting down thousands of definitions of the beautiful, one comes to believe that what most people mean by beauty is the most perfect adaptation of means to ends, the most perfect adaptation of an object to its uses, and to the needs of its user or beholder. This point may land us in quagmires of discussion, but let it stand.

If beauty be the most perfect adaptation of means to ends, then industry is as full of art and beauty as the Milky Way is full of stars. And if art means anything at all, it means so much that we must have it in everything from the cup and saucer to the skyscraper. Here as elsewhere the activity of mankind outstrips its theorizing. We produce art long before we recognize it and label it as such.

We reached that conclusion fairly early in Newark. We came to believe that art in articles of wear, in articles of daily use, in household goods, in furniture, and in mechanical contrivances, is the art of the greatest importance. When people have the right attitude to this most popular art, then they will also have the right attitude toward the fine arts, toward painting, sculpture, and architecture. In choosing articles to wear, in choosing furniture, in choosing the leather with which an automobile is to be upholstered, average men and women get their most pervasive aesthetic experiences and form habits of criticism and judgment.

✦

The Newark Museum began its career with small exhibits of fine arts and arts and crafts, with the idea of discovering and showing the industrial art of its city. The New Jersey pottery and porcelain exhibit shown by the Newark Museum in 1915 and the textile exhibit of 1916 were full of the beauty of the machine. In the textile show of 1916 we had a Greek woman spinning with a distaff and spindle, and we showed the primitive elements of weaving. We also showed modern methods of spinning, weaving on Jacquard looms, and the more modern machine processes. People were interested in both the ancient and the modern processes. The Greek woman spinning showed them something of the poetry of the past. The modern machine processes had in them the poetry of youth, and it was about these processes that we had the most inquiries.

In the pottery and porcelain exhibit of 1915, people in large groups, and especially the children, stood in fascination before a potter at work. They saw the relation between ancient and modern processes, traced through tools, designs, forms, and objects, the primitive bowl and jar, the modern teacup and bathtub. In this light the bathtub became to them an object of beauty and adventure.

The Newark Museum has consistently tried to show the beauty of the machine, and has tried to discover the articles in local manufacture, whether in the shop or in the factory, which exhibit the most careful research into the adaptation of means to ends. It has done this as its part of the adventure of living in America in our day, believing that not only will these exhibits have a salutary effect in improving the quality of design in the articles produced, but that Newarkers who have seen these exhibits will show a more respectful interest in the men and the municipality which are giving these things to the world. So the museum has instituted an annual show of ceramics and ceramic design, featuring the work of local designers and craftsmen, arranging special exhibits of ceramic design sources from the history of ceramics in Europe and Asia, and also illustrating sources of ceramic and textile design sources from the history of ceramics in Europe and Asia, and also illustrating sources of ceramic and textile design in other arts as, for instance, in our Chinese exhibition of 1923 we showed a collection of Chinese embroidery which proved a mine of suggestion to the ceramic designer, and to the textile designer as well.

We have showed Newark-made jewelry, Newark-made buttons and medallions, leather goods, textiles, and whatnot in certain galleries—and paintings, sculpture, and arts and crafts in others—with the aim to show Newarkers that beauty and fitness are, and should be, basic elements in all the useful artifacts made by man, just as much as they are in the fine arts.

In its new building, when it opens this month, the Newark museum is stressing these sides of the adventure of living in America today: the adventure of machine production in a great leather exhibit, and the adventure in the field of fine arts in an exhibit of more than a score of paintings by living American artists purchased during the past year. This stately building, admirably adapted to its purpose, bears the name and is the gift of Louis Bamberger—the most modest of men, of whom one can say a word of praise only when he is ignorant of one's intent to do so. The marvelous success of the enterprise is ample testimony to the fact that he looks well into the future; and the sympathetic interest he has for years taken in the project for a museum in the city of his adoption has seemed to compel him to apply generously of his money to make his vision of a Newark museum come true. The building stands on a central plot of land bought by the city of Newark, and the city has appropriated approximately $100,000 for the support of the museum this year.

The museum emphasizes American industrial art and American fine art, but not

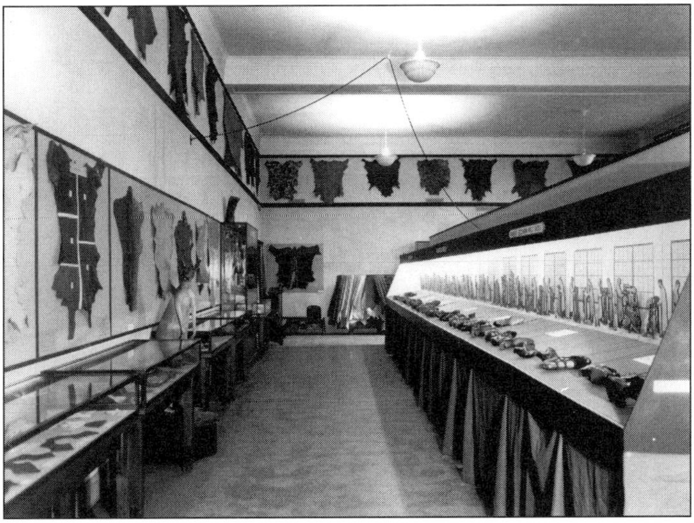

"Leather: A Newark Industry," one of the exhibitions on display at the Newark Museum in 1926.

exclusively—it has already showed a number of European exhibits of industrial art, Hungarian, German, Czechloslovak, and exhibits of the Orient, particularly, China, Japan, and Tibet. It is acquiring typical objects of fine art, both painting and sculpture, particularly the work of American artists; the best obtainable reproductions of some of the world's leading creations in these fields; and examples of applied art and of material illustrative of history and of the sciences, for the museum has scientific and educational departments in addition to the art and the industrial arts departments.

✦

Designers and craftsmen from Newark jewelry factories, leather embossers, linoleum makers, and other manufacturing plans come to us for objects and pictures to be used in designing. It is no rare thing to see groups of men in working clothes studying exhibits in the Newark Museum during the noon hour, on Saturday afternoons, and after the whistles blow at night. One jewelry designer has been coming to the museum for years, borrowing plates, designs, and often actual objects. This spring his employer, who has just returned from Europe, said to him: "Guess you'd better take a few months off this summer and go to Europe to brush up on design."

The designer, in telling a member of the museum staff of the incident, added: "You bet I didn't tell him of all the lovely stuff I get right here at the museum. He'd tell me I didn't need to go to Europe."

Small collections of objects are also lent to individuals, groups and societies, stores, factories, and others whenever these things are useful to the community when thus lent. It is the aim of the Newark Museum to establish numerous branches throughout the city in easily accessible rooms, in libraries, in business houses, and in special rooms with separate entrances in school buildings, and in other places. Some of these branches have been established, and to them have been sent from the museum's collections such things, for example, as a fine painting with descriptive leaflet; a bronze, also with descriptive leaflet; plaster casts, prints, wood carvings, textiles, woods, stones, animals, birds, insects, local industry exhibits, etc., all with labels which explain and describe, and often with leaflets which visitors can take away. Groups of interested persons in all New Jersey communities are encouraged to borrow these branch museum exhibits. Department stores in Newark and several of the leading department stores of New York ask the Newark Museum for exhibits from time to time, and always send members of their sales staffs to study exhibits such as the textile, ceramics, and leather shows.

The Newark Museum is becoming a center for collectors of all New Jersey, old and young, and for specialists, through a state-wide collectors' league, which is being made up of museums, libraries, individual collectors, and art and science lovers. In return for the use of the museum's resources, these collectors and specialists cooperate with the museum in adding to its collections and in helping to identify and describe specimens and in preparing labels and leaflets.

In many of the fields in which the Newark Museum is showing and expounding its collections it can hope to do no more than to arouse a new or awaken an old interest. It is therefore doubly keen to arouse active interests by its methods of presentation, and it is adding simple devices for informing visitors where they can best continue their studies on the lines to which Newark's museum has moved them.

All this is a large program. But, even though time may show that it is far too large to be carried out by such an institution as Newark is willing to support, it is well that we should try to carry it out, or at least that we should set it down. Every public institution should always have before it an ideal of public service far above that which it dares hope attain. It should not have its eyes on the ground or be for a moment satisfied with what it has done.

And, for my part, the growth of Newark's willingness to strive for a city's excellence—a growth that we have so plainly seen in the past 20 odd years—added to her ability to supply the essential backing for her strivings, compels me to believe that it will do more than make come true any prophecies that can be set forth of the future of her museum and of the part it is to play in the life of the community.

The New Museum Opens Its Doors: It Aims to Enrich the Life of the Community by Stimulating an Interest in Creative Design

Small beginnings are best. That is the idea which I find illustrated in the story of the Newark Museum, and in the development of the new museum movement in this country. The museum is like any other individual in society. It must be born quite small and, in its early days, struggle for growth in constant reaction to its environment, and in the end find its proper niche in the life of its community. The deadly gloom and boredom, the glacial fixity of the old museum, resulted from the fact that it sprang full-armed from the past, bringing with it the barren mass of tradition and an aloofness which made any further growth or any response to its environment impossible.

It has been the good fortune of the Newark Museum to begin in a small way, with no inheritance of tradition or dignity to prevent its going out into the streets to ask Newarkers what they would like to have in their museum. From the first we have had to ask ourselves, Why do we want a museum in Newark? What can the museum do for the community? What pleasure can it add to everyday life? How can it help Newark in its work and in its play?

In trying to answer these questions, and to find our way along the unchartered paths of the new museum, we discovered that Newark did not want a museum of a specific kind, an art museum, a science museum, a museum of natural history, of industry, of education, or what not. The Newark Museum begin in the art field by borrowing and showing watercolors, engravings, etchings, oil paintings, bookplates, and posters. In the field of science it received gifts of rocks, minerals, soils, plants, seeds, flowers, leaves, shells, fossils, and allied objects, and we arranged them for an exhibit. At the same time we began acquiring applied art objects of colonial times and, from the Far East, utensils, costumes, and furniture.

As we went on, the question was always present, Is the museum bringing to the

The Newark Museum Association, 1926. Reprinted from Charm.

people of Newark a little more of experience and giving them each day some new pleasure in the life and activities of their city?

We had no great and expensive collections to show, no old masters, priceless rarities, or antiques. But we had a city around us, an industrial and manufacturing city, which every day was making thousands of articles for everyday use, for convenience, for enjoyment. And the thought came to us that we could show some of these things, and the processes by which they are made, and that we might discover in them some of the creating and designing talent which has made the masterpieces of the past. We proceeded to show the clay products and textiles of the state; we even had a showing of bathtubs made in New Jersey.

The people of Newark responded. They were interested, and they came in droves to increase their knowledge of the things made in their city. They discovered that into the making of the most ordinary things of everyday life, cups and saucers, pottery jars, rugs, textiles, went creative talent of a kind similar to that which produced the objects of vast prestige and price usually shown in museums. The result was that art and science and industry were made to seem more closely related to everyday life. Man's creating, making, designing talent was here, something they could understand, something near home and intimate. They got a new vision of what art is and to see that it is simply one phase of man's struggle to shape his environment in accordance with his needs and desires.

In many ways, the influence of museums has been pernicious, particularly in the field of art. They have served to make people think of art as oil paintings and sculpture, usually made by great masters long ago, objects far out of the ken of everyday life. They have devoted themselves to things so far removed by rarity and price from everyday life that they seemed to observers to demand mere wonder, and not to convey any suggestions for improvement in taste. The result of this has been that people have put these things aside as not for them, becoming reconciled to ugly utensils, ugly clothes, ugly houses, in the belief that art is something sacred and highfalutin. And they put aside attempts to beautify their immediate environment with a sigh, in the belief that real, genuine, high-brow beauty is not for them, that it resides only in museums, in studios, and in the homes of the rich.

The old art museum has stressed the idea that art and beauty must be rare, must be high in price, and must, in most cases, be antique. The Newark Museum, in looking around for ways to interest the people of its city, has definitely broken with this idea. It has never tried to collect the old, the curious, the rare, as such. It values its exhibits not on the basis of antiquity, rarity, or curiosity, but upon their usefulness; that is, it asks itself if its exhibits inspire by their beauty, stimulate creative design or creative ideas, or have an educational value.

The Newark Museum has consistently followed a policy of acquiring and using only what can be made effective in the life of its community, remembering always that within an hour's journey of Newark, in New York City, are some of the greatest museums in the world. Since Newark is a producer of countless types of manufactured goods into which an element of design enters—such as jewelry, medals, leather goods—the museum has acquired objects, designs, pictures, and illustrated books which might be helpful in industrial design. That these exhibits have been of value in this field may be judged by the number of designers and producers who have made use of them, and by the number of articles in trade journals which have appeared about these collections.

From showing the arts and the manufactures of Newark and of New Jersey, the museum branched out into other countries and times. One of the early exhibits of this kind was the "Colonial Kitchen," which made vivid and understandable a part of American history. In it were displayed utensils, furniture, and costumes used in colonial times, and lecturers in colonial costume were present daily to explain the exhibit to visitors.

Next we began to show some of our neighbors, the first exhibit being that of the Republic of Colombia, in South America. We borrowed articles from Colombia, from officials in Washington, and from travelers, supplementing the objects shown with pictures, maps, charts, and legends. The interest taken in the Colombian exhibit, which showed the life and the resources of our sister republic, encouraged us to go on with this sort of exhibit and showed us the value of pictures in arranging museum exhibits. A group of pictures well selected, briefly but fully labeled, and supplemented with a small collection of actual objects will make a vivid story and give as complete a picture as many a more pretentious exhibit could give.

The Colombian exhibit also set us thinking about the problem and the meaning of museum exhibits of other lands. Were they simply to show geography, resources, costumes and customs, industry, with a little art and handicraft? What about promoting understanding and sympathy between nations? Would exhibits of the life, the customs, the problems, and the ideals of a neighbor people lead us to a better understanding of that people? Would it help break down hostility and open up paths to friendship? We answered these questions in the affirmative, and the most ambitious result of our faith in this function of museum exhibits was the "China: The Land and the People" exhibit of 1923. We tried in this exhibit to show, through objects, pictures, maps, and legends, that the problem of China, and of the good relations of the rest of the world with China, is one of the world's greatest problems, and that the right solution of that problem can come only through a sympathetic understanding of the Chinese by the Western peoples and of the Western peoples by the Chinese. The Chinese exhibit had assistance from every province of China, from Chinese students in this country, departments of the United States government and the Chinese government, American consular representatives in China, and Chinese diplomatic representatives in this country. The exhibit was shown in Newark for two months, and was then sent, in a number of small exhibits, to many of the leading cities of the country, where it was shown in museums, libraries, and colleges.

Our policy of beginning at home before going far afield has led the museum to acquire, on the side of fine and applied arts, works by American painters, sculptors, and designers first, and then, later, characteristic works from abroad. We have been very fortunate in acquiring a number of works by distinguished Americans, and these will be seen to advantage in the new museum. But our begin-at-home policy has not prevented our acquiring small collections of classic and Renaissance art; copies and originals of works of famous European artists; arts and crafts of Germany, Czechoslovakia, Scandinavia, Russia, France, and other countries; and objects illustrating the life and customs of the various civilized nations; as well as ethnographic collections showing the life of primitive man in all parts of the world.

Through the gift of a distinguished Newarker and through other gifts and purchases, we acquired a scientific collection which contains upwards of 100,000 specimens and which has been called one of the best small working science collections in the country.

Study of the needs of teachers and designers led us to institute a liberal policy of lending. We were led to this policy also because our museum was reared in a public library, one of the primary functions of which is to lend books. The lending collections have grown by leaps and bounds, and the use of them has grown, too. At the beginning there were few requests, but as the years went on school-teachers, students, and others discovered the value of these objects, with the result that we lent in 1924 more than 18,000 of them, and in the first months of 1925 their circulation was over 2,000 a month. These objects in the lending collections are used mostly by the schools. Requests come in daily, and three times a week a motor van delivers the objects asked for. Today the lending collection consists of about 6,000 objects brought from all parts of the world, illustrative of the life and arts of the various races of man, including the man of our own very complex era and civilization.

Our experience in Newark indicates that a few simple objects and pictures, united with the idea of service, make a good beginning for a museum. No expensive collections, no objects rare and costly and or aristocratic history are necessary. The museum should attract, entertain, arouse curiosity, lead to questionings—and thus promote learning. To do these things a museum can very well use simple, common, and inexpensive objects, just as daily life uses wayside flowers and trees; sheep, cattle, ploughs, and hoes on the farm; pavements, motors, and shop windows in cities; and man and his doings everywhere to awaken young and old to interest and inquiry about the world outside themselves. To use simple things to promote an intelligent and particular interest, a museum needs only to look around for what is near at hand, and then apply to these things the best skill it can acquire, infinite tact, and constant sympathy.

VI. Museums and Education

How Museum and Schools May Aid Good Workmanship

There is only one opinion about museums: It is that they are large, ornate, and expensive buildings, standing in a public park on the outskirts of their respective cities, containing in solemn rows, or in cold and glittering cases, objects which ought to be admired because they are in the museum—all visited in a sort of Sunday-school spirit when Aunt Mary and the boys come to the city for a few days.

This is the one and only popular opinion on museums. Other ideas are on the way. In a few places they are being tried and heartily approved. Here is an attempt to give a hint as to what these other museum ideas are like:

Skilled labor in a town helps to make the town peaceful, progressive, and prosperous. This is because men who do work that calls for skill are men who are naturally brainy, steady, persevering, and of long experience. They like their jobs, they want homes of their own, and they favor town improvements because those improvements make their property worth more and make the town a better place for their children to grow up in.

Newark is a town of skilled labor, but not so much so as she might be. Every manufacturer in the city wishes he could find steady, settled citizens of Newark, of good education, and with solid training in their trade to come and work in his shop. The steady, skilled workman is always in demand.

Newark has probably gone backward rather than forward in the matter of skilled labor in the past 20 years. This is because good workers stopped coming from Europe and Newark did not raise a supply of her own. Her schools kept the children until they were about 12 or 14. The streets called them for most of a year or two, and then they went into shops, and in the shops was no system of selection and training.

This is to be changed. When the high schools are well underway they will do three things: They will make work in the grades better, they will make children want to stay in school longer, and they will every year turn into the city's population more than a thousand young people who have been kept at systematic study until they are 19 years old. To the high schools as aids in producing skilled workers the new idea adds museums.

This new idea seems to say to Newark that her museums will be something like this:

Near the center of the city is a tall building 10 to 15 stories high, modern in all its arrangements of elevators, fireproofing, lighting, sanitation, and general convenience.

Within this building are shown, in a few large rooms, small collections, not crowded, of paintings, engravings, lithographs, printing, marbles, bronzes, vases, textiles, ironwork, ivories, rocks, minerals, jewels, birds, animals, plants, insects, raw material of manufacture, things illustrating the life of the American Indian, and a historical collection on Newark and New Jersey.

These and similar things, carefully arranged, fully labeled, and with descriptive lists and handbooks, form the least important part of the museum, but the part which popular opinion now says is all there is to a museum—rare, curious, unique, and so-called beautiful and usually costly objects, gathered by a city to give it standing among aesthetics as a patron of art. Save to satisfy this demand for a museum of the exclusive, expensive, warehouse curio type, these objects will be of not much use.

In other rooms will be large collections of the kinds of things which the people of Newark make and sell and wear and use daily in their homes. The best products of the city, of hundreds of kinds, will here be placed side by side with the best products—in originals or in copies—of other cities in the world; and of the present and other times.

Of many of these there will be many examples, and aside from a small proportion kept with care because of fragility or rarity or cost, they will be lent to inquirers or men from workshops, to teachers for school use, to all comers for enjoyment, comparison, and study in the home.

In botany, geology, zoology, and other fields of science and in all the handwork subjects which can well be illustrated by actual objects, there will be, as in the field of applied arts, collections in duplicate, as demand may indicate and funds permit.

With all these things there will be the largest collection in the world of pictures. These will illustrate art, fine and applied, in thousands of examples; the history, the social development, the industrial life of Newark and thousands of other topics; they will be closely classified, easily accessible, open to all, and lent freely. It is possible that this collection of pictorial material will be the most valuable part of the

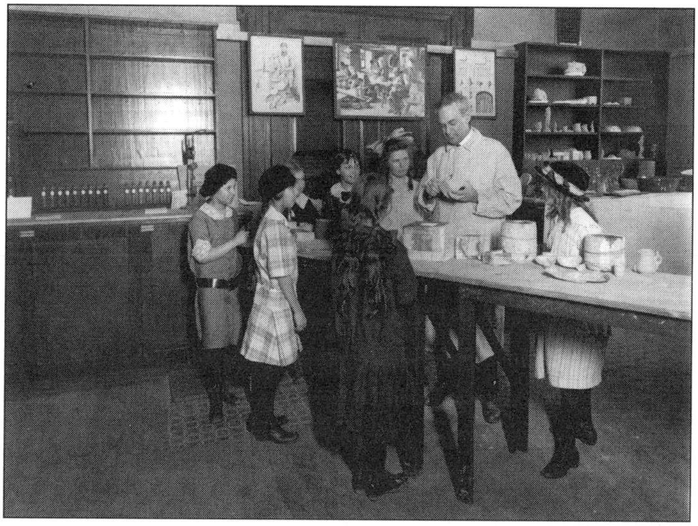

An instructor demonstrates the art of making pottery, 1915.

whole museum.

In the building is room, of course, for all the city's educational work in drawing and design, and for much besides. Art societies will meet here, and so will scientific societies and many of the organizations designed to promote the efficiency of the members as workers and citizens.

Visitors will find attendants ready to guide groups and to explain collections. To the teachers in all schools will be given courses of lessons on the use in the classroom of illustrative material of whatever kind they need and the museum can furnish.

In every schoolhouse there will be a branch museum, containing a changing series of appropriate collections of objects. Besides the things of more immediate interest, illustrating the studies in each school, there will always be found in appropriate places in every building beautiful statues in bronze or marble, fine paintings, originals or facsimiles, engravings, brocades, vases, and whatever other objects the central collection can for a time well spare and the neighborhood can best appreciate and most enjoy.

It is this new kind of a museum that would interest many in good workmanship, would broaden and refine the taste of many, and would greatly help Newark's other educational agencies in making her, more notably than now, a city of skilled workers.

Schools and Museums

The museum that helps a teacher to make her lessons easier for herself and more interesting and more instructive to pupils, and that does this constantly, day in and day out, and on every subject in the curriculum—that is the only museum worth speaking of in the same breath with schools.

Let me qualify that a little by saying that non-lending, study museums of medicine, of Spanish history, of natural science, of safety appliances, of textiles; and mere gazing museums of oil paintings, or Egyptian antiquities, or rare and costly curios—that all these and many other kinds of museums may be worth an annual visit by teacher and class, and may, through that one visit, give very definite help to classroom work. But if a museum is used by pupils to the extent only of a visit or two each year, it is not a museum that can be properly alluded to as an aid to schools.

The museum that really affects schooling, then, being one that teachers use daily, ought to be in the schoolhouse itself? By no means.

The objects which teachers can profitably use in classes of all grades must be many in number and of almost infinite variety; they are not easily found; they often need to be cased, mounted, or strengthened for handling, and always need to be labeled and often to be described in accompanying leaflets. To collect and prepare these many things is work which calls for space, tools, appliances, and skilled workers. It would be a great waste of money to gather all this museum apparatus into every building in a system; and doing that would mean a wasteful duplication of money, material, and labor; and the collections in any one school building would be of little value to the others.

These statements, also, may be qualified. The one large central school building of a small town can quite wisely gather materials for its own use unless there is in the

Public Libraries (Library Bureau, Chicago) 23, no. 2 (February 1918).

same town a museum or some other educational organization that will undertake the work. The teacher in a remote country schoolhouse may advantageously collect a few things which will, in effect, form a small museum and be useful to her and her successors. A rich friend of education may put into a schoolhouse a collection of objects which, being widely labeled, arranged, and cased, may help the teachers in that particular building; though it should be called a school's museum and not a museum for schools. It could not be a live, growing, daily-used museum, for it would have no staff of workers to handle it and keep it alive. It would, in most cases, be what Mr. Goode called a dead museum, being as finished and unchanging as an Egyptian mummy.

In telling what a museum for schools is not, I have quite clearly stated what it is. It is a central, lending collection of objects useful in teaching. St. Louis has precisely this thing, and all reports tell us that it is very helpful. Few cities are wise enough to know that they should have a like institution. And few superintendents would recommend that its city spend, as St. Louis does, $12,000 to $15,000 per year on the upkeep of a school museum.

This lending museum for schools is very much like a lending library. Before we had many large central libraries, and before they were as liberally administered, especially for children and teachers, as they are now, it was quite a common thing, and a very good thing in its day, to find libraries in schoolhouses. These schoolhouse libraries had two serious disadvantages. They were not well administered; that is, no one person made it her business to know them, to learn what subjects each teacher taught and when, and what books most helped and entertained both teachers and pupils and, knowing these things, proceeded to bring books, teachers, and pupils together at just the right point of need. The other and quite overwhelming disadvantage was that the collection of books, not being constantly and wisely added to, soon went out of date and became almost worthless.

As it was with school libraries—set up independently in each building and not cared for and kept up through the ministrations of a central bureau and storehouse like a main public library—so would it be with museums in school buildings. The objects in them would gather dust, decay, and become broken, lose their labels, lack interest for pupils and teachers alike, and come to the proper end of non-managed, non-growing, unchanging, dead museums.

Shall we say, then, that the museum a school system most needs is merely a central storage warehouse, containing as many as can be secured of the countless things which teachers use to advantage in adding object teaching to their methods, with facilities for shipping the things to and from schools as requested? Far from it.

The storehouse is needed; but before the storehouse of objects useful in visual instruction can be called a museum for schools, two things must be added to it: one, a staff of skilled workers; the other, collections of not-lent objects, attractively and instructively installed, and occasionally changed; together with frequent special, temporary exhibits which are either borrowed or brought together by the museum itself.

Here it will be the part of wisdom to say that I am writing of museums as if there were in existence a well-thought-out and clearly expressed museum doctrine. Neither of these assumptions is correct. The art and science of museums are at about the same stage of development today as were the art and science of libraries 40 years ago; and, in view of the fact that I am in the habit of censuring my library colleagues when they seem to assume that certain qualities and functions of libraries are even now known and thoroughly understood, it should be easy for me to clear myself of the charge that I pretend to know much about museums!

The fact is that, just as libraries have grown inevitably out of peculiar qualities of modern society, being truly far more products of our manner of self-education than factors in that education; so have our museums come—the old type from our habit of imitating older people in the collection of curios, and the new type, and especially our educationally oriented museums, from an increase of visual instruction in our schools.

Now, no one has yet pointed out clearly any large and definite service rendered to society by either the older type of gazing museum or the more recent type of school-object-teaching museum. From this we may not conclude that either the old or the new kind of museum is not a good and useful thing and worthy of being fostered. But from it we must conclude that of the proper manner of setting up museums of any kind—and by setting up I mean doing all that concerns them, from site and character of building to the details of the smallest label—we know very little, and can learn only by study, experiment, and observation, and even then must draw merely tentative conclusions and act as if we were sure of our way only for purposes of immediate administration. It is as important today that we have museums which, though not sure of their way, nevertheless do things, as it was 35 or 40 years ago that we have libraries of that same character. The museum that does things because it is quite sure that they are the only right things to do is quite harmful to museum development. In a new and largely unexplored field, only the inquirer who is not only bold but is also fully conscious that the field is unexplored can give us useful data for mapping that which is as yet unknown.

So much by way of apology for, and explanation of, a certain assurance of expression.

Returning now to the skilled workers and the permanent and changing exhibits which must be added to a collection of lending objects for visual instruction before that collection can properly be called a school museum: The idea of the teaching museum, or of a museum as a definite aid to current educational work, has developed slowly. This is because the museum theory became fixed in practice long before the public-supported educational work had become more than a dream of the student of society and of the alms-giving rich. Museum collections, and collections that later formed the bases of museums, were at first made almost solely by rulers and nobles. To them the objects collected, plus personal pride and selfish enjoyment, were all in all. The objects, having been acquired and placed in proper receptacles, called for nothing more of service. They were not to be used, handled, examined, and studied by artists, artisans, or lovers of art or of its history. This tradition of the all-sufficiency of the ancient, the rare, and the costly as the constituents of a museum has continued, down to the present day, to dominate largely the activities of nearly all museums of the fine arts, and to color the activities of museums of other kinds.

Now comes the theory, slowly rising into reasoned belief and being developed, also slowly, in actual practice, that publicly owned or publicly supported collections of valuable objects should be made demonstrably useful. When a museum accepts this theory, it finds that it must at once equip its collection with brains. Among these brains there should be, obviously, those of experts in art and its history and in science; also, and still more obviously, those of the administrator, of the student, and of the expert in current educational work, and of deft workers.

The conclusion seems inevitable. Put concretely it is that a collection of lending objects to be used by teachers and pupils needs for its useful and economic handling an accompanying corps of diligent and intelligent workers.

Our own modest experience in this type of school museum in Newark has led us to the conclusion that a collection of objects costing, say, $1,000, plus the activities of a group of museum workers costing $10,000 per year, would be of far more value to a community, chiefly through its use by schools, than would a collection which cost $100,000 and is merely presided over in the ancient manner by a few curators.

As to the argument for permanent exhibits, accompanied by others constantly changing, it is summed up in the statement that a museum for schools, a collection of lending objects of use in visual instruction, should be attached to and form a component part of a public museum of art, science, history, and industry. For this there are many reasons which can here be only suggested.

The large public museum, holding collections of rare and precious things in the fields of art, science, industry, and history—too fragile or too precious or too large to lend, beautifully installed and visited by the public in its idle moments, by citizens as an agreeable stimulant to local pride and by occasional students—is probably a good thing for a community to construct for itself and will surely continue to be constructed by one community after another for many years to come. As such a museum is, or is to be, in almost every city, and as its fundamental purpose is already avowedly and soon will be actually that of promoting education, it is clear that it should take up into itself the material and work of a school museum, properly so called. From it will come much material not fit for the purposes of a gazing museum, but admirably suited to form part of the group of lending things. In it will be found experts who can give the school-lending staff assistance in identifying, arranging, and presenting, through label and leaflet, the objects they are handling. And, perhaps most important of all, it can offer in its permanent and changing and borrowed exhibits a sufficient reason for receiving from school pupils, singly and in classes in school hours, one or more visits each year.

These visits may often arouse interests, incentives, and suggestions that will add much to the value of borrowed objects seen only in schoolrooms.

To summarize: The good school museum is a collection of lending objects useful in school work; prepared by a corps of workers who are in close touch with the schools; and forming part of a general public museum of art, science, industry, and history.

What Can Be Said of a Museum's "Educational" Work?

The word "education" is almost universally used to mean formal instruction by a teacher or lecturer, with textbook, course of study, and examination. If the educational work of museums is considered in that meaning of the phrase, we cannot include in it the selection of its objects, the arrangement of its home, its methods of installation, its labels, catalogues, reports, and handbooks; its guards, preparators, and curators. And yet a very large part of all that a museum does in interesting, stimulating, and informing the people of its community is due to the peculiar excellences of its environment, its acquisitions, and its management.

If we limit the education done by museums to that kind of education which demands a teacher, textbook, and course of study, we find it almost negligible. It seems quite impossible for museums to continue to expand, as they all quite inevitably do, along the lines of acquisition, installation, and labeling; and of guidebooks, bulletins, and reports; and at the same time acquire funds that they can use to employ teachers, construct classrooms, and in general carry on the activities proper to "education," in the usual meaning of that word. Even lectures, which are generally thought to be quite the most ineffective form of educational effort, if adequate in quality and number would put on a museum a greater financial burden than it could carry.

We conclude, therefore, that the growth of a museum's educational work must consist chiefly of the development and improvement of such work as lies within the activities which museums have already found to be proper to their construction, their equipment, and their incomes. Museums can neither turn themselves into schools of free education nor add free public schools to their equipment and their work. Even docenting—that is, the teaching by clever perambulating lecturers of random and casual groups of visitors, now so much in vogue—will surely be found to have, as educa-

Twentieth Annual Report, 1928 (The Newark Museum Association, 1929).

tional work, great limitations; and as factors of expense, great possibilities of growth.

A museum is not a school; it cannot afford to become a school; and by its own unaided powers it can do little educational work of the formal kind. Fortunately it has close at hand a multitude of educational institutions: schools—public, private, and parochial; universities, technical institutes; professional and business colleges. Cooperation of museums with them has been tried in many places to a moderate extent, notably in Newark, and always with fair success. The museum as an aid to teaching institutions of every kind seems to be in its proper position.

But there are two things that stand in the way of the use of museums as aids to formal educational institutions: the first, that museums insist on keeping all their objects and activities in one place, making it quite impossible for them to be used by more than a very small fraction of teachers and students in a city of fair size; and, next, that museums are universally opposed to the lending, for teaching purposes, of more than a small fraction of their collections. I believe that both these tendencies, though they are natural and even inevitable to museums as we know them today, should be checked and modified. If museums are to look to existing educational institutions as the proper means of extending their own educational work, it would seem that they must do it by equipping themselves with far more lending material and a far larger staff for the management of lending than they have at present. This will be expensive, quite. Also it would seem that they must add to their general equipment, especially in large cities, branch museums. This will also be expensive. Yet both these things should, I believe, be done by Newark's museum.

It will at once be said that it is exceedingly difficult to persuade towns and cities so to increase the appropriations they now make to museums, as to enable them to carry on their present very essential activities of acquisition, preparation, and installation and the new work of cooperation with existing schools and universities. To this one may reply that, just as the money needed to carry on our schools has increased, per capita, each year, as their work, growing in range and quality and in public esteem, has seemed to demand that increase; so will the income of museums from public funds be increased, as the aid they give to education in their respective communities is seen to grow in extent and quality.

VII. Museums and Art

Relation of Art to American Life

Art is a fine large word. It shares with liberty the task of serving as an excuse for many crimes. It is used without any meaning; to mean several things at once; to conceal thought, and to conceal the want of thought. It is one of those words of emotional connotation which so fills you with feeling that you feel you are full of thought. It is a dangerous word. Define it, limit it, don't be fooled by it, and don't fool your pupils with it.

You hold that if a boy learns to draw, he learns to observe, to use his eyes better; but only a few can learn to observe in the way you mean, and only a few of these few can learn to draw what they observe, or ever care to, or ever need to.

Also, you say, drawing helps the brain to develop by bringing into close relations the centers for eye and hand. Probably it does a little. But very little, if keen interest is absent, and it usually is, and still less if it is for only an hour and a half a week for only three weeks out of five for a few years. And when you compare the manual training with that of the base-ball field, it becomes in most cases quite negligible. There are proven benefits of drawing and manual training in special cases, of course. The race has rightly put faith in the manual arts since the day it learned to flex its thumb. But a little of it formally taught in the schools affects little.

You may sum up the matter thus:

1. A little drawing is of very little use to most; and we need only a few good drafts men.
2. What is learned on the play-ground comes out in the classroom; and your pupils may be growing skillful in spite of you.
3. The boy who has learned to draw may not have one artistic fiber in him.

Address before the Eastern Art Teachers Association, Brooklyn, June 1906. Published in the Newark Sunday Call, June 24, 1906, and Schools Arts Book 6, no. 1 (September 1906).

Were there time I could, and would, speak of color-work, modeling, paper-folding, weaving, wood-work, and other activities which come into your field in this same inquiring way. I think your work, anybody's professional work, is in continual need of catechizing, and I would help you to a little of it. I'm sure you should ask yourself oftener, "Is public school education just naturally improving while we stand by, or are we helping it?"

Let me add that you would do well also to appoint a "Committee on an Index Expurgatorus," which shall draw up a list of words which may not be used in any paper read to you for at least two years from date, save under extreme provocation and with precise definition. The committee would include, of course, "uplift," "inspirational," "vital," "true," "balance," "harmony," "rhythm," and some others.

We return now to your boy who has learned to draw, and yet is not artistic. He is so common that I need not enlarge on him. The like remark holds true of any other of the many technical operations involved in the production of beautiful things. In effect, one does not become artistic by acquiring skill of hand. It is worthwhile to remind ourselves of this now and then.

Moreover, one does not become artistic by reading about painters and sculptors and their works; or by learning to tell Gothic from Grecian architecture, or Moorish from Celtic ornament; or by doing or learning most of the other things the doing or learning of which is usually designated as "Art Study."

And here I return to my first warning about this word, art. Because it covers such a multitude of meanings, many who proclaim that they are enrolled beneath its banners and march in the front ranks really are just clerks in the commissary department of life. Moreover, again, these clerks make a great deal of noise, and the outsider's eye and ear are caught by them, and he says, "If these be Art's soldiers, let us have peace!" Most who think they are studying art are simply gathering facts. Let us approach a little nearer to our definition, though chiefly by negations: Art is not skill, though the artist must have it. Art is not knowledge, though the artist must have it. Art is what the artist gives us in his product which is a permanent possibility of an agreeable thrill. And to be artistic is to be easily thrilled by what the artist gives us. And to study art is to strengthen the habit, by exposure, suggestion, and practice, of being thus thrilled. And here in America this habit is so weak when found and so rarely found that the subject, the Relation of Art to American Life, may almost be treated as was the classic topic of snakes in Ireland.

A nation gets the kind of government it deserves. The same is true of its insurance, its beef, its cities, and its artists. We are a numerous and active people, possessing a very rich and fruitful country. Were we far less skillful than we are, wealth would still have crowned our labors. Being new, mixed, eager, and as greedy as any, we have produced, perforce, a nation of spendthrift mediocrities. In art, in letters, in government, in invention, in science, in organization we have done few great things and produced few great men. We adequately support hardly one journal of serious thought of the kind which England has a score. We are 80 millions and rich as Croesus and still import the magazine of art we cannot produce ourselves. In our greatest and richest city, the stigmata of the leisure class, conspicuous consumption, and conspicuous waste are assumed with frenzied eagerness and quite banish those foster parents of refinement, simplicity, and restraint. Our great museum of art is but a prophecy. Henry James epitomizes its history and its near future. He is noting his impressions as he looked upon the museum: "There was money in the air! ever so much money that was, grossly expressed, the sense of the whole intimation. And the money was to be all for the most exquisite things. The thought of acres of canvas and the tons of marble to be turned out into the cold world as the penalty of old error and the warrant for a clean slate ought to have drawn tears from the eyes. But these impending incidents affected me, in fact, on the spot, as quite radiant demonstrations. The Museum, in short, was going to be great, and in the geniality of the life to come such sacrifices, though resembling those of the funeral-pile of Sardanapalus, dwindled to nothing." In a word, we had money; convention said we should have objects of art, and we bought them by the acre and the ton.

If we look to those who have been taught for something to relieve the flamboyancy of those who have taught and made themselves, we find in our great club-house of the college-bred the intrusive insignia of the spendthrift rich. It says at once to the visitor, "We men of books also can indulge in conspicuous waste."

Pausing for a moment we will reflect that, being librarians and teachers of art and manual training, fate makes none of us insultingly wealthy and plainly marks us out as those who will save the rest from the evils wealth breeds.

For my purpose this morning, I have said enough on the topic you gave me. I have tried to intimate that American Life is essentially laborious, productive, money-getting; that the people consequently think a little, work much, and, like all hard workers among crops of either gold or potatoes, are not quick or nice in their emotions. They wish their colors strong, their stories crude, and their humor broad. They think the picture good if it cost much, the statue if it makes much talk. They are keen on esthetics when convention says to them that they should be; but then only. Why, some of your members trip daily past the disheveled ash box and the fragrant can of garbage on the sidewalk of their cities and move swiftly on to school to teach the children how to spot and how to spatter by the laws of balance, harmony, and rhythm.

Like the rest of us, they are esthetic only at the appointed time and place.

We are commonplace. Our people are not artistic. If they were artistic, they would have thrills over our American cities, and not all of them agreeable ones. If they could all draw and color and model and weave and bend iron to make boxes they might produce no more art than now. And my conclusion is, that if you wish to hasten the day when there shall be some Relation between Art and Life in America, you must, so far as your own work is concerned, make sure that it does something other than give a little more skill to those who are born skillful; that it breed, by exposure, suggestion, and practice, the habit of having feelings about all that they see.

II. You are not more surprised than I am at my temerity in venturing to criticize your attitude or methods. And now I accentuate that joint surprise by proceeding to speak of some of my own efforts at art promotion. I am not an artist, or a teacher of art, or a student of art, or a collector of art. My excuse for this venture lies in my interest in your efforts, and in a measure in the opportunities I have had, rather unusual for a layman, to observe you at your work.

My interest began in Denver nearly 17 years ago. My duties as a librarian brought me into close touch then, as it always has since, with teachers and their pupils in the schools, and especially, though my own special tastes, with drawing and manual training. My first colleague was your Mr. Collins, then drawing supervisor in Denver, now here in the public schools of Brooklyn. He was fresh from art school in Paris, and I was fresh from a ranch in western Colorado. We soon found that what he did not know about art I did! Being rather detached from the world, out there on the other side of the Great American Desert, with no distractions to speak of in the way of art in any of its forms, we could, and I think we did, take a somewhat independent view of things, and found it pleasant to settle out of hand many of the questions that I see from the reports of your meetings you are still puzzling over. You may well envy the advantage this earthly detachment gave us. It would do many teachers of art much good to withdraw from eastern realms of artistic law and order and commune with themselves for a time on the farther edge of the desert region of things unknown in esthetics.

We seem to have had at this time, Collins and I, two things in view as of considerable importance in the field of which we are speaking:

1. Helping children to discover their peripheries, that is, to use their hands and to see things clearly.
2. Helping adults to see with discrimination, to like or dislike what they see; help ing them, that is, to make life more interesting.

My work was, of course, chiefly with the adults. It must have been then that I discovered in my efforts to induce them to observe with feeling, that is to "taste," the everyday things about them—that people think art is something quite apart from daily life; that they are, to put it more technically, consciously esthetic only when they look on art that has been duly certified as such. This, too, in spite of the training in taste almost daily undergone by most in the processes of planning dresses, trimming hats, decorating rooms, selecting furniture, and choosing pictures. But this daily training in taste does not, for most, seem to pass over all into the field of art. This latter is something, as I have said, consciously connected in their minds only with accredited artworks. I concluded that one of the greatest obstacles to the growth of the esthetic habit I have spoken of, the habit gained, by exposure, practice, and suggestion, of liking and disliking, judging emotionally, what you see, is the "masterpiece"; I am of the same opinion still. And let me say here that if I succeed at all in my talk with you today, it will be, in my opinion, because I lead you once again to see the importance of this habit of looking with interest, with inquiry, with the question ever in your mind: "Do I like it?" "Has it charm?" "Wherein lies its charm?" upon the thousand and one of the handiworks of man that come hourly under our observation. The house, the common everyday house, the chair, the table, the pitcher, the cup, the door, the molding by the door, the picture in the Sunday paper, in the magazine, on the bill-boards, these are the things you daily and hourly see; here is where, if anywhere, you can try your skill in tasting; these are the things you should teach the children to see clearly, to have a feeling for or against. In these everyday objects we can show good taste; and on them whether good or bad, we can practice ourselves in tasting.

The children should know the masterpieces, of course. It is in a measure one of their rights that they be taught something about them, taught to recognize them, to know the stories of them, and the poetry and romance they epitomize. But to acquire this knowledge about masterpieces in art is hardly nearer to acquiring the esthetic habit than is the acquisition of knowledge about the sources of the Mississippi or the length of the Brooklyn Bridge. Moreover, you can't practice the children's taste on the masterpieces. They are not here, and those we have of our own make are few and to be seen but seldom and then with difficulty. We have photographs of them, which are good for imparting knowledge, but not as good for cultivating taste as are the thousand common objects I have alluded to. The photographs are mere shadows; and the best of these shadows are rare. Like masterpieces themselves, they are not in our homes; they are not where we can constantly see them and try our judgement on them.

In this matter, my conclusion is—and I have already said it—point out the good and bad in everyday things. You make too much of the fine photographs and casts you put in the schools and not enough of the things that every hour and minute assail the children's eyes. You lament over the character of the pictures in the Sunday papers, and you seem—I hate even to hint at such stupidity—but you seem to hope to counteract their assumed influence for bad taste by a few photographs on the schoolroom walls and a few 20-minute lessons in color and design. Why not tie the brief moments of your influence to things as they are? Give a few lessons on our Sunday cartoons. Don't affect to ignore what countless thousands of children every day delight in, but preach from them, as texts against them where you must, with them where you can. The children are living with the houses and the furniture and the wall-paper (God help them!) and the Buster Browns and Nervy Nats of today, and the ever-present influence of these will not be overcome by ignoring them and summoning Giotto and Velasquez for 10 minutes from the past.

Of all picture books, the one which, in my observation, has the strongest appeal for children is a bound volume of Puck and Judge. There are reasons why. If you discover those reasons, and then proceed from the known to the unknown, your influence for good taste may be more weighty. Surely this is safe to say, that you can point a lesson in drawing, in vigor, in directness, in color, far better from a cartoon in Puck and Judge than from most of the shadowy prints of paintings which you ask the children to admire.

To say a word about my own efforts, which have been sufficiently feeble and fruitless to satisfy any among you who may be inclined to scoff at the suggestions I offer: Collins began it in Denver with a collection of initials and head and tail pieces from old books and magazines. I furnished the material from the library's extra supply, also sheets of manila paper for mounting. Teachers and pupils clipped, sorted, and mounted, and the result soon was a large and useful pile of material, such as money can scarcely buy.

From the magazines and journals, again, by the same process, soon came illustrations of many kinds, used for many purposes. In those days I thought chiefly of the pictorial part of art, which, as I have since come to see, forms only a small and rather unimportant part of the whole esthetic field. We learned that children of 12 can soon distinguish illustrators by their respective works and like to do it. They clipped and mounted and arranged by artists in many schoolrooms many thousands of illustrations other than the stories. Similar collections in decoration, furniture, tableware, and a score of other subjects could easily be gathered in the same way, and the habit of judging—of liking and disliking—cultivated for use in daily life.

Our library collection grew rapidly. We held exhibitions of things cut from current journals, and admirable they were; and they were enjoyed, too, by many hundreds of young of old. Schoolroom decoration came our way about this time, and we began to put up in rooms these inexpensive prints, colored and black and white, cheaply framed and unframed. We held that it is well to show, in the school room, not only the best obtainable photographs of paintings, or buildings on which time has set the seal of approval, but also inexpensive things, things such as almost the poorest child can hope to have in his own home. In how many homes today hang lithographic, crayon, and steel-plated horrors! They are often gorgeous in color, and thereby hands a lesson for you, the same lesson you ought to find in the popularity of the Sunday supplement and Puck and Judge. Begin with a yard of roses and the unfortunate Washington and his family, not with a Madonna and a Stuart baby, and you will find that you are getting right down where the children are at home. High price and great remoteness are no real virtue in a work of art. We live, day by day, not with the best things the greatest men have wrought. We live with the common ugly things, chiefly, but mixed with these and also common and gloriously cheap are the many things that are good. Help the children to pick out these everyday good things and enjoy them.

As the years have gone by and I have tried my hand in other cities, I have pursued in some measure this same plan of collecting illustrations of objects of art—of nature and science, also—and have pressed them into use wherever opportunity offered. We can illustrate very form of picture-reproducing process. We can show the poor print of the great painting and beautiful wood engravings by masters in the art. We have bad lithographs and those wonderful modern ones that fairly shout to you to enjoy them, now made in France and Germany. We have thousands of portraits, pictures of furniture of every kind, and designs for everything under the sun. And we hope to have only begun. We believe these things will grow in favor and gain more use, and that they will help many to realize that good is sitting here in their doorways and calling them from the daily and monthly press, as well as standing by the Seine and hanging on the walls of the Louvre.

We have exhibits of good things, expensive things, the best things, when we can get them. But we have the exhibits anyway—and when they are cheap, we are sure they are not all bad. We show the work of the schools, of course, and wish we had more opportunities to show it.

The details would make another long chapter. Our objectives are not all esthetic. We furnish much illustrative material for geography, history, and storytelling; and our portraits, of course, are chiefly for history and biography. But all the time we have in mind the exaltation of the obvious and everyday thing, the opening of eyes to it, the practice of having an opinion on it, of feeling about it, and tasting it, and so of forming the esthetic habit.

III. You will expect me, as a librarian, to say something about books, of course, and I shall recommend to you two. They have to do chiefly with the manual training side of your work, an aspect of it which my remarks may seem, on the surface, to have scarcely touched. But if I have read your papers and proceedings and your journals aright, then you are bringing into very close relations the two subjects, drawing, design, color, "art," and handwork. This is as it should be. You are finding strength in union here. And I am sure that most of you can read into my remarks references to the handicraftsman which do not appear on the surface. This is already evident, that the teacher of drawing and art in the schools is going to get the strongest and best argument for the continuance and the expansion of her work from the relations it will have with things made with the hands.

The two books, then, though both industrial, are not here out of place. They are:

1. *Report of the Commission on Industrial Education,* made to the Massachusetts Legislature this year. This is published by the state of Massachusetts and is obtainable, I suppose, free on request. It is a very important document, one sure to have much influence. It contains a very able and interesting letter by one of your members, Mr. Warner of the Springfield, Massachusetts, Manual Training High School.
2. *Industrial Efficiency*—a comparative study of industrial life in England, Germany, and America. By A. Shadwell, Longmans. '06, 2v. $7.00. The first and the last chapters are especially worthy of attention. They will be found excellent for tempering one's national pride.

IV. In conclusion, let me ask: If you could control the art teaching in the United States, and had a moderate amount of money and a few good teachers, what would you do? This is your question. I think you would look with favor on the suggestion that you begin in the homes. You would encourage in them restraint, simplicity, strength. You would begin with those things seen by most people and most dear to them. Does your work reach the home sufficiently? As much as it can? This step taken, the successive ones are obvious.

But, you will say, you are in the schools and are there held down to certain definite work. In this work, it would seem you should aim to do these things:

1. Teach a *few* (perhaps one in 40) to draw well.
2. Teach a *few* to use color well.
3. Teach a *few* to model well.
4. Teach a *few* to draw for construction well.
5. Teach a *few* to design well.
6. Teach a *few* to use tools well.

The others, the majority, you should test occasionally to see if they have developed either the taste or skill and then let them alone as far as technique of hand or eye is concerned. You should also:

7. Give all some skill in reading pictures.
8. Invite all to observe with care.
9. Teach a few to observe well.
10. Urge all to question their likes and dislikes.
11. Teach a few to criticize keenly.

The sum of this is, do not waste time, yours or the students, in training in a special line those not born to be trained in that line.

As I have said, I have read your proceedings and find nearly all I have been saying in them, and many other good things also. You have helped modern education very much. If you had done nothing but add to it a certain breadth and humanity which before it sadly lacked you would have earned your meager stipends many times over.

In view of the limitations under which you have worked your progress has been most gratifying; every unprejudiced observer will say this: I think the European critics of our institutions frankly admit it.

Just one every day suggestion: You have a special advantage in your propaganda work in that the results of your efforts are visible. The teacher who helps a class to master addition cannot hang her pupils' little brains on a burlap screen and point with pride to their arithmetic lobes! While the teacher who can show rows and garlands of boxes and flowers and designs and mats is thought to have done wonders with the little dears. You should make more of this advantage. You need more publicity. The people don't know what you are aiming at. Keep telling them. Frequent expositions in print and frequent displays of work will help us to realize that you are trying to teach children to see clearly, to discriminate, to feel; and will help to cultivate in the people themselves that practice of liking and disliking common things which is, in effect, the habit of being esthetic.

American Art: How It Can Be Made to Flourish

There Is Very Little of It

When I reflect on the words American art, many things come into my mind: such, for example, as tableware, cutlery, table linen, chairs, and tables; draperies and wallpapers; houses, churches, banks, office buildings, and railway stations; medals and statues; books, journals, signs, and posters; lamp posts and fountains; jewelry, silverware, clocks, and lamps; carpets and rugs; laces, embroideries, and ribbons; vases and candlesticks; etchings, engravings, drawings—and paintings.

Then I ask myself, do we in America, when we make these things, commonly give them that indescribable touch which turns each of them into an object of art, an object, that is, which gives continuing pleasure to discriminating persons of experience in such matters? And I answer my question by saying no.

Though we are very numerous, very prosperous, and very rich; though we spend millions on education and on the whole are perhaps the most competent people on earth, we do not yet produce much that the calm observer may call beautiful. We buy our objects of art from other countries; we educate our artists in other countries; we borrow designs for decorating almost everything we make, or we import foreign-made designers; and for an art journal we steal a corner of one published in England, call the whole thing international to hide the theft, and publish none of our own worthy of the name.

Do I say there is no American art? By no means. I say that of art objects pure and simple, of our own make, and of objects made beautiful by the application of ornament of our own designing and applied by our own artisans, we produce, in spite of our numbers, prosperity, and wealth, very, very few.

Hill-of-Corn Series, no. 1. Woodstock, Vt.: The Elm Tree Press, first printing, 1914; second printing, 1929.

II. Why There Is So Little American Art

I have hinted at what I include in the term American art. Before attempting to make that statement clearer, let me say that there are sufficient reasons for our failure to produce more than a few art objects which are worthy of note. The reasons are simply these: (1) we are too busy, and (2) our rich buy art objects elsewhere!

We are rather energetic. We began life with a picked lot of stiff-necked and rebellious people, people who found irksome the curbs that the conventions of their old home put on them, and were quite ready and willing to accept hardships and serious toil if they could thereby win a living and meanwhile be free of those curbs. Even to this day our numbers are almost hourly recruited by those who have chafed under the discipline of ancient circumstance and have come here ready to be tireless in accomplishment, if only they can acquire. We are born, that is, to wish to do—if thereby we can earn. Nature has set a very fertile country here before us, and we are now busily at work therein, with quite admirable results.

III. Play and Art

We have at last put our affairs in such good order that we can spare a little time for play. But a people may take quite freely of recreation and still not find itself ready for the enjoyment and patronage of art. Play represents the agreeable release of certain surplus energy; art appreciation seems to represent the agreeable release of certain rather definitely trained surplus emotions.

The surplus energy is ours by reason by our nature, our high standard of living, and our abundant and easily conquered resources. The surplus emotions are perhaps ours also, but it has not yet occurred to us so to train them that their exercise will give us deep and varied pleasures.

Our rich and learned, and especially the women of the rich and learned class, can spare time and strength for the opera, but hardly for a discriminating study of music. They can find time for visits to an art museum when such visits are the mode, but not for the development of the aesthetic sense by the careful study of any of the thousands of classes of objects there displayed. They can find time for art lectures at a club, but not to read a sound book on any art topic, or to collect with discretion and taste art objects of any kind.

We seem to have been born with the work habit and with endless opportunity and some press of need for its exercise; we are acquiring the play habit as our gains begin to outrun our needs; but we have slight leanings yet toward that art habit which calls for a careful training of our unexpended fund of feelings. This is not because we are less artistic than other peoples, but because we have not had time and inclination to give heed to objects of art.

IV. Artists and Artisans Are Here, But Are Not Paid to Produce

Among us, as among all other peoples, a few men and women are born with the desire to spend their lives in acquiring high skill in some craft and in applying that skill to the production of useless objects of beauty and the adornment of objects of daily use. These persons are born and live among us; but, while the consummate genius among them may survive and prove his powers in spite of lack of support and sympathy, the most of them are either never stimulated to serious endeavor, or are never aroused to an appreciation of their talent by any atmosphere of art patronage that we supply.

V. Genius and Talent Remain Hidden Until They Are Called Forth

Some say there never was a mute, inglorious Milton—that all high talent inevitably finds its way to accomplishment. But can we believe that if we gave as loud and insistent a call, and one as profitable to those who answer it, for sculpture, or for autumn landscapes in oil, or for tapestries, or for porcelains, as we have given in recent years for automobiles, we would not have found an ample response from men and women of notable talent? The rich among us have, in recent years, spent many millions for paintings by foreign painters and for rare and ancient curios of other lands. Had that money been offered for worthy products of native talent, would not the worthy products have appeared? No one can give any sound reason for believing they would not. It is easy to show by example that they would.

VI. The Italian Renaissance Came When It Was Paid to Come

The rich and powerful leaders of men and affairs in Italian cities 400 and 500 years ago found that they must mark themselves as a distinct and superior class, not merely by showing that they possessed high intellectual powers through their conduct of war and affairs, but also by a certain display of wealth. They found that to hold their standing as persons peculiarly blessed by providence—as notoriously good, great, and noble—they must do certain things and possess certain things, the doing of which and the possession of which would be accepted as honorific by the common people. They acted upon this conclusion, just as have all the groups of rich, great, and powerful men of historic times. They demanded palaces for homes. They took up pastimes which only the rich and powerful could take part in. They acquired rich and costly clothing. They built and endowed churches and erected elaborate and costly shrines and altars. They made collections of paintings, marbles, bronzes, and curios of a thousand kinds.

Some of these things they could cause to be brought from other countries, and those thus obtained, especially if rare, costly, and unobtainable by others, acquired thereby an added honor-giving power. For to the desire to do and to possess things which gave them distinction in the eyes of the populace, was added the desire to outdo their wealthy and powerful rivals in the pursuit of that same distinction.

Thus far the case of the Italian aristocrats runs parallel with that of our own. Here and today the wealthy are impelled, first, to distinguish themselves from the common, poorer people by conspicuous consumption and conspicuous waste and, next, to outdo their equals in wealth by the acquisition of costly and curious objects, so rare that their colleagues in wealth cannot acquire the counterparts thereof.

The use of wealth in enhancing distinction has followed a like custom with Italian nobles and rich Americans. But the former found that the supply of honor-bringing curios was small and its source remote. He was soon compelled to call on the people of his own country to create those elaborate labor-consuming products which he needed to serve as stigmata of social distinction. He asked for tapestries, silks, wood carvings, ironwork, bronzes, silverware, jewelry, and a thousand other things. He insisted that these be larger, finer, more costly, more bizarre, more glorious, and more labor consuming and skill demanding than those his rivals, in the search for honor-bringing possessions, had yet discovered and acquired. These were not to be found in the east or in France; or, if found, were not sufficient to the special needs of his own person or his own palace. He proceeded straightway to command Italian artists and Italian artisans to produce them, and the renaissance in fine arts was forthwith on its way.

VII. The American Renaissance Is Not Even Courteously Invited to Appear

With us the conditions are far different. Our rich find an ample supply of honorific curios in the relics of European and Asiatic civilizations. They buy the Barbizon painting and the Gothic shrine; they enrich the forger and they rifle the ancient temple. Modern methods of trade and transportation bring within range of their purses the choicest of the remains of a dozen civilizations, in each of which conditions like those in Italy in 1500 persuaded genius and skill to produce art objects in countless curious forms.

Indeed, so ample is the supply of honor-bringing curios that the race for distinction in art patronage among our very rich long since ceased to be one of taste and has become one merely of length of purse.

Meanwhile, it is not as it was in Italy with artists and artisans. They were commanded to produce, and at times the commands were even guided by a discriminating taste. Here our artists and artisans are continuously ignored. Their products are not needed as prizes in the race for distinction in curio-acquisition; genius, talent, and patiently acquired skill are not called forth, and America has neither artists nor artisans—and there is very little American art!

VIII. Our View of What Is Art Is Much Too Narrow

Returning to the things that the phrase American art brings to mind, I would say that I named them because I wish to show that we habitually take far too narrow a view of the art field.

Most of us like to work. But work does not exhaust the possibilities of enjoyment, and idling has large and continued possibilities of pleasure only for the unfortunate few. Play has narrow limits to its powers of pleasing. Only by making a game serious and letting it ape the manners of a task can we long tolerate it; and, lacking productive or creative features, it does not, even when masked as labor, long entirely satisfy. But our nature is such that—even after we have brought body and brain measurably near to the point of exhaustion either by work or by play masquerading as work—we still have on hand a surplus of feeling. This surplus we can, if we will, use for the production of high and simple pleasures in the contemplation of what, for lack of a better phrase, we call objects of art.

I venture to restate the thought in other words: To get the maximum out of this short life, we must take delight in our feelings. We can work, and win the race, and add house to house and land to land; but if we do not at the same time have the daily and hourly pleasure of alert and intelligent response to the fine and delicate and thoughtful and genius-born design, ornament, and decoration which are always before us, then we live only a fraction of the life it is possible to live.

Granted that there are degrees among us as to the possibilities of cultivating this emotion. Some can delight gloriously in a bit of machine-made molding in the jamb of a door or the sill of a window if they find its curves evince thought and refined taste in the one who designed it; while some are unmoved even before a splendid bronze or a glowing canvas.

IX. The Oil Painting Fetish

But in general this is true: that life is measured by its thrills. His good day's work, his game well played, and the art that genius sets before him—each of these should furnish delights, and the latter can give easily the most, and some of the deepest, and some of the most lasting.

Now, genius sets art before us in many forms. One of these forms, painting, has long received more than its due share of attention. Few men of art genius have the special genius for painting. The number of wood paintings produced in a generation is consequently small; being much in demand they are high in price and are bought only by the wealthy. The result is that few can see good paintings save by making visits to a distant museum.

If it is true that it is well to broaden and enrich life by agreeable reactions, and that these may best be acquired by educating ourselves to respond eagerly when we look upon objects of art, then it is also true that we should learn how to secure those reactions in and by the presence of objects of art which are of less rarity and of less cost than paintings.

In other words, if you wish to get all the enjoyment that your capacities permit out of the beautiful creations of your fellow men, you must learn to see and feel the beauty that lies in the good engraving, etching, tapestry, bronze, wood carving, chair, table, lace, molding, façade, and countless other objects of pure or applied art.

X. The Study of American Art Defined

To learn to know and feel this beauty in everyday objects which have been produced in America—this is to study American art. It is not to read works on aesthetics or on the history of art production, though such reading may prove entertaining and even helpful in your study proper. It is not, save in slight degree, to make an occasional pilgrimage to an art gallery, though this may be worthwhile if only to enable you to keep up with that conversational procession in which at times we all must march. It is not to parade with guidebook, guide, or professional aesthete through the art galleries of Europe, though this may give us some of the peace that comes with consciousness of duty done.

It is, first, to observe with care one or several of the many classes of objects which our artists and artisans are producing and trying to make beautiful in line, form, arrangement, and color; to observe them with care; to decide if, regardless of price, they please a little, or much, or not at all; to learn of their many kinds; of the manner of their making; of the skill that goes into their production; of the changes they have undergone in their development, and, finally—always finally—to learn what is said of them by those competent to speak thereon.

XI. The Importance of Being Interested and Critical

In art matters, it is more important to be sensitive than to be knowing; it is better worthwhile to feel that a thing is right for you and to get pleasure with the feeling than it is to know who made it and when, where it was made and under what conditions, who has owned it, who now owns it, what he paid for it, and what great critics have said of it.

If you cultivate your sensibilities by the keen observation and careful criticism of everyday, familiar objects, you cultivate thereby the whole aesthetic side of your nature almost as effectively—and in view of the multiplicity of opportunities which these ever-present objects offer, even more effectively and certainly more rapidly—than by the observation, for example, of the world's masterpieces of painting.

At the bottom of all visual arts are certain elements—line, form, arrangement, let us say—which may be studied in the simple pen-and-ink sketch which appears in a monthly journal or in the cup which serves its humble purpose on the breakfast table, almost as well as in the façade of a cathedral, in the glory of a splendid painting, or in the glow of an ancient porcelain.

XII. Art Study Should Be Domesticated

Furthermore, if you school yourself with moderate effort to look for beauty and for ugliness also—for it is in seeing both the wrong and the right in art objects that emotional discipline and art culture come—if you look with care for the good and the ill in the objects that lie about you daily, you do it without the distractions that encompass you on a visit to a gallery of art. For here you are conscious of 10,000 votes already cast in praise of what you see, and you cannot set your judgment free of them. You see with others' eyes, not with your own. Even if you dare be true to yourself and secretly admit your failure to find the pleasure that others find in a Monet or Cézanne or an Italian primitive, you probably have not the courage of expression; and you come away not more acutely sensitive to good painting, but simply more sinful in pretense.

And again, even if you are able to look at a painting, fair and true, and to say to yourself that regardless of the world's judgment, this and that are what you find it to add to your enjoyment, you quite probably are so taken up with what the painting tells, what sort of a person the painter of it was, how he looked and what his morals were, when he lived and where, and, especially, how much the painting cost, that, hedged in by questions of morals, history, biography, and finance, you have no fair look whatever at the painting itself.

The study of American art, then—the study of how to develop one's appreciation and enjoyment of American-made art objects—properly begins with the collection, the careful study, the critical observation of all objects of art—and they not necessarily the best—which are made in America.

One need not complain that American art is a mere copy of the art of other countries, for art is always largely a copy of what has preceded it, plus the something which makes it art. One need not lament the lack of sincerity in American art and its contrast in that respect with the art, for example, of the Italian Renaissance; for the sincerity is not lacking now and here and was not notably present in the days of Raphael.

The thesis here laid down is simply this: Art has a wider field and therefore offers more possibilities of pleasure than most of us have recognized. We in America have not produced much good art because we have been too busy adjusting a growing colony to a new land, and because our rich acquire distinction in curios bought in other countries. We can best study art to the end of becoming sensitive to it, which means becoming aesthetic, by observing it and criticizing it, and especially in all its more familiar forms.

XIII. How to Become Patrons of American Art

If what I have ventured to affirm is true, it is easy to learn from it how we may promote American art, how we may become worthy and helpful patrons of it in the best sense of the word.

The formula is very simple: First, we must buy it; next we must study it; next we must criticize it, adversely where we feel compelled; and, finally, we must praise it where we can.

In buying, with the patronage of art in view, we must of course discriminate. To be able to discriminate to good purpose, to the end that we may encourage the serious and accomplished artist, and, by neglect, discourage the pretender, we must seriously study our subject. Unless one is rarely gifted and has an intuitive knowledge of what is fine and sound and wholesome and enduring in all departments of art—and very few are so gifted—one must select a narrow field, study it, master it as far as ability and opportunity permit, become in it an expert, or, better, become in it what we may call, to render freely the French phrase, an honest amateur.

XIV. The Great Obstacle to Becoming an Honest Art Patron

Now, if any chance to feel tempted to take up art in this simple, honest, everyday sense and, holding themselves in all other fields to the acquisition of objects of the simplest and most frankly utilitarian kind, devote themselves to one special field, inform themselves concerning it, buy objects in it with some freedom, always expecting to learn from each purchase how to select more wisely for the next one—if any do this with the hope of becoming one of the blessed and ever-joyful company of honest amateurs, they will find at least one serious obstacle to progress.

This obstacle is the result of the combination of some of the factors already spoken of: our native energy and our natural resources. These have worked together to make us, as it were, wealthy before our desserts. There is, no doubt, a time for riches; but it were well for art if that time did not so often come so soon. With us the power of acquisition has outpaced the growth of capacity for appreciation and enjoyment. We like to get things; but, having them, it often happens that the only form of enjoyment in them that occurs to us is to show them. To put it another way, our mental and aesthetic equipment is not up to the level of our wealth. We have been so busy sowing and hoeing and garnering in nature's garden that we have not taken time to practice intensive agriculture on our own intellects. As a nation, we are as smart as we think we are, I guess; surely we are not as wise.

XV. A Definite Suggestion for Art Patronage

The phrase which describes quite well the obstacle to the art study and art patronage which I have recommended is "spendthrift mediocrity." It denotes a national tendency. It does not make for the promotion of good art.

Abundant suggestions are at hand for guidance in the task of patronizing American art. Here is one: Study your teacups. The drinking vessel of everyday use is an object on which those endowed with the creative art faculty have spent time, care, labor, and high skill for many thousands of years. It has taken a million forms and has been adorned in a million ways. The whole field of drinking vessels is too large for anyone to attempt to master; but the teacup of today, as made in America, and better still as made in America in the last 10 years, would be an object about which one might hope in time to learn something.

To study art as exemplified in teacups of today may sound a trivial suggestion. Surely it is not. It can open up the wide topics of line, form, color, and arrangement, and help one to become discriminating in all art fields, if one has capacity for discrimination. Remember, also, that if even a few only of our citizens were to give time, thought, and a modicum of money to the purchase and study of present-day teacups, the designers in our potteries would know it and would be encouraged thereby. These designers must chiefly design what will appeal to spendthrift mediocrity, but that is not the kind of work for which inspired designers feel they are born; and for them to learn that even a few of their fellows have determined to master the elements of good taste as they may be exemplified in the products of their skill, will give them encouragement akin to that which the nobles gave to artist and artisans in Florence 500 years ago.

Art has always flourished where it was asked to flourish, and never elsewhere. If we wish for a renaissance of art in America, we must be students and patrons of endeavors which seem humble but are in truth of the utmost importance, here at home. If American art does not flourish, it will not be because we are too rich, or unduly sordid, or insincere; but because we refuse to become discriminating patrons of the everyday good things our fellow citizens can produce if a kindly interest stimulate them thereto.

The Use of Museums

Our art museums do not teach us to recognize good art and to like it; they do not help to improve the design of our manufactured products; they do not encourage such of our people as are born with talent or genius for drawing, painting, and designing to give their lives to the development and training of that talent or genius.

Let me hasten to say that art museums do encourage the collection and preservation of valuable objects; and that the objects they collect will someday probably be of definite aesthetic influence.

A recent magazine article written by a worker in and a special pleader for the Metropolitan Museum of Art in New York says very truly that we are in error when we set apart fine arts and applied; that in fact both are noble. He adds, not quite so truly, that machine production of applied art objects has, in the minds of the critical, in some degree degraded applied arts. Then he says, truly, that we can ennoble the applied arts once again by the slow process of education in taste, with accompanying production of such designers as will teach our machines to produce applied art objects which are in fact of the fine art brotherhood.

It is his next step which parts him from me, and, I even dare say, from common sense; for he goes on to a description of the influence of art museum collections on design, and arrives at the opinion, which is, I must confess, rather cryptically expressed, that only in the objects of a museum of art like the Metropolitan can designs be found which, being made the bases of designs for machine-made goods, can cause our machines to produce applied art objects that are veritably in the fine art field.

Do I make clear the essential point in the Metropolitan's claim? It is that no design is good unless it is based upon study of old designs which are themselves good; and that good old designs, which will alone lead the student to the making

---

The Nation 115, no. 2988 (October 11, 1922).

of good new ones, are found almost solely in art museums, and notably in the Metropolitan. To put it more bluntly: The Metropolitan management, if one may judge of its opinions from the essay alluded to and from other written expressions by the same official, seems to hold that the only real, true, and holy art is found in the objects it has gathered; that it is conferring a blessing on manufacturers in permitting their designers to visit the Metropolitan and there draw real art motives from its treasures; and that it is this studying and copying and adapting of designs found in its objects by agents from a few of our tens of thousands of factories that is leading to improvement in our applied art products.

These assumptions ignore the facts of manufacture and trade. To name only one group of these facts, our own department stores alone sell thousands of millions of dollars worth of goods each year. These goods are "objects," the vast majority of which are "designed" to be attractive. Whence come the "motives" for all these thousands of designs? From other objects and from suggestions in books and journals, of course; all being somewhat affected by the ideas in the heads of buyers for big corporations, of sellers, of the general buying public, and of the foremen, owners, and hired designers in mills. What is the motive power behind all the millions of choices made by millions of our fellows, of shape, pattern, design, color, and whatnot in the objects they buy? The taste of the buying public, of course.

Every maker of things in this country, and every buyer for big stores, and every salesman of things made, never forgets for a moment that the goods they produce or buy or sell depend for their success in the market on their fitting the choice or taste of that market. And that market is the people of these United States. Every day into thousands of planning and forecasting minds comes the question, "What shall we do to our products to make them more alluring to our market? We must, of course, simplify our tools, produce goods at less cost, transport them more easily and more cheaply; but—and this is of chief importance—we must also make them more 'tasty'; that is, we must fit them more closely to the likes, the wishes, the opinions of our buying public."

And what is the chief factor in the formation of the taste of the buying public? It is fashion, convention, what "they say," of course. And how is this fashion modified, for modified it is every day and hour and notably every year? By the goods themselves, which the public sees disposed before their eyes in shops, in pictured advertisements, including fashion papers, and set forth in millions of journals and daily papers every year, and by other factors too numerous to mention here, of which the study of rare and costly objects in museums of art is so slight as to be entirely negligible.

Every year the buying public of this country learns more of the ways of the world. In movies, in illustrated advertisements, in picture journals, and by travel in trains and motors, in walks by shop windows, and in daily conversations, this buying public acquires a wider and fuller knowledge of what the world has produced for its pleasure and for the adornment of life. Every year this buying public brings to its judgment of what is new in the design of things offered to it for selection a fuller background of observations and experience; and every year—if increase of knowledge does in truth modify favorably, as we all assume it does, the fine art of choice—the buying public selects, on the whole, things that are a little finer than were those they selected the year before. Hence good design finds more often an appreciative observer, and hence design in the products of American mills improves.

The current assumption of those who think the objects in museums of art are powerful factors in improving public taste ignores the mighty flood of impulse for better things which pours daily through the nationwide process of selection just outlined. That assumption bases itself on the facts that in museums of art are objects which, having been approved by the few who are expert in such matters, are working wonders in the improvement of public taste.

In passing we do well to remind ourselves that the expert few are lamentably prone to think knowledge of things ancient is synonymous with a heaven-born sensibility to their beauty, and are inevitably touched by that affection for the old, the rare, and the costly which belongs of right only to the archaeologist, the ethnologist, the scientist, the historian, and the wealthy amateur.

The man who has much faith in art museums may even go so far as to assert that better design can come forth and win recognition in a country such as is our own today only by and through the processes of persuading all producers to base the designs of their products on the designs of the past; and to assert, further, that as the best designs of the past are found only in the objects in his museum, it is only by a careful adherence in design today to the motives found in the objects in his museum that any progress toward making fine art of our applied art products can be secured.

It may be true that most designing has a fairly well-defined history; that it passed on from Egypt, Crete, Assyria, and Persia to Greece and to Rome and to the Renaissance, and even to the Gothic. It may be true that he designs best who knows the most of what has been well esteemed in design prior to his day. Design has passed from hand to hand, it is true; but whence the new touches therein? Why did it widen its range? When did it pass from temple column and sacrificial knife to ship's prow and water container? Surely all design for all things did not come forth complete as one grand gift of the thoughts and passions of one man of genius. To it 10,000 times 10,000 originating brains added here a new thing and there another and another, up to millions of motives, plans, arrangements, colors, outlines, and masses. Did China bend the knee of copyist and modifier to the products of Egypt and Assyria and Greece that it might produce its millions of alluring objects? Did Japan add nothing fundamental to the lessons learned of Korea and China? Where did the Maori of New Zealand get the laws and principles of historic ornament in obedience to which he wrought his decorations? And the same query jumps to the mind as one considers the Maya temples of Yucatan, and the textiles of the Peruvian graves, and the potteries and basketry of our Indians. And to come to a homely query born of our times and our own products: "If the International Harvester Company wishes to beautify by colored paints the marvelous mechanism which, in marching across a field of wheat, reaps and threshes and cleans and bags and ties and drops the ripened grain, where, in the history of design, will it get the motives, tried and true and infallible, which, being duly used as a guide, will disclose the ornamentation divinely appointed for an American Harvester of 1922?"

In this country there are born each year, one may safely assume, as many persons in each 10,000 who are by nature capable of adding somewhat to the joy of life by giving a new and welcome touch of difference to objects of daily use as were ever born among any people in any age. But we are heirs of all past ages and borrowers from all other people to greater degree than was ever any people before. At first we brought all our "art" from other countries. When we learned to make things, we borrowed the art of decorating them. Then riches came, and inevitably those who had them used them to bring here those veritable objects of art, approved by experts, which gave distinction to their owners. Then came the rich endowed museums, in which things other than the old and rare and costly are anathema. And soon the keepers of these objects, which time had hallowed and the student had sanctified and the price had made to speak with tongues—these keepers said: "By the study of our objects you get the secret of beauty, and only by and through that study can you learn how to give to the products of your mills and the gift of that beauty." And thereby they did all that they could, though fortunately little, to suppress the creative and designing mind, and art did not here flourish, because art does not thrive except in freedom of restraint and cannot thrive unless it is encouraged by patronage.

But fortunately the museum is but a tiny thing in the midst of our vast movement of production and consumption; while in and by that movement is growing steadily a skill in choice backed by wider and fuller knowledge; which is but another way of saying that our taste is improving.

In the hope that I may make a little clearer the special point of my criticism, I add three things. First, this: As a nation we ignore our own artistic powers, not entirely but greatly. Being inheritors of all that artists have ever done, we are not interested in pro-

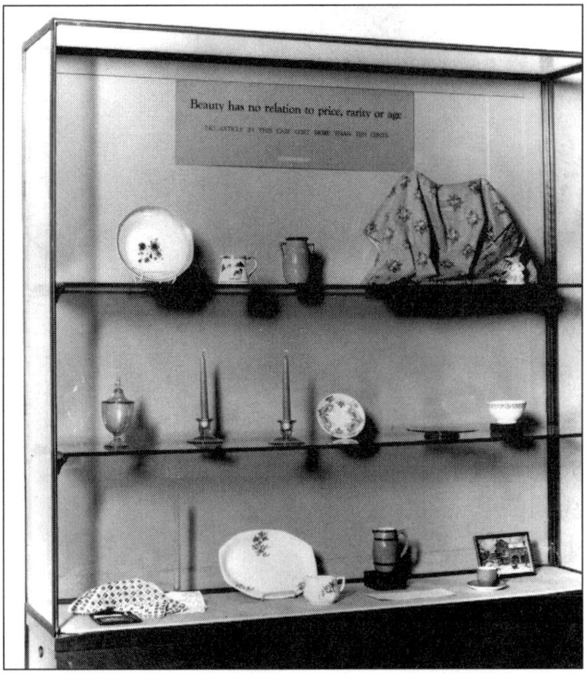

John Cotton Dana believed that "beauty has no relation to price, rarity, or age." These objects were on display at the Newark Museum in 1928.

ducing artists ourselves. For example, one of our skillful potters makes beautiful china; but to sell it he must refuse credit for himself, his designers, and his artisans and permit it to be marked as "French Ware." A silk manufacturer does the same, and we may easily believe thousands of others do like things in some degree. In the mere matter of production the resulting evil here is slight; but in the field of artistry, in the matter of giving our designers and craftsmen a fair chance, it is serious in the extreme. It betokens a sad state of mind; a state of mind which the museum that devotes its collecting powers almost solely to things produced in other lands, and to products of native talent not at all, does its utmost to make permanent and universal.

Second, this: That nearly all talk of art, as it comes out in the public press and is exuded from museum experts, is first and foremost about oil paintings and next of things rare, old, and costly. Now, taste is something to be bettered by exercise. The general feeling is that taste may be exercised only in the presence of real art. But if taste is to be bettered for our general aesthetic welfare, the average citizen must be helped to realize that taste is not a rare and recondite thing to be brought forth and used only when he enters a gallery of paintings or a museum of art; but is merely a certain aspect of the process of choosing which he constantly practices. He should be led to see and feel that he is dealing in "art" matters, is exercising aesthetic emotions, is learning to be a "critic of art," is strengthening his "taste," just as much when he selects a cravat or a table cover or a rug or a chair as when he goes to a museum and looks at rare, curious, costly, and confessedly beautiful things. Having thus come to realize that art concerns him daily and almost hourly, he will see how remote from daily life is most art talk; how near to daily life is design; how important in daily life is the born designer; and he will transfer to the designer of good umbrella handles some of the veneration and worship which he has been accustomed to give only to oil paintings and rare, old, and costly objects.

Third, this: Two mental movements, by some called habits, are of great social importance: one, imitation, which fits the average child to his social environment, giving him the politics, morals, and religion of his fathers, all to be held pertinaciously through life though backed by no reasons why; the other, curiosity, which leads to inquiry, acceptance or rejection of things, to discovery, invention, adaptation, and design. Imitation leads to copying; curiosity leads to thinking. Imitation is the stronger movement, and usually prevails; and in the guise of conservatism forbids modifications of manners and beliefs. Curiosity and resulting thought, insofar as they may prevail, permit us to pass on. A people which accepts its art from its forebears as a finished thing and forbids all the invention and design that thinking inevitably begets—such a people is purely imitative. It likes to think that the book of design is closed; it puts what has been done in a museum and says to the curious, inquiring, inventive, and designing: "You may come here and borrow ideas; those you may give birth to yourselves are not the children of imitation and should be throttled at birth."

In a land where what has already been done in art is enshrined as the last word, where imitation is encouraged, and the product of inquiry is condemned because it is not the child of convention and conservatism, what chance has the artisan, the designer, the artist who are creators—or nothing?

The Museum as an Art Patron

Some museums have grown; others have been made to order.

In Munich is the National Museum of Bavaria. It has a beautiful home into which have been gathered objects illustrating the story of the life of man in what is now Bavaria for nearly 3,000 years.

How the objects that form the museum came to be brought together I do not know; but one sees at a glance that here is no made-to-order collection, but one that has come out of the very life of the Bavarian people as they have slowly climbed to their present high estate.

The museum that is made to order, not being a natural product of the activities of the community in which it appears, is the child of a passing fashion; is built about a fixed idea of what a museum should be; does not represent or issue from the life of the people by whom it is brought into being. The National Museum of Bavaria is a series of original documents produced in Bavaria and picturing its history for 3,000 years, and can be truly said to have grown. Of many of the museums in Europe the same thing may be said. They present, through the objects in them displayed, much of the domestic, civil, religious, and martial life of the communities in which they are found.

They are by no means all of equal interest, at all times, to the people whose ancestors they owe their existence. This is partly because the interest taken by any community in the life of previous generations varies from time to time, both in intensity and direction. But a museum that is made of objects which were wrought out, in the course of years, by the hands of a given group of people is each year almost inevitably of increasing value to that group, even if it be, at any given period, not of wide popular interest.

The willful queen of Frank Stockton's story made a collection of buttonholes, they being artifacts in which she was herself intensely interested.[1] She placed them in a

Creative Art 4, no. 3 (March 1929).

museum building and insisted that her subjects visit them, enjoy them, and take profit from seeing them. She carried her theory so far that most of her subjects, having found her museum a quite intolerable bore, cheerfully chose to live in jail rather than make a second visit to it.

That queen is fairly typical of the creators of the made-to-order museum. They do not ask what a community wishes to see in a museum. They assume to know what it will do a community good to see, and proceed to supply it. Their collecting proclivities are almost purely the children of precedent. They have noted that the cities of Europe have made vast collections of objects which are ancient, rare, and often beyond price. These collections give prestige to the cities which possess them, are visited by tourists from other countries, and are of value to a few students of the histories of the arts. Those who direct museums in this new country of ours quite illogically draw from the existence of such foreign museums two erroneous conclusions. The first is that these collections have stimulated art production in the communities which have made them, and are the prime predisposing reason why art production has flourished in those communities. The second error follows naturally from the first, and is that similar collections, arbitrarily made in the new cities of a new world, will be primary causes of art production in those new countries. Hence we have in America made-to-order museum collections imitating similar collections in Europe. As one American city after another becomes the home of wealthy citizens, they hasten to gather valuable collections and to house them in buildings of great cost and of a style that convention demands, with the unfortunate result that each newly filled American museum has a collection of ancient, unique, and highly priced objects which is inferior to the one that last preceded it in the collecting process.

II. I venture to repeat my statement. The people of the Old World have, each in that period of its life when the urge for the production of beautiful things was upon it, brought forth art objects, in one or many fields, that still arouse joy in those capable of appreciating them. By many and varied ways, certain of these beautiful productions came into museums and were there preserved. The proponents of "museums of museum pieces" for American cities say, in effect, "What has been done in the Old World can be done in the New. Museum collections of things old, unique, and costly have there been one of the great proximate causes of the production of art; they will be with us like agencies developing taste and calling forth talent."

The absurdity of this assumption surely need not be presented. No one knows why a people have a desire for beautiful things and an accompanying ability to create them. Even of the Renaissance in Italy it cannot be said that it was caused by the sight of such beauty, fashioned by the Greeks, as came within reach of Italy's vision in the early days of her awakening. Of this, on the other hand, we can be fairly well assured that artist and craftsman come forth and create and construct only when they can gain, by so doing, a certain due esteem and perhaps also a living wage. If the eyes of a people are turned eagerly toward things that have been wrought out in other lands and in ancient times; if the purses of a people are opened wide for the purchase and the fashionable and costly installation of the products of artists of other days, and are opened grudgingly, if at all, for the patronage of men and women of the present day and hour who wish to create beautiful things and ask only for an opportunity to try so to do—then the age of art for that people is surely not at hand.

III. It is not necessary to name any of the cities that have in recent years given hostages to the art productions of the past by the erection of ornate and costly buildings in which the past only is to be given space, and thus have cut themselves off from rendering any aid whatever to the artists of today and tomorrow. They are easily found. It may be wise to try to correct, at this point, the impression which these notes may give, that they are purely critical and in no way constructive, by making a few suggestions.

If any American city wishes to be a promoter of interest in, enjoyment of, and appreciation of things in the art field, and thus to stimulate the production of art objects and the development of high technical skill in the arts, let it proceed somewhat as follows:

In the museum building of the city—or if it is already crowded or is remote from the center of the city's daily movement of population or is not adapted to changing displays, then in buildings constructed or rented for the purpose, conveniently located for visitation by average citizens—let it set up a series of exhibits of things currently produced by the artists and workers of its own city and country. Precede and accompany these exhibits by ample statements, in the public press and otherwise, of the reasons why they are to be made and what is hoped to be accomplished by them. This statement can say that the museum of the city is no longer to be simply an object lesson on the achievement of artists, designers, and artisans of other countries and other times; but aims to become also a stimulant to improvement in the arts as practiced in our city and our land today and tomorrow. It hopes it can add to the story, which has long been told by its collections, of what patronage has induced aspiring artists to produce in other times and other conditions, a series of object lessons telling what art is bringing forth in our own time, by reason of the patronage which is here and now offered to that art. It is aware that popular opinion on art is the child of fashion and convention, and that both fashion and convention in this field are, in the main, prod-

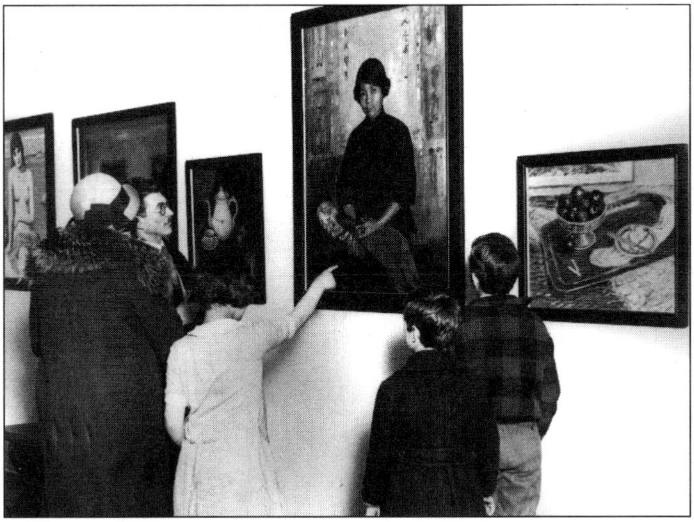

Visitors view an exhibit of works by "Living American Artists" at the Newark Museum, 1927.

ucts of self-constituted connoisseurs who have imbued with their opinions first the wealthy and then the people at large. It has long known that while the outgivings of our own studios and workshops are purchased, used, and enjoyed by the people at large, those same outgivings are frankly looked upon as merely American, as not truly artistic, and to be tolerated only until a product entirely in harmony with rare and costly objects found in our museums can be substituted for them. It seems that while our own output may enjoy a certain passing vogue and may be quite freely purchased, it is not put in the same class with objects which have been heretofore shown in the museum; does not arouse the respect granted freely to the latter; calls forth no special respect for the artists, designers, and artisans who have brought it into being; and leads to no special interest in, and no desire to aid the development of, the practice of the arts in our land.

And, the statement of the museum's new purpose can go on to say, the museum feels that it can, by the plan it is here outlining, persuade a few of our fellow citizens to realize that objects produced for enjoyment and use by any people are always capable of being made more interesting, more attractive, and more completely satisfying—and that the way to make them so is for those who purchase and use them, and live with them, to look upon them more critically; to evaluate more often their qualities; to condemn what they find in them that is silly, meaningless, and mere surplus; to praise in them what they can; and to keep in mind the fact that improvement in design and craftsmanship for objects of any kind never comes as a chance gift of the gods, but out of the desires of the people who are to use them.

IV. Those sentences merely suggest some of the many things that the museum can properly say in its preliminary statements.

As to the things shown in the special exhibits which the museum will hold for the purpose of awakening interest in things designed and made in the city which supports it and in the country of which that city is a part, they will be of such nature and size as conditions indicate. As oil paintings and sculpture come most commonly to the minds of nearly all people when the word "art" is used, and as they involve the fundamentals of well-nigh all of the applied arts, the exhibits may well begin with them. Local artists will be invited to contribute. For some exhibits, a jury of selection may be appointed; for others, not. In a large city which has many artists, each exhibit may be confined to a certain range of subjects. The museum should be able to buy at least a few works from each exhibit, if any are found worthy of purchase. If it cannot do this, it can at least award prizes, even if they are no more than written praises of the best critics obtainable. The museum's purpose is, of course, not to support artists who are not worthy of support; but to stimulate interest in, and in due course intelligent appreciation of, the arts of painting and sculpture as practiced in our land. Most American museums of art seem to spend their money and their efforts in any attempt to suppress as far as possible all demonstrations of the presence in their respective cities of interest in painting by local artists.

The last statement applies to interest in local art production of any kind; also it suggests, better than can any enumeration of details, proper methods of exhibiting, or of the selection of objects for exhibit, in what may be called the museum's "art opportunities." "Opportunities"—this is the word which the unrecognized art worker has chiefly in mind when he asks for a little more than downright ignoring. He is not wishing to be supported in his days of effort, on the chance that he may make good his hopes; but only that he be not considered by the museum of the town and proponents of its methods as being unworthy of notice simply because he is a product of his town.

V. The museum exhibits here suggested may begin with painting and sculpture, and go on to the decorative arts, furniture, textiles, ceramics, and all types of manufactured goods in which beauty and use may go hand in hand. It would be an error to go further into the subject of the kind of things that can be shown in a museum which tries to be a product of present-day artists, designers, and craftsmen. The exhibits should not be large. They should be carefully selected, and so labeled, described, catalogued as to make them easily seen, and their good qualities quickly discovered. The annual expositions of so many different kinds of things as can be crowded into a huge building and are open for a few days only—these have at times been exceedingly useful; but they are not at all what I am trying to suggest.

In almost every line of art and manufacture there is rivalry, not only in the race for cheapness of production, for wearing, and other qualities in the products, but also in the search for looks. It is this endeavor of manufacturers to make their output pleasing to the eye that naturally and necessarily brings machine-made goods into the field of art. We are too prone to think that art is an indefinable somewhat which infects the objects gathered in a museum, and that to the touch of art the products of our factories are quite immune! This curious notion prevails in spite of the fact that the persons in a city, who may be moved to appreciation of the rare and costly object which has been acclaimed as artistic, are at most but a few thousand; whereas the persons who examine with keen interest and with intelligent criticism the countless products of our factories, which are displayed in our stores, are counted by millions. The fact is, of course, that we are as a people studying art, learning to judge and discriminate and choose in well-nigh every moment of our waking lives—and especially when we are selecting things for purchase. But, unfortunately, we do not associate this unceasing practice in art criticism with art, largely, if not chiefly, because we have for so long stupidly accepted as true the claims of the guardians of our museums, and alas! of most of our writers on the arts, that art is something which has attached itself only to the productions of the past, plus a few, a very few, of the things turned out by practicing artists of our own times.

What I have tried to say is that we should cause museums to grow out of the activities that we are now engaged in; and that we should so manage these new museums as to make them a component and helpful part of the efforts of our present-day artists, designers, craftsmen, shop workers, and manufacturers to produce beautiful things, and to add to useful things the somewhat which makes them attractive to the eye. In so doing we shall put into the very field of art the examination, the criticism we all exercise, and the choice we all make in selecting even the humblest of pots and pans.

Editor's note:

1. "The Queen's Museum" by Frank Stockton (1834-1902). Reprinted in *The Storyteller's Pack: A Frank Stockton Reader* (New York: Scribner, 1968).

VIII. Bibliography

John Cotton Dana, Museum Master:
An Annotated Bibliography of Selected Museum Writings

Compiled by Hugh H. Genoways and Mary Anne Andrei

Introduction

Most current museum professionals probably know John Cotton Dana primarily through the writing of Edward Alexander (1983) in *Museum Masters*. As we pursued our interests in the history of museums and museology, we were surprised to find how difficult it was to access many of Dana's original writings. This led us to explore more fully his career and particularly his writing concerning museums. Most of Dana's book-length contributions were published by The Elm Tree Press in Woodstock, Vt., which was operated by Dana and his brothers. Only 300 copies of these books were issued. Many of Dana's shorter contributions appeared in the popular press and literature of the day. These tend to be rather ephemeral in their preservation and present a challenge to bibliographers. However, Dana's ideas were not ephemeral, and many still speak to us today. When we came to know John Cotton Dana better, we realized that these were exactly the types of publishers that he would seek to use. He wanted his ideas to reach the largest possible audience, and he used the popular media of his day to accomplish this goal.

John Cotton Dana came to the museum profession relatively late in his career. He did not have charge of a museum until 1902, when he came to Newark, and his earliest writing on museums appeared in 1905. In 1878 Dana graduated from Dartmouth College. In subsequent years he moved to Colorado for health reasons, then returned to New York to study law. He then moved to Minnesota, where he practiced law for a brief period before returning to Colorado. He engaged in "some insurance and real estate business, some surveying, some preaching in the Unitarian Church, some writing, some reading, and some drafting and construction work" (Lipton 1979, 17). In 1887 he bought a small ranch near Glenwood Springs, Colo., where he farmed and continued to read and write until 1889. In 1888, Dana assumed the position of head librarian of a library established both for students and adults in a new high school building. For the remainder of his life, he served as a librarian. Dana remained in Denver until the end of 1897, when he became the head of the Springfield, Mass., Public Library. A museum of science and a museum of art were associated with this library, but confusion and tension over Dana's relationship with the directors of these units led him to leave at the end of 1901. He took up the position of the librarian of The

Hugh Genoways is chair and professor, Museum Studies Program, and professor, School of Natural Resource Sciences, University of Nebraska-Lincoln. Mary Anne Andrei is currently a Ph.D. candidate in the History of Science and Technology Program, University of Minnesota. At the time this bibliography was compiled, Andrei was a research assistant, The Papers of Geoge Washington, University of Virginia.

Newark Free Public Library at the beginning of 1902, where he remained until his death in 1929. In this position he had a new library building with space for an embryonic museum, thus presenting the opportunity for him to enter the museum profession.

Many of Dana's contributions to museology were first used in the libraries that he directed. He was a leader in the move to open library stacks, to open the library building for community functions, to advertise the library, and to simplify cataloguing techniques. He made library books more available to the public by establishing branch libraries throughout the community. He also created specialized libraries, such as the first business branch library and the first children's reading room (Lipton 1979). Several important biographies of Dana have been written since his death that explore in far more depth the dual careers of this complex and energetic man. Among these biographies (Wisner 1930; Johnson 1937; Kingdon 1940; Hadley 1943; Coffey 1956), we found the one written by Barbara Lipton in 1979 to be the most balanced and insightful.

Dana was a prolific writer, but his publications were primarily in library science and related areas. We would not have been able to draw up our list of Dana's publications in museology without the bibliography prepared by Johnson and Wisner (1937), and not even this extensive list is complete. In selecting the items to be listed herein, we had to make some difficult decisions because some of the papers, particularly those concerning art, are borderline in their importance to museology. We hope that this is a useable list that leads museologists to the rich contributions of John Cotton Dana.

Because Dana's publications are not highly accessible, we have given brief annotations for each so that users can more easily find relevant papers. In recent years, only the four books in the New Museum Series have received extensive review (Cushman 1985). Those readers who devote the time to find and read Dana's original work will discover a store of ideas, many of which did not find widespread acceptance until after his death. Readers will find themes that are repeated in many of Dana's publications, such as museums are educational institutions, museums should be of service to their communities, museums should advertise, the location and architecture of museum buildings should be changed, and applied and industrial arts should be included in museum exhibitions. He pushed the ideas of the establishment of branch museums, the relationship between museums and libraries, and the relationship between museums and schools. In the latter relationship, Dana believed that museums did not have the resources to become a primary provider of formal education; therefore, they should support their local schools through the lending of museum objects. One of his more famous quotes was: "The worth of a museum object is in its use."

His criticism of certain parts of the museum field, particularly art museums and oil paintings by the Old Masters, was harsh. However, upon Dana's death, Robert W. DeForest, president of the Metropolitan Museum of Art, wrote, "The art museums of the country have suffered an irreparable loss in the death of John Cotton Dana. He was an inspiring and redoubtable leader in awakening our art museums and libraries to their real opportunities and in inspiring effective action." At the same time, The Art Center of New York City passed a resolution that stated, in part: "It is known to all that John Cotton Dana was a really important personage in the field of Art in America; that he was esteemed by the best of its leaders; and that his counsel was taken seriously always, and, when followed, as in the creation of The Newark Museum, has produced even epoch-making results in the art world" (Wisner 1930). The ultimate judgment of time has been even stronger, for he is now considered to be one of the founders of the modern museum movement (Coffey 1956; Alexander 1983).

Annotated Bibliography

Undated

"What Ought The Newark Museum to Do?" N.p., n.d. 1 p. The contents of this one-column undated piece would indicate that it was written fairly early in Dana's tenure in Newark. It should be remembered that Dana was a printer himself, and this piece has the look of an item that could have been printed by him to stimulate ideas from visitors to The Newark Free Public Library. Dana states that Newark should be looking for a museum that would be most useful to its community. He believes that there was no model to be followed. The museum should be one that moves Newark toward greater skill in "[t]he arts of living." Dana calls for people to get beyond their preconceived ideas of a museum to find a model that did not fit the old mold.

1905

The Newark Science Museum in The Free Public Library. Newark, N.J.: The Newark Free Public Library, internal date of February 25. 8 pp. This paper gives a brief history of the early development of the science museum and some of Dana's ideas on how the museum should develop. When the new Newark Free Public Library was built, two rooms of about 1,400 square feet each on the fourth floor were left empty and labeled "Science Museum" and "Art Museum." The trustees of the library hoped in this way to stimulate the development of museums, which were not present in Newark. The Science Museum was now ready to open with cases purchased by the library and with collections in botany and mineralogy as the primary display material. Dana points out that Newark did not need a large museum but "a small, practical museum." He calls for a regional museum with illustrative collections rather than comprehensive research collections. Dana also proposes to use duplicates in the collections in portable boxes to be lent to schools. He believes: "A complete museum is an impossibility" because a museum that is alive is "always in the making. . . . A growing museum, even though it is small, stimulates the interest from which it gets its growth."

1906

"The Relation of Art to the Everyday Life." *Newark Sunday Call,* June 24, and "Relation of Art to American Life." *School Arts Book* 6, no. 1 (September): 3-15. Dana discusses the advantages of using common objects to cultivate an aesthetic habit in the art student. He imagines American life as a limitless source of the aesthetic, providing the art teacher with the necessary tools to develop in the student a habit of thinking and feeling critically about art. Dana sees the "masterpiece" as the greatest obstacle to the development of an aesthetic because it had already been judged as good art. Through exposure to, practice with, and suggestion about all the common objects that surround students, the art teacher gives them an opportunity to judge emotionally and critically what they see in doorways and in the daily and monthly newspapers, as well as that hanging on the walls of the Louvre.

1909

"Americans Too Busy to Appreciate Art." *Newark Sunday Call,* December 5. This article is the text of a speech given by Dana to the Woman's Club of Orange, N.J. Dana's main thesis is that Americans had gained wealth, which gave them the "power of acquisition," faster than the growth of their "capacity for appreciation and enjoyment." The primary reason for this problem was that Americans had been too busy making their wealth. Because Americans had not cultivated their sensibilities by "keen observation and careful criticism," they had not encouraged American artists and artisans. Dana urges his listeners to avoid trying to learn about paintings because the only place that they could see them was at "distant museums."

Dana tells his audience to begin learning about American art by studying and collecting teacups. He believes that this would reveal to them such topics as line, form, color, and arrangement. Dana believes that such interest in teacups would encourage the designers of teacups, particularly those in New Jersey, to improve their craft. Dana suggests that other items equally appropriate to collect and study would be wood engravings, door knockers, and the printed book.

1910

"The Beginning of Art in Italy and America." *The Independent* 68 (April 14): 807-810. A visit to Italy confirmed Dana's belief that there has never been an artistic culture. Everywhere in churches, palaces, and public buildings, he saw a lack of originality and an adherence to fashion. Dana is convinced of Veblen's assertion in *The Theory of the Leisure Class* that the development of art in Italy arose from the desire of the rich to make a display of their wealth and education and not a spontaneous emergence of passion for art and learning. This trip further clarifies to Dana that art collecting is a distinctive diversion, separating the recreations of the lower classes from those of the wealthy. Given that the rich possess large and expensive residences, Dana believes that they are compelled to adorn them with elaborate objects. The demand, then, for architects, painters, sculptors, goldsmiths and silversmiths, and other artisans is directly related to this need to acquire unique objects. Patronage determines the supply of art, and good art is determined by the current fashion among the rich. Artists give the rich what they desire. Dana argues that artists and artisans in America would be forthcoming if the current trend would simply shift from ancient European art, which is valued by the rich in America not because it is good art, but because it is difficult to acquire and thus expensive. Dana concludes that art created during the Italian Renaissance should be enjoyed and not worshipped, and that American artists could produce such art if they were afforded more opportunities, esteem, and monetary rewards.

1912

"The German Exhibit of Applied Art: To Be in the Library." *The Newarker* (The Newark Free Public Library) 1, no. 4 (February): 57. Dana announces the coming of an exhibit of German manufactured goods or applied arts. Dana makes the case for having museums or exhibits of applied arts in New Jersey because it is a manufacturing state and returns to the theme of the connection between museums and industries in later papers. Dana makes the point that because the public is learning to discriminate in favor of artistically designed manufactured goods, it is important that Newark manufacturers learn to give their products creative designs or improve them through the applied arts. Dana ends the brief paper with a list of 13 museums in New Jersey that were published in a survey of American museums conducted by the Buffalo Museum of Natural Science.

"Newark's Museums: The Story of Their Development." *The Newarker* (The Newark Free Public Library) 1, no. 5 (March): 76-77. Dana discusses the origin of The Newark Museum. Interest in a museum was generated when The Newark Public Library hosted an exhibit of the George T. Rockwell collection of Japanese art objects. The city of Newark agreed to purchase the collection and to establish a museum association. The association first met on April 29, 1909, and formed a Museum of Science and Art. The objective of the museum was to receive and exhibit articles of art, science, history, and technology.

"Museums Come Because the Public Library Building Came." *The Newarker* (The Newark Free Public Library) 1, no. 10 (August): 164-165. Dana gives a brief history of the first 10 years of The Newark Museum. A private collector, using one of the vacant rooms in The Newark Public Library, founded the museum. After 10 years the museum is occupying several rooms in the library, is presenting public exhibits, and is being operated by The Newark Museum Association. The library purchased such objects as pictures, bronzes, and vases for the collection, which at this time consists primarily of art objects.

"Art Museum Palaces." *New York Times*, October 31, p. 12, col. 7. Dana's thesis in this newspaper article is that American art museums are ineffective. He attributes the look of these museums to the fact that art was originally the property of royalty and therefore housed in palaces. As the art objects passed into new hands, it was placed into old palaces or buildings imitating Greek temples or Italian palaces. American museums not only mimicked the character of European museums, but they also were located outside the city proper, preferably in an open space such as a park, as were European museums. Dana believes American museums house largely second-rate original art along with historical and archaeological artifacts of little or no value. The museum buildings housing these objects are expensive to maintain; therefore, they could be open only on a limited basis. All of these factors are leading museums to be available to the very few and therefore are not fulfilling their purpose. Dana urges that, as future museums are established, they not follow this old idea, and he hopes that existing museums could be changed over time.

1913

"Live Museums." *New York Times*, February 11, p. 12, col. 7. Dana presents his ideas against art museums acquiring oil paintings and Egyptian artifacts. His main argument is that they have no relevance to the lives of average people and that items of the applied arts are more appropriate for American art museums. These items would be of interest to the average visitor and would promote the results of manufacturing of the local city. Dana believes that museums collect expensive items to enhance the status of the museum and its staff, which do not serve the people. Dana recommends that for a museum to be alive it must do two things: teach and advertise. The museum would become connected to its community by teaching and would make decisions based on the uses of its resources.

"How Museum and Schools May Aid Good Workmanship." *Newark Evening News*, August 23. Dana believes that cities are based on their skilled labor and that Newark needs more skilled labor. The museum would work with educational institutions in Newark to improve this situation. He states that the museum would build collections in the applied arts, the sciences, and "the largest collection in the world of pictures" illustrating the fine and applied arts. Material from the collections would be lent freely to schools, to workshops, and "to all comers for enjoyment, comparison, and study in the home." To aid education the museum also would serve as a community center for groups and organizations with interests related to the collections of the museum and library. Dana also proposes that "[i]n every schoolhouse there will be a branch museum." The museum would provide changing materials to support this activity, which also could be used by the local neighborhood. Through these methods the museum could aid other educational agencies in making Newark "a city of skilled workers."

"The Gloom of the Museum, with Suggestions for Removing It." *The Newarker* (The Newark Free Public Library) 2, no. 12 (October): 389-404. See the annotations for the book of this same title published in 1917.

1914

American Art: How It Can Be Made to Flourish. Hill-of-Corn Series, no. 1. Woodstock, Vt.: The Elm Tree Press, first printing, 1914; second printing, 1929. 31 pp. This is Dana's most complete and direct statement on the need to develop American art in its broadest possible meaning. It is a recurring theme in publications throughout the remainder of his career, and this book had a second printing in 1929, clearly indicating Dana's continuing interest in the topic. This book incorporates and extends the article that appeared in the *Newark Sunday Call* on December 5, 1909.

Dana presents the thesis that there is very little American art primarily because American artists are not being patronized by the wealthy in the United States. He uses the Italian Renaissance as an example of how the wealthy can call forth art by purchasing the art produced locally. Dana criticizes the wealthy in America because they use their resources to purchase "an ample supply of honorific curios in the relics of European and Asiatic civilizations" while "our artists and artisans are continuously ignored." Dana reserves his sharpest criticism for the "oil painting fetish" because oil painting "has long received more than its due share of attention." He believes that people could not learn about art from studying oil paintings because, since they are expensive, they can only be viewed and studied in art museums. By the time a painting is placed in a museum, it has already been praised by thousands of others and is, therefore, not truly open for honest evaluation. Dana believes that "[i]n art matters it is more important to be sensitive than to be knowing. At the bottom of all visual arts are certain elements—line, form, arrangement, let us say. . . . [Y]ou cultivate your sensibilities by keen observation and careful criticism of everyday, familiar objects." Dana returns to his earlier idea of people collecting and studying teacups or other products of the applied arts thereby to increase their appreciation and enjoyment of all forms of art. He finally concludes: "Art has always flourished where it was asked to flourish, and never elsewhere. If we wish for a renaissance of art in America, we must be students and patrons of endeavors which seem humble, but are in truth of the utmost importance."

1915

"An Industrial Exhibit in a Municipal Museum." *The American City* 13, no. 1 (July): 20-22. This paper describes a six-week exhibition at The Newark Museum entitled "New Jersey Clay Products Industrial Exhibition." The exhibit included such manufactured goods as china, porcelains, decorative pottery, sanitary ware, electrical ware, brick, and terra cotta. Forty-two firms contributed to the exhibit. The museum added 150 pieces of pottery made in New Jersey before 1876, featured the process of manufacturing pottery, and displayed materials used in the process. The exhibit was accompanied by a catalogue. A potter presented demonstrations each afternoon. There were 25,000 visitors during the six weeks. Dana judges the exhibit to be a success in promoting the clay industry in New Jersey and in educating the people of New Jersey about one of the state's products.

1916

"Increasing the Usefulness of Museums." Paper presented at the annual meeting of the American Association of Museums, Washington, D.C., May 15-16. In *Proceedings of the American Association of Museums* 10: 80-87. This paper outlines Dana's vision for a new museum, which he calls "the institute of visual instruction."

He calls for the end of the museum, especially the art museum, as a monument to social conventions or community fashions. He sees these "institutions of visual instruction" as justifying their existence by being "effective agencies in the intellectual, aesthetic, industrial, and moral progress of their respective communities." The new museum would house not only paintings, sculptures, and prints, but also a selection of goods made in the community: objects of clay and glass, textiles, leather, metal objects, jewelry, wood, and foods; habitat groups of small animals; science collections; a library; and a moving picture room. Instructors would teach workshops using the collections. Most compelling is Dana's idea of creating branch museums in shops, churches, factories, and schools, and loaning them objects from the main museum.

Artistic Posters and a Step-by-Step Exhibition of the Production of Printed Publicity. Newark, N.J.: The Newark Museum Association, April 23. 6 pp. This pamphlet was to accompany a traveling exhibit coming to The Newark Museum from the Municipal Art Gallery of New York City. The exhibit was "designed to show particularly the steps in the process of making a lithographic poster in colors for out-of-door use." The Newark Museum added new labels and new posters from Germany, France, England, and Japan. The organizers of the exhibit hope to educate the consumers of posters, if only slightly, because they believe that those American purchasers of printed publicity in color are unappreciative of the best poster artists in the world. In addition, the organizers hope to teach more print and picture buyers to exercise good taste when purchasing objects and to be willing to pay for quality. Finally, they wish to "make the printer himself more conscious of the dignity of his craft."

1917

The New Museum. The New Museum Series, no. 1. Woodstock, Vt.: The Elm Tree Press. 52 pp. This is the first in a series of self-published books by Dana in what was called the New Museum Series. Dana presents some of his fundamental beliefs about the goals and ideals of museums as well as practical suggestions for establishing a new museum in a community. The book is based primarily upon Dana's experience in developing The Newark Museum within The Newark Public Library. Dana opposes what he perceives to be the primary mission of the traditional museums of his era. He speaks against the "art-gallery type of museums" that are "temples to dead gods." The Newark Museum defined as its mission the adding to the general efficiency of the businesses and work lives of the people of Newark. Dana emphasizes the education and entertainment of visitors rather than the building of research collections. He endorses creating branch museums that exhibit objects in locations that are convenient for the public and the lending of objects to schools, individuals, and community groups.

Dana describes the traditional museum as a storage warehouse or community attic with an atmosphere that is "depressing and numbing to the sensitive visitor in direct ratio to the self-conscious grandeur and refinement of its architectural container." The museum that Dana envisions is responsive to the needs of the community. It is actively involved in the community and dedicated to a mission of public service and education.

Museum professionals today may find some of Dana's ideas unusual. He seemed to have little concern for the innate value of objects; he supported museums acquiring inexpensive pictures as the basis for a collection; he recommended that museums accept any and all donations that come without conditions attached; and he placed little emphasis on the preservation of objects in smaller community-based museums. However, Dana's ideas concerning the primary mission of museums as educational and responsive to community needs will sound like products of the 1990s to many in the museum profession.

Part III of this book is "Museums That Can Help You," which is a list of 51 museums that agreed to help new museums get started. The list may be of historical interest to museologists, but the only museum listed west of the Nebraska State Museum, Lincoln, and the North Dakota State Historical Society, Bismarck, is the State Museum, University of Washington, Seattle. Part IV is "A Few Books and Articles on the Elements of Museum Management," which lists 22 publications and journals that will be of historical interest to museologists.

The Gloom of the Museum. The New Museum Series, no. 2. Woodstock, Vt.: The Elm Tree Press. 45 pp. In this book, Dana presents his criticisms of the traditional museums of his day and offers suggestions and predictions for museums in the future. Dana addresses primarily "art" museums; however, his is a broad definition including not only traditional art museums, but also museums that collected antiquities and other cultural objects. He writes that the collection of art objects as well as fine houses, higher education, and leisurely pursuits have long been the privileges of the wealthy. The wealthy set the trend for acceptable artwork in America. Since they look to Europe and Asia for what they consider true art, American artists and craftsmen are receiving little patronage from the wealthy. Dana believes that if the wealthy gained an appreciation for American art, they would encourage artists and artisans, increase prices and wages through competition, increase the study of art, attract artists from abroad, and "begin our own renaissance." Dana holds that art museums are part of the problem because they exhibit works primarily of European artists. In particular, rare and expensive works are what museums tended to collect. He argues that the primary mission of American art museums should be "to discover talent and encourage its development here at home." Dana promotes a greater interaction with the public, and he sees the purpose of museums as promoting a betterment of manner and feeling. Dana believes that to accomplish this objective, museums should show comparative types of similar objects, modern objects, and regional objects.

Dana is concerned that museums in this country are being designed on a European model in which museums tend to be in grand palaces or temples surrounded by extensive park land. Dana observes that American museums often are on the edge of a city, surrounded by gardens and separated from the people. He feels that designers are more concerned with the appearance of the building than its location or functionality. The space within the building is not being built for proper storage or exhibition of objects. Dana proposes that the "modern" museum should follow the department store model. In this model, the museum would be centrally located near the transportation hub of the city, providing access for all segments of the population. As in department stores, museums should be "easily reached," be "open to all at all the hours when patrons wish to visit," receive "all courteously," give "information freely," exhibit the "most attractive and interesting objects," classify collections according to the "knowledge and needs of its patrons," be well lit, have good restrooms, supply free guides, advertise "widely and continuously," and change exhibits to meet trends and demands.

Part III of this book is "The Literature of Museum Management," which is a very interesting 15-page list of early museum management publications.

"Notes." *The Museum* (The Newark Museum Association) 1, no. 1: 1-12. "Notes" basically serves as the foreword to volume 1, number 1, of *The Museum.* This journal was put together by the staff of The Newark

Museum to test whether it would be worthwhile to establish a museum journal. The journal was intended for museum workers, covering areas that we would call museology today, and not scientific treatises. It is worthwhile noting today that the only museum journal extant in the American museum profession is *Curator, The Museum Journal.*

The final brief note begins, "A museum is an educational institution." In order for museums to fulfill this mission, they must be used. "To be useful it [the museum] must advertise itself—advertising, that is, of the very essence of the useful activity of any museum."

"The Little Red School House: An Exhibit and a Museum." *The Museum* (The Newark Museum Association) 1, no. 1: 4-7. Dana discusses and describes a schoolhouse that was being constructed in St. Louis, Mo., as a replica of historic schoolhouses used in the United States. Within the schoolhouse was to be "a modest museum, a collection of books, and other materials illustrative of the school life" of America since its founding. This paper is another affirmation of Dana's belief in the educational value of museum exhibits and the value of education.

"Wood Engravings in Color by Rudolph Ruzicka: An Exhibit." *The Museum* (The Newark Museum Association) 1, no. 1: 36-38. This publication describes in some detail a temporary exhibit mounted by The Newark Museum. Interest for museologists will be primarily historical in nature, although the description of this exhibit does give insight into Dana's thinking about what made a good exhibit. The artist was from New York City and was doing a project for a private group in Newark. Ruzicka was thought to be the most accomplished painter-graver in the country. The exhibit consisted of 60 of Ruzicka's wood engravings in color and black and white, and 55 examples of wood engravings from the 15th century to the time of the exhibit. The engravings were arranged in chronological order, with Ruzicka's at the end. The curator of prints at the Metropolitan Museum wrote material that was printed in a 20-page leaflet to accompany the exhibit. An exhibit of 90 engravings was arranged to travel to museums, universities, and libraries, along with a brief descriptive catalogue.

"Printing Presses in Museums and Libraries." *The Museum* (The Newark Museum Association) 1, no. 1: 40-42. Reprint, *The Library Journal* 42, no. 7 (July): 538-539. This article concerning the value of printing presses in museums and libraries will only be of historical interest to museologists. Dana claims that having a printing press available to print signs, labels, and other printed matter would save time and money as well as allowing better control of the quality of the final product. A similar article probably could be written today about having a computer and a high-quality printer available in museums to produce signs and labels.

1918

"Schools and Museums." *Public Libraries* (Library Bureau, Chicago) 23, no. 2 (February): 60-63. In our opinion, this is one of Dana's most important statements on the educational role of museums, especially in the area that we currently would term "outreach programs." We urge anyone with an interest in museology to read and study this paper. To summarize this publication in Dana's own words: "The good school museum is a collection of lending objects useful in school work, prepared by a corps of workers who are in close touch with the schools, and forming part of a general public museum of art, science, industry, and history." Dana emphasizes that it is important for a school museum to be associated with a larger public museum because "[i]n it will be found experts who can give the school-lending staff assistance in identifying, arranging, and presenting, through label and leaflet, the objects they are handling."

Another important point that Dana makes in this paper is that the state of museology is about 40 years behind that of libraries. He points out that "we know very little, and can learn only by study, experiment, and observation, and even then must draw merely tentative conclusions." Dana continues, "In a new and largely unexplored field, only the inquirer who is not only bold but is also fully conscious that the field is unexplored can give us useful data for mapping that which is as yet unknown." Unfortunately, the field of museology has had few "inquirers" in Dana's sense, and few that have been "bold" and conscious "that the field is unexplored."

"Libraries and Museums for Business." *Bulletin of Bibliography* 10, no. 3 (July, August, September). Dana briefly discusses the "little-known 'museums' in business houses," which were generally used to advertise a business. Dana also cites the Philadelphia Commercial Museum as one of the few large museums dedicated entirely to business interests. He describes the "Exhibition of the Republic of Colombia," which was prepared by The Newark Library and Museum "as a practical demonstration of the use of library and museum to the businessman." One of the exhibit's special attractions was a series of small exhibits prepared by Newark manufacturers featuring objects exported from Newark to Colombia. These exhibits were rotated through the Business Branch of The Newark Public Library.

Installation of a Speaker and Accompanying Exhibits. The New Museum Series, no. 3. Woodstock, Vt.: The Elm Tree Press. 25 pp. Dana applies his management ideas for the "new museum" to the "real world" outside the museum. He suggests how non-museum individuals could apply museum techniques in areas such as public speaking, displaying objects, and interior decorating. Through this discussion, Dana expresses his ideas on designing museum displays and incorporating speakers into museums. He presents his ideas by drawing a parallel between a speaker and an object on exhibit. As with a successful exhibit, he believes that the success of a speaker depends upon the skill with which she is "installed." Dana believes that much thought, care, and attention to detail should be given to the installation of objects and speakers in museums. All of this preparation is done for the benefit of visitors so that they could "gain the maximum of profit and pleasure" from the experience of hearing a speaker or viewing an object. In Dana's opinion, a neatly arranged, uncluttered, well-lit exhibit with clear labels is infinitely more desirable than one that is poorly designed; the same principles apply to speakers in any setting.

1919

The New Relations of Museums and Industries: The Story of the First Ten Years of a Group of Experimental Museums. Newark, N.J.: The Newark Museum Association. 23 pp. Dana gives a brief overview of his 10 years of service to The Newark Museum Association. In keeping with Dana's museum philosophy, The Newark Museum Association parted from the conventional museum concept. The nature of The Newark Museum was experimental, based on Dana's vision of "the institute of visual learning." The museum was housed in the public library building; it was this close association that made it easy to realize Dana's vision of the museum as a component of the library. The marriage of museum and library, coupled with the fact that Newark was a city of industries, made this the perfect testing ground for Dana's new museum. The pioneering work of the museum began with an exhibition of the commercial products of Germany. The museum then collected the applied arts of Newark, and other American museums followed, collecting and exhibiting objects made in their respective cities.

1920

A Plan for a New Museum: The Kind of Museum It Will Profit a City to Maintain. The New Museum Series, no. 4. Woodstock, Vt.: The Elm Tree Press. 57 pp. In the last of his four self-published books in the New Museum Series, Dana outlines his concept of a "useful" museum. Dana's vision differs considerably from the notion of a traditional museum in that he stresses that museums are institutions of public service. He was a pioneer of museum education and even goes so far as to suggest that institutions that fit his vision may not even be properly called museums, but rather "Institutes of Visual Learning." Dana reserves his harshest criticism for the "fine art" museum. He contests the popular idea that the mere sight of fine art or "curios" is enough to uplift the average museum visitor and believes instead that only through interpretation and appreciation of everyday objects or the "applied arts" could the world of the average person be broadened or improved.

Dana believes that the value of a museum is measured by its use; thus the museum needs to be accessible to its audience. However, Dana envisions an accessibility that goes far beyond the physical location of the museum building. He encourages museums to establish (what we would call today) outreach programs such as lending collections, branch museums, and cooperative programs with schools, libraries, and public parks—anywhere people could be reached. The fact that the term outreach has been added to the museum lexicon is a testament to Dana's success.

A concept that many museum professionals will find controversial even today is Dana's belief that reproductions of museum objects are, in most circumstances, just as valuable as the original object. He believed that museum objects should not inspire wonder or awe, but should be valued for their ability to educate.

1921

"Newark's Museums." *The Library and the Museum Therein* (Newark Public Library) 1, no. 7 (February): 13-14. Dana makes the point that the collections of The Newark Museum each represent the beginning of a museum; thus he refers to "Newark's museums" rather than "The Newark Museum." Among these "museums" he lists "Fine Art," "Applied Art," "Science," "Industrial," "Anthropological," and "Educational."

The second part of this brief contribution is Dana's quotable quotes on his ideas concerning museums. Our favorite (because we believe that it is still true) is: "All museum work is today experimental and should be frankly regarded as such, even by those who are developing and managing our largest and richest museums."

"Libraries and Museums: How Museums Came to Be So Deadly Dull." *The Library Journal* 46 (May 15): 455-456. This paper enumerates a few factors that have contributed to the dullness of museums, art museums in particular. Dana begins with his usual castigation of the wealthy as stupid and unimaginative, obedient as always to fashion, traditionally regarding museums as "temples to dead gods of art and science." Another factor is the exaltation of oil paintings. Dana believes that the endless galleries of oil paintings lead only to "soul-and-body-tiring" and suggest nothing of how to make daily life more enjoyable or beautiful. Dana's major complaint is that the museum's representation of art is isolated and completely unrelated to everyday life. In the end he concedes that many museums are attempting to become more interesting and useful, a precedent he hopes will continue.

"Libraries and Museums: The Functions of a Museum." *The Library Journal* 46 (June 15): 539-540. Dana addresses the question of how to make museums useful, so as to aid in the happiness, increased intelligence, and general well-being of the community. The new museum would be most useful to the entire community by maintaining a diverse collection of objects from the diverse fields of art, science, industry, and history. Dana makes the argument that public libraries are the proper place to lay the foundation for a new museum and that librarians are well suited to found and direct such a museum. He sets forth four forms of activity that the new museum should conduct: lending its objects for use in schools, shops, or homes; placing its objects in branch museums; publishing information about the collection that will aid the community; and teaching citizens about objects as they relate to the spoken and written activities of the community. Dana argues that the public library is already well equipped to accomplish the four activities of the modern museum and that the modern library is the basis on which he developed his vision of the new museum.

"Libraries and Museums: First Steps Toward Museum Founding." *The Library Journal* 46 (September 1): 697-699. The third paper in this series aims to set forth the process of founding a new museum. Dana instructs those interested in founding a museum of this type first to examine thoroughly the museum field and research the museums and libraries that may already exist in the community. He urges them to examine their contents, their administrative apparatus, their finances, and their annual cost to the city relative to the services that they offer the citizens, young and old, of the community. After critically analyzing the need for the new museum, Dana suggests meeting with the teachers and the superintendent of schools to discuss the usefulness of the new museum based on the fact that it would maintain a teaching collection that would be loaned to area schools, adding that the museum would adapt as it grows to the needs and wishes of the entire community. Dana encourages the museum director to realize that the new museum will never be completed and "to think of it always as a beginning, as an ever-changing series of collections, administered in ever-changing ways."

"Libraries and Museums: The Literature of Museum Management." *The Library Journal* 46 (October 15): 839-842. This paper is a brief review of literature from the early 20th century relating primarily to the museum's educational mission. Dana reviews several of his own early books and pamphlets. He quotes extensively from British literature concerning museums, especially the works of Professor William Rothenstein, whose ideas closely paralleled Dana's. Dana cites several museums that produced museum educational material that were of interest, including the Commercial Museum of Philadelphia, American Museum of Natural History, Metropolitan Museum of Art, Children's Museum of Boston, and Art Institute of Chicago.

Dana visits one of his common themes in the conclusion of this paper: "'Institute of Visual Instruction' is the name which should be given to what we now call museums." Museums should at least strive to live up to such a name.

Dana also concludes that "[t]he literature of museums is meager." In addition to the material already cited above, Dana discusses the proceedings of the American Association of Museums published between 1907-1917 and the later *Museum Work*. Unfortunately, Dana's conclusion can still be applied to the museum field today, which still lags behind many related disciplines.

A Small American Museum: Its Efforts Toward Public Utility. Newark, N.J.: The Newark Museum Association, November 1. 15 pp. Dana reports on the results of The Newark Museum's many experiments in museum management. He expresses his hope that the experiments would serve as the epitome of the educational work undertaken by American museums. He begins with a brief history of The Newark Museum and provides reasons for creating a general museum. In this discussion, Dana reveals the underlying cause that compelled The Newark Museum Association to conduct experiments in museum practice. After a careful study of the current museum literature and on-site investigations of other museums, the association saw that there were a few museums, all the time increasing in number, that were making efforts to serve better the public through loans, lectures, publications, and docents. The study also revealed that although these museums were moving in the direction of change, none had made a careful study of the needs of their respective communities. To serve its community better, The Newark Museum began a series of "experiments" that tested the public's reaction to particular exhibition topics. While many of the exhibits focused on the products produced by various New Jersey industries and the processes involved in manufacturing these products, art and design were fundamental to every exhibit. Other exhibit topics included geography, commerce, history, the applied arts of Germany, and cultural issues. Each exhibit disseminated knowledge through exhibit labels that revealed a definite narrative when read in sequence, leaflets and pamphlets, and docents. Another aspect of experimentation involved the museum's loaning of objects to the public school system to facilitate a harmonious relationship between the museum and Newark's educational system.

1922

"A Small American Museum: Its Efforts Toward Public Utility." *Museum Work* 4, no. 3-4 (November-December 1921, January-February 1922): 144-150. See previous annotation.

"Libraries and Museums: Pictures in Place of Objects." *The Library Journal* 47 (September 1): 705-708. Dana wrote this piece specifically for librarians who were considering expanding their libraries into museums. He suggests that a library with ambitions of becoming a museum must begin with a carefully arranged collection of pictures, as they are inexpensive and have wide public appeal and great utility. Dana defines a collection of pictures, or illustrations, as a museum in and of itself, and offers a Paris museum that housed a collection of pictures with no accompanying objects as an illustration of his point. Dana explains that he chose the term "pictures" carefully to emphasize the utility of such collections. To add credence to his argument, he provides a few examples of the public (from ivory carvers to architects and designers) and their particular inquiries to which the picture collection at The Newark Public Library had provided answers.

The fifth article in this series is not missing, but was authored by Louise Connolly, with only a brief introduction by Dana ["Libraries and Museums: The Museum Idea at Pinnacle." *The Library Journal* 47 (January 1, 1922): 23-24.]

"The Use of Museums." *The Nation* 115, no. 2988 (October 11): 374-376. After reading an article written by a worker as a special pleader for the Metropolitan Museum of Art in New York, Dana writes a response in which he argues against the major premise of the article. Although Dana agrees with the first part of the writer's thesis—that fine and applied arts are both noble—he takes issue with the notion that only art museum collections could influence design. Dana argues that art museums do not teach the public to recognize good art; do not influence the design of manufactured products; and do not encourage those with artistic talent to devote their lives to developing that talent. Dana asserts that art museums simply encourage the collecting of fine art and that these objects would inevitably influence the aesthetic sensibilities of the culture. He adds that art museums and the objects contained therein are only one source out of the many found within the motif of daily life that provide inspiration for good design and ultimately good art.

"The Public Utility of Museums." *The American City* 26, no. 4: 359-360. This paper serves as a brief explanation of Dana's premise that museums should be of public utility. Dana makes the point that the mission of The Newark Museum always had been to serve the educational interests of the people of Newark by establishing a collection of objects that would reflect the values and interests of the community. He explains that cooperation with public service agencies, such as county park commissions and scientific clubs, to promote interest in natural history and related subjects, is fundamental to The Newark Museum's "theory of public utility." Dana emphasizes that to produce tangible results in utility, museums also must work with educators in both public and private schools to determine the scope of the museum's collection. Such input is critical to creating a collection that would best serve the community. Dana explains that value is another essential aspect of public utility. He believes that museums could maximize their value by exhibiting their community's manufactured goods and the processes that created them in such a way that would demonstrate the value of the community as an organization functioning for production. Because a community does not exist in a vacuum, Dana suggests exhibiting objects produced by foreign cultures that would be of interest to farmers, workers, manufacturers, and distributors. Dana concludes by listing a few museums, such as the American Museum of Natural History in New York and the Educational Museum in St. Louis, which had successfully employed the theory of public utility.

1923

"A Museum of Service." *The Survey: Graphic Number* 49, no. 9 (February 1): 581-585. Published separately by The Newark Museum Association. Dana tells the story of the development of The Newark Museum—a story that he sees as representative of the developments taking place in museums everywhere. The new museum, serviceable to the community, was an idea that profoundly affected the museum field, and Dana led the way for American museum institutions. Dana sees The Newark Museum as a small laboratory for experimenting with new museum methods. The laboratory is a ripe testing ground for Dana's ideas, eventually leading him to draw several conclusions about museum management. He finds that the act of gazing at paintings, sculpture, and graphic art rarely goes beyond mere gazing, and Dana offers the docent as a solution to this problem—a new museum method that was slowly coming into general use. Another conclusion was reached after The Newark Museum showed two successful exhibitions, one about clay products and the other about textiles, both produced in New Jersey. Rather than simply displaying objects, these exhibits were designed to reveal the processes that produced these objects. Dana concludes that the museum of the future would include exhibits that revealed processes such as the painter painting, the weaver weaving, and a sculptor modeling rather than simply showing objects statically arranged in glass cases. Dana also concludes that publishing labels, legends, leaflets, catalogues, and descriptive pamphlets as part of the museum exhibition are absolutely essential to the dissemination of visual knowledge. He does, however, caution that the museum could not function as a formal educational institution given that the income of most public school systems far surpassed that of any museum. Dana believes that museums should function instead as a service to the public school system, providing material for visual learning.

1924

"Art for the People's Sake: The Newark Museum's Idea." *New York Times*, April 20, sec. 9, p. 12, col. 1. This *New York Times* article is about a new kind of museum that was quickly becoming fashionable: a museum of direct service to the general public. The Newark Museum serves as an example of the new museum, and Dana, as director of The Newark Museum, is quoted extensively. The success of the museum and the popularity of Dana's ideas with the citizens of Newark are also discussed.

"Note to the Staff of Library and Museum, from the Librarian." *The Library and the Museum Therein* (Newark Public Library) 1, no. 10 (August): 12-13. This short publication is based upon a note posted in The Newark Library and Museum, which began, "It is whispered about that ours is a peculiar library; that our museum is more peculiar; and that the librarian and director and his immediate aides are more peculiar." Dana proceeds to tell his staff that this is what they have wanted to achieve and that they should be proud of their institutions. He writes that only through change could institutions continue to improve and that those institutions that strove to be different through change would be seen as "peculiar." The only measure of the success of changes is whether or not their audiences used the institutions more.

The remainder of the paper discusses changes in the library and museum as a major new addition was added to the library. Brief mention of a major Chinese exhibit completed and arranged by the museum is also made.

1925

"A Museum of Everyday Life." *Woman's Home Companion* 52, no. 1 (January): 29, 72, 97. Dana uses the experimental Newark Museum as a model for the new museum, a model that could be adapted by any town or city for the purpose of founding a museum. Dana uses the lending library as the foundation for the new museum. The practice of loaning books to patrons sparked in Dana the idea that the new museum would maintain a diverse collection of objects to lend to schools. He uses The Newark Museum's bathtub exhibit as an example of the down-to-earth quality of the new museum. He writes that every new museum would exhibit the products produced by their local industries to promote an understanding of the industry, its history, its technique, its management, its workers, and its problems. Dana believes that such exhibits raise the consciousness of the community by bringing "the life around us into a more vivid relief." Every new museum must also consider how to maximize its usefulness at a minimum cost. To that end, new museums would make use of simple and inexpensive pictures and objects in their exhibits. He believes that much could be revealed about a subject through the careful selection, arrangement, and labeling of inexpensive pictures and objects. The new museum would also serve as a means to promote understanding between nations.

1926

"A Museum Of, For, and By Newark." *The Survey: Graphic Number* 55, no. 11 (March 1): 613-617. Published separately by The Newark Museum Association. Dana synthesizes the meaning and purpose of the new museum in this article. His ideal of the museum and the city working together to disseminate knowledge was realized in The Newark Museum. Dana begins by describing the many services provided by The Newark Museum to the community, particularly the schools. He then sets out to answer the question, "What is the meaning of these deviations from the traditional museum pattern?" Dana believes that the deviations—most notably the mission to serve the community as a "workshop of education" and to assist all educational enterprises throughout the city—are necessary if the general public is to understand the aesthetic and apply it to their everyday lives. Dana defines beauty as "the most perfect adaptation of a means to ends, the most perfect adaptation of an object to its uses, and to the needs of its user or beholder." His ability to see art in industry, in the objects of everyday life, creates a sense that America had an aesthetic that deviated from that of Europe. Dana sees the new museum as providing a venue for exhibiting and understanding American industrial art. "The Newark Museum had consistently . . . tried to discover the articles in local manufacture . . . which exhibit the most careful research into the adaptation of means to ends."

"Art in Industry." *New York Times*, April 15, p. 26, col. 7. In this newspaper article, Dana praises the Metropolitan Museum of Art for presenting exhibits of the applied arts. He traces the history of the acceptance of these types of exhibits in art museums to the exhibit of German applied arts organized by The Newark Museum, which had been rejected by the Metropolitan Museum. In the interim, the Metropolitan Museum had hired a "liaison officer" to work with manufacturers in getting access to the "vast store of impeccable designs to be found in and on the Metropolitan's ancient, rare, and costly objects." The Metropolitan also acquired products of American factories, but only those with old designs, which were believed to be the only truly good designs. This policy had changed, but Dana calls for a "more generous appreciation of the products of American machines." Finally, Dana concludes, "Native talent we have in abundance. Appreciation in the form of practical patronage would call it into use. The Metropolitan has followed the trend of the day by its admission of the American machine-made to its galleries."

"In a Changing World, Should Museums Change?" Paper presented at the annual meeting of the American Association of Museums, New York, N.Y., May 17-19. In *Publications of the American Association of Museums*, New Series 1: 17-22, and *The Museum* (The Newark Museum Association), September. Dana charges art museums with having remained static for the last 50 years, while society had undergone tremendous change. He finds the old tradition of displaying works of art in long galleries as having little to no effect on the visitor. Dana takes issue with the theory that real art could only be found in art museums. It is unsettling to him to think that a woman from a western state who had never traveled east to the great art museums of New York had, therefore, never seen art. Dana insists that "good art is wherever the interested and intelligent open their eyes and find color, form, line, and light and shade." He believes that the coming of the department store had greatly exposed the public to the art of design and had thus taught them more about art and beauty than art museums. Dana offers The Newark Museum as an experiment in popularizing art and in drawing the aesthetic out of daily life; for example, he suggests exhibiting a half-full glass of water. In Dana's museum, the visitor would be encouraged to view this utilitarian object in a new light, to see the line and mass and the reflective qualities in the glass and water. A response to Dana's paper, written by Mr. Howard of the Cleveland Museum of Art, follows Dana's discussion. Mr. Howard refers to the glass of water exhibit as a common experience and says that art museums, given that they have limited space, time, and funding, should only exhibit fine art that the visitor could not find at his own table.

He insists that the school systems could more adequately provide experience in the beauty of common objects, given that resources were limited and art museums had to focus their resources on the particular mission of exhibiting fine works of art.

"Muses in a Museum: At a Casual Glance It Looks Like a Poem." Newark, N.J.: The Newark Museum, June 21. 3 pp. This bit of light verse is wonderfully and "intentionally" bad. Written in "halting lines of dull and deadly verse" (by the poem's own description), "Muses in a Museum" was read at "The Passing of the Apprentices" at The Newark Museum on June 21, 1926. The poem was intended to commemorate the service of the student apprentices to the museum, but Dana also takes the opportunity to spoof museums and the "noxious gloom" that pervades them. As one would expect, he takes particular aim at the art museum, writing: "Jugs, busts, and pictures here and there appeared; / Most called them 'Arty'; few were those who jeered. / Some kindly said, 'We really like to see 'um, / 'Our libr'y now is almost a museum!'" The poem ends by noting that six of the nine student apprentices would return the following year, "so, 'Salve,' not 'Alas!'"

The New Museum Opens Its Doors. Newark, N.J.: The Newark Museum Association. 3 pp. Reprinted from *Charm*. On the occasion of the opening of the new Newark Museum, Dana reviews the history and philosophy of the museum since its founding. He emphasizes that the "experience in Newark indicates that a few simple objects and pictures, united with the idea of service, make a good beginning for a museum. . . . The museum should attract, entertain, arouse curiosity, lead to questionings—and thus promote learning." The Newark Museum designed early exhibits that highlighted the applied arts of Newark and New Jersey and Dana believes that this "beginning at home," especially with the applied arts to which the local audience could relate, had led to the success of the museum. Eventually the museum was able to broaden its exhibits with programs such as "Colonial Kitchen," "Republic of Colombia," and "China: The Land and the People." The museum was also able to increase its collections in such areas as fine arts, science, ethnography, and especially the lending collection.

1927

"The Museum and Library Combination in Newark." *The Library* (The Newark Public Library) 2, no. 7 (January): 97-99. In light of the relatively recent formation of the Institute of Museum and Library Services, modern museum professionals may be surprised that Dana discussed this relationship nearly 75 years ago. Dana states that Newark had "made her library just as much a part of her museums as her museum is of her library." Dana sees the activities of the museum and library as being complementary and extending each other, especially through their lending of items to the public. In his view, "the library of the city is the library of the museum." He sees the mission of each as promoting their use, providing service to the community, and presenting educational opportunities.

"Should Museums Be Useful?" *The Museum* (The Newark Museum Association). 22 pp. Dana concedes in this paper that the best imaginings of the museum enthusiast had not yet formed a clear picture of a museum rich in utility. He defines utility as "moving a community toward greater skill in all the arts of living." Dana considers the challenge of creating more useful museums by first asking the following questions: Why museums at all? Which of their activities in fact pay for their cost? and, Of those that do pay, which would be the most profitable in the average city of this country? In seeking out the answers to these questions, Dana reaches a few conclusions. He first notes that countless societal changes had in effect outdated the old-style museum. Progress in the printing industry and department stores had flooded the culture with objects and images of art that formerly came from museums alone. Dana observes that in comparison to the public's daily exposure to the objects and images of popular culture, museums enjoyed few visitors. He dislikes the current practice of adding music to the art galleries in an attempt to attract more visitors. He sees this as an ineffective means of increasing museum patronage, since the influence of fashion magazines, papers, and journals far outweighed such minor attempts at change. Dana goes further to charge art museums with quelling the creative spirit by exhibiting old masterpieces as the final word in all the arts; he believes that the art museum should be viewed as an effect rather than a cause.

Dana identifies particular problems that hindered change, specifically that art museums were restricted in their ability to change because the majority of their resources were tied up in the flood of gifts that must be identified, labeled, restored, exhibited, and because space must be dedicated to the proper storage of such objects. He notes that museums are underfunded and that donors often earmark their gifts for particular purposes, further restricting the museum's ability to make effective financial decisions. Dana identifies preserving, researching, labeling, cataloguing, and exhibiting as principles particular to museum management and as the factors that overwhelm museum resources, causing museums to cease functioning. Dana argues that museums could be more effective if they were managed as a business. He wants the board of directors to function as a governing body that merely sets standards to guide the museum in its fundamental purpose, allowing the director to use his imagination, skill, and expertise to discover the best way to maximize the museum's utility.

Dana concludes by comparing art museums to museums of natural history and industry. The science museum, Dana explains, "collects, identifies, classifies, notes relations, searches for sequence and causes, and arranges things collected, with the student and inquirer in view." The industrial museum illustrates the development of manufactured goods and the history of invention, using docents to instruct and inspire interest in the public, particularly the young. It is this element of education that Dana echoes time and again. Clearly he believed that education, which functioned to arouse in visitors a profound interest in the visual arts, defined a museum's utility.

The Industrialist Is an Artist. Hill-of-Corn Series, no. 2. Newark, N.J.: The Newark Public Library. 8 pp. This publication is basically a philosophical treatise about what constitutes the artistic and as such is only marginally applicable to museums. Two statements can summarize Dana's thesis: "All creators of things are artists" and "All creative genius is artistic." Dana argues that we should consider great industrialists, scientists, mathematicians, inventors, and businessmen as artists because they have created things that perfectly fit the purpose for which they were created. Dana writes that the notion of artistic creativity should not be limited to "music, poetry, writing, painting, sculpture, decoration, design, architecture."

1928

"Museums of Design Without Objects." *The American Magazine of Art* 19, no. 8 (August): 433-435.
In this article, Dana enumerates the benefits of what he calls "museums of design," or picture collections. After visiting the Forney Municipal Library of Art and Industry in Paris, Dana is satisfied that the work of The Newark Museum had not been in vain. This French museum was created for the purpose of helping artisans

complete their education, improving the taste of artists engaged in applied arts, and promoting better relations between artists, artisans, and designers and businessmen, shopkeepers, and factory workers. Dana sees the success of this museum as a direct endorsement of The Newark Museum's picture collection, and it provides him with a vision of what the future might hold for The Newark Museum.

"The Newark Museum Today: A Museum of Art, of Industry, and of Science." *Charm* 76 (August): 24-25, 76. Dana determines that "the gazing museum is fast losing its power to charm or to teach," at least in part because of the competition from department stores, movie theaters, and newspapers. By a "gazing museum," Dana is referring to "a collection of mere things, silent, motionless things." In contemplation of the utility of The Newark Museum, Dana uses the remainder of this article to describe the activities of the museum in the two years after it moved to a new building in 1926. The first floor of the building was occupied by art exhibits, a children's museum, and a lending museum. Featured art exhibits included a display of "paintings by contemporary American artists acquired during 1925-26" and "Living American Painters," which was restricted to artists living outside the New York metropolitan area. The second floor of the museum building was occupied by a national leather exhibit, which told the story of leather historically, industrially, and artistically. The third floor was devoted to science and industry and showed the artistic side of industry. Dana concludes with remarks about European visitors, commenting on children's interest "in exhibits, in lectures, in meetings, and in borrowing museum objects."

Is the Department Store a Museum?" *The Museum* (The Newark Museum Association) 2, no. 1 (July-August): 1-2. "A great city department store of the first class is perhaps more like a good museum of art than are any of the museums we have yet established." In this paper, which followed another that Dana wrote 15 years earlier, he enumerates the ways in which department stores are like museums, but concludes that "[a] department store is not a museum." Dana writes that museums also are not fulfilling their missions very well. He believes that museums "should teach as well as preserve." He again promotes the thesis that art museums should not confine their exhibits to the "old, rare, and expensive; that must be masterpieces." Dana states that art museums "must add to their masterpieces those productions of the day"—that is, the results of manufacturing and the applied arts. He concludes, "Art-in-industry is coming at last to its own."

1929

"What Can Be Said of a Museum's "Educational" Work?" In *Twentieth Annual Report, 1928.* Newark, N.J.: The Newark Museum Association. This is an important statement by Dana from late in his career concerning his philosophy about the role of museums in education. "A museum is not a school; it cannot afford to become a school, and by its own unaided powers it can do little educational work of the formal kind." Dana believes that museums could best fulfill their educational mission through cooperating with "formal educational institutions." Dana recommends actions that we would today classify as informal learning and outreach programs—lending materials to schools, increasing staff to manage the lending material, branch museums, and docents in the galleries. Dana believes that museums could increase the aid that they received primarily by increasing their involvement in the "education in their respective communities."

"Is a Museum Good for Anything?" *The Museum* (The Newark Museum Association) 2, no. 5 (February): 34, and "Is a Museum Good for Anything?" *The American Magazine of Art* 20, no. 10 (October): 584. Dana answers the question "yes" if it means that museums are "helpful in keeping us alive and healthy." He believes that if the museum did its service for the community, then the community would come to understand "that as a mild sort of tonic to the art of living it is well worth far more than the few cents per person that it costs." He believes that the new museum that had opened only two years earlier in Newark had "won approval as a tree bearing the good fruit of wisdom and beauty, of science, of art; adding to the city's excellences."

"American Applied Art and the Department Store." *The Museum* (The Newark Museum Association) 2, no. 6 (March): 42-43. This brief note serves as an update to the ideas Dana first expressed in his 1912 paper "The German Exhibit of Applied Art. . ." and the small 1914 book *American Art: How It Can Be Made to Flourish.* Although he does not feel that the work was completed, he finds that American designs, art, and inventions were flourishing. Department stores and other shops were selling with confidence products of American applied arts. He proudly notes that department stores and shops were "using all that museums have learned of the arts of presentation and adding freely thereto." He believes that Americans were getting more free time, "so they turn some of their thought and energy to adornment, to beauty, to art in everyday things."

"Museums Have Not Kept Up with Changes in Conditions." *New York Times*, June 2, sec. 3, p. 5, col. 1. Dana summarizes what he considers the failure of museums by stating: "Their trustees, directors, experts, and curators, absorbed in acquisition, identification, labeling, and preservation, came to think that what they had done was all that museums should be asked to do." He compares museums of his day to libraries 40 years earlier, before they had open shelves and freely loaned their materials. Dana's believes museums should "look upon their collections as means to certain ends and not as ends themselves." He urges museums to advertise so that people would know about their location, collections, and programs. In larger cities, he believes, branch museums should be established so that the museum could bring collections and programs nearer to where people lived. He also recommends that museums remain open evenings and lend objects not only to schools, where formal education occurs, but also to churches, hospitals, parks, and gardens. Dana believes that museums had learned to preserve things, but he urges "here is the suggestion that they use things."

"The Museum as an Art Patron." *Creative Art* 4, no. 3 (March): xxiii-xxvi. Dana explains that the American museum tradition had evolved out of two misconceptions: first, that fine art in European art museums directly stimulated the production of art in Europe and were thus the primary reason why art production had flourished there; second, that similar collections brought to museums in America would directly affect art production in the cities that housed them. Dana offers a few suggestions for avoiding the erroneous made-to-order collection and for establishing museums that reflected the community's interests. He urges any city that wished to promote the arts by establishing an art museum to find a space that was conducive to temporary exhibitions. Dana writes that the museum staff should design exhibitions that reflect the range of objects produced by the artists and workers of its local, state, and national community. He urges the museum to begin by exhibiting sculpture and oil paintings, as these objects are most commonly considered "art," and then move on to decorative arts, furniture, textiles, ceramics, and other manufactured objects. Dana is confident that careful labeling, description, and cataloguing would facilitate the visitor's understanding of objects and their aesthetic value. He establishes these principles as a framework for creating a museum that would ultimately grow out of the activities of the community and serve as an integral component of art education.

Acknowledgments

We wish to gratefully acknowledge Dr. William A. Peniston, librarian of The Newark Museum, for his help in obtaining many of the more obscure papers annotated herein. Our efforts were also aided by Charles Cummings, The Newark Public Library, and the Interlibrary Loan Division, University Libraries, University of Nebraska-Lincoln. We would like to thank Ted Genoways for his insight into Dana's poem.

Literature Cited

Alexander, E. P. *Museum Masters: Their Museums and Their Influence.* Nashville, Tenn.: American Association for State and Local History, 1983. x + 428 pp.

Coffey, K. *John Cotton Dana's Basic Philosophy of Museums.* Newark, N.J.: Board of Trustees, The Newark Museum, October 23, 1956. 5 pp. (unnumbered).

Cushman, K. "Four Books by John Cotton Dana." *Museum Studies Journal* (John F. Kennedy University) 1 (1985): 49-52.

Hadley, C. *John Cotton Dana: A Sketch.* Chicago: American Library Association, 1943. 105 pp.

Johnson, H. A. "John Cotton Dana." *The Library Quarterly* 7 (1937): 50-68.

Johnson, H., and B. Wisner. "Bibliography: John Cotton Dana." *The Library Quarterly* 7 (1937): 68-98.

Kingdon, F. *John Cotton Dana: A Life.* Newark, N.J.: The Public Library and Museum, 1940. 175 pp.

Lipton, B. "John Cotton Dana and The Newark Museum." *The Newark Museum Quarterly* 30, no. 2/3 (1979): 1-58.

Wisner, B. (ed.). *John Cotton Dana, 1856-1929.* Newark, N.J.: The Newark Public Library and Museum, 1930. 125 pp.

Index

A

B

C

D

E

N

O

P

U

V

W